John Safi is an Afghan and American hero who risked his life at a young age to try to bring peace to his home country and safely return Americans home after their tours. Fighting in the one of the most dangerous areas of the war for multiple years straight with little relief, Safi, is a giant among men. He is already a model US citizen and has an amazing story to tell.
-Jason Criss Howk, writer, editor, publisher, and Afghan War Veteran

An inspiring story of courage, dedication to duty, and resilience. Safi's journey provides an awe-inspiring insight to the lives Afghan interpreters who risked everything to keep American Soldiers safe, and the harrowing paths they had to take to become American citizens.
-Cris Gasperini, Major, U.S. Army

An excellent read that takes you into the struggle of growing up, surviving, and improving a divided war-torn country."
-Joshua Miller, U.S. Army

A superb account of the day-to-day life and combat experiences of an Afghan interpreter. Readers are introduced to the harsh reality and dangers that many of our Afghan partners face. John's journey from child into manhood is essential reading for those wishing to understand the dynamic culture and dangers facing US/Afghan interpreters. A vivid and introspective glimpse into the life of my best interpreter. Safi's story is hilarious, terrifying and sorrowing and he is a true voice of the Afghan war.
-Sergeant First Class (retired) Pat Flanagan, Infantry Platoon Sergeant, U.S. Army

A well-written book that shows the struggles of a family stuck under the Taliban rule and one man's journey to help his family, country, and the United States of America.
-Staff Sergeant David Benson, former U.S. Army

His story is truly unbelievable, and it's important that people hear it. John was my platoon's interpreter in Afghanistan and I can say for certain, that without him, we would have not been as successful. He risked everything in supporting the United States' mission in Afghanistan.
-Captain Justin Renken, former U.S. Army

As much as we all face our own turmoil, and sacrifices, I can't imagine living through some of these situations. John is an amazing human being, so genuine in every way, with a smile and warmness he exudes to bring joy wherever he goes. No matter what he has had to face in life, he hasn't allowed that to harden his soul. I am proud to know him.
-Jenny Jordon, Musician

John is a true American patriot. His work as an interpreter has affected and saved many soldiers' lives on hundreds of missions outside the wire. If John tells you something it is the absolute truth!
-Oran Roberts, former U.S. Army

John is a true Hero that sacrificed his own safety and country to serve the United States of America during an Afghanistan wartime. He dedicated and sacrificed his life to help fight the Taliban not knowing what the final outcome for himself would be. Not many people would even lay their life on the line for their own country as John and many other interpreters have done over the past 20 years.

-Michelle Benson, Human Resources assistant, Fort Drum

Over the course of my Army career, John was my first and best interpreter. Most importantly, he was one of us. More often than I care to remember, I was charged with leading men into places and situations we should not have walked away from. When all the other interpreters would refuse to go, John was already waiting for the birds to come get us. And it's because he was one of us that he did so without hesitation...then he did it for eight more years. His story is the realest, most accurate and unbiased dialog you can read today.

-Major Jacob Kerr, U.S. Army

Nasirullah "John" Safi embodies the thousands of Afghans who risked their lives to support the men and women who fought, negotiated, supported, built, and worked tirelessly for better way of life in Afghanistan after the Taliban. His personal commitment to a better life in America, leaving behind all that had meaning in his world, echoes the early 20th century immigrant experience. Our country needs future citizens like John to make our country, and his native land, better.

He delivers his message the Afghan way, through a series of stories, just like history has been passed from generation to generation in Afghanistan. You can almost hear the words on the pages speak to you.

-Stephen Magennis, Lieutenant Colonel, U.S. Army

I became fascinated with John's story from the moment we met, and knew it needed to be told. The details of his journey from Afghan child under Taliban rule to being a hero to our soldiers and making a life in America are enchanting, horrifying, and inspiring.
-Dawn Brower, Friend and Mentor

The personal life experiences that John shares are not very descriptive but also highly entertaining. I would never imagine John growing up to be the man he is today, yet we are still good friends and his stories continue."
-Justin Anderson, former U.S. Army

After 20+ years as an English language instructor in a variety of settings, I thought I knew the meanings of terms like patriot, honor, and United States of America. The experience of working with and learning more about John through his stories broadened my understanding of these not-so-simple terms in life-changing ways. Learning more about the US military's role in Afghanistan through John's unforgettable experiences will forever enhance your knowledge of these nations and their people, too.
-Laura Fister, MS, Former Chemeketa Community College English Language Instructor

Must Read. Extremely fascinating view of life through the eyes of an Afghan interpreter. There are one in a million encounters in life where you meet people that you know are going to change the world or someone's outlook in life. The American government and our allies owe him a debt of gratitude for the thousands of lives he has saved due to his experience and knowledge. Absolutely grateful for our friendship and family addition.

-Kevin Devine, Command Sergeant Major, U.S. Army

This book should be a movie! Readers are taken to the front lines seeing the harsh realities of war and life growing up in Afghanistan. Nasirullah shares the rough truths about the brutality of living under the shadow of the Taliban regime through compelling vignettes about his life from developing the dream to learn English as a child to becoming an interpreter with the US military. Nasirullah's sincere and engaging style of writing lets readers experience the brightness of the human spirit in the darkest of places.

-Mary Hughes, MS, Chemeketa Community College

John at heart is a U.S. Army grunt who risked everything to fight with American soldiers.

-Bing West, Former Assistant Secretary of Defense, Marine combat veteran, and *New York Times* bestselling author

Get the Terp Up Here!

War as an Interpreter to U.S. Forces in Afghanistan

Nasirullah "John" Safi
Pre-Medical Student, Oregon
Afghan War Interpreter/Veteran

Tamarisk Press

North Carolina, USA

"Get the Terp Up Here!"
War as an Interpreter to U.S. Forces in Afghanistan

Published by Tamarisk Press
an imprint of AYM LLC North Carolina USA

"Get the Terp Up Here!"
War as an Interpreter to U.S. Forces in Afghanistan

ISBN paperback 9798459644104
Published in USA

Contents

Acronyms

1SG: First Sergeant (E-8, NCO leader of a Company)

Abai: Mom

ABP: Afghan Border Police

AK: Refers to Kalashnikov rifles developed in the Soviet Union dating back to 1949. "Avtomát Kaláshnikova"

ANA: Afghan National Army

ANDSF: Afghan National Defense and Security Forces

AO: Area of operation

BN: Battalion (Kandak in ANA). Unit commanded by a LTC

CAS: Close air support

CDE: Collateral damage estimate

CF: Coalition Forces

CO: Commanding officer

COIN: Counterinsurgency

COP: Combat Outpost

CPT: Captain (officer grade O-3 in most ground forces)

CSM: Command Sergeant Major (senior enlisted leader)

CTOC: Combined tactical operation center

Dadda: Dad

DFAC: Dining facility (mess hall or chow hall)

FO: Forward observer, calls in artillery/mortars

FSO: Fire support officer

HCT: Human collection team

GIRoA: Government of the Islamic Republic of Afghanistan

HG or HiG: Hizbi-Islami-Gulbudin terrorist organization that made peace with the Afghan government in 2016.

HLZ: Helicopter landing zone

HQ: Headquarters

ISAF: International Security and Assistance Force (NATO forces)

OP: Observation post

ISR: Intelligence surveillance and reconnaissance

JTAC: Joint tactical air controller

KDK: Kandak (Battalion in US military)

Kafir/Kufar: Arabic word for persons who do not believe in Islam as the truest religion, and used as justification to kill people by radicalized violent Islamists

KIA: Killed in action

Lala: Older brother

LLVI: Low-level voice intercept

LT: Lieutenant (2nd or 1st Lieutenants, often Platoon Leaders)

Malak: Community/village leader

MEP: Mission essential personnel

MREs: Meal Ready to Eat

MSR: Main supply route

NCO: Non-commissioned officer (Corporals through Sergeants Major-enlisted leaders in the Army)

Nasara (Nusara): Quranic term for Christians (Nazarenes)

NVG: Night-vision goggles

OGA: Other government agency, most often CIA

PFC: Private First Class (E-3, Enlisted rank level 3 of 9)

PL: Platoon Leader

PSG: Platoon Sergeant

RPG: Rocket propelled grenade

SFAT: Security Force Assistance Team

SFC: Sergeant First Class (E-7, often a platoon sergeant)

SGT: Sergeant (E-5)

Shaheed: a martyr, Muslim who died honorably

SPC: Specialist (E-4)

SSG: Staff Sergeant (E-6)

TBN: Taliban

Terp: Interpreter, slang

TOC: Tactical operation command center

Toop danda: Sport that is closer to baseball than cricket

WIA: Wounded in action

Yahood (Yahud): Arabic word for Jewish people in Qur'an

I wrote this book for my parents because there was not a single word that I put down without thinking of them, as well as my youngest sister who was shot multiple times and is now living in exile.

I also dedicate this book to my brother in-law and his 7-year-old son who were both brutally killed by the Taliban.

These stories are for my brothers-in-arms who were tragically killed during the war against terrorists in Afghanistan.

Thank you, Kevin and Pat. I would not be here today without your support. You are my brothers in every sense of the word.

1st Platoon, 1-32 Charlie Company, Nuristan Province, Afghanistan August 28, 2009

Last day picture during a hellish operation in Barge-Matal District of Nuristan Province on August 28th, 2009. 1st Platoon, 1-32 Infantry.

Preface: A Letter to My English Teacher

Salaam Hamza, peace and blessings be upon you.
My dearest English teacher,

I would like to begin this letter with something that I always wanted to tell you, but uncertainty in life, violence, poverty, sadness, loneliness, lack of communication, created obstacles to reach out to you. I neither had the phone to call you nor could I come back to visit you even though I wanted to so badly. I didn't want to put you and your family at risk because the Taliban already planned to target you, kill you, cut off your head, burn your body, harm your children, wife and elderly father, who had a broken back, and who was always there to say, "How're your parents doing, Safi?" I miss his conversation, kind words and stories of his tough life as an orphan and of Russian soldiers. I didn't know why your father always hesitated to talk about Russians and got very emotional unlike you. You were always a proud Mujahidin who fought the Russians with honor and dignity. You had lost two brothers who were buried just a couple of miles away from the house at the cemetery by the school.

We both spoke Pashto[1], our mother tongue, but neither of us spoke Dari[2]. It is weird to think that my English teacher could speak English, the language of infidels, as the *Mullahs* described it, but not Dari. I even heard you speak Arabic, the language chosen by Allah, the language of the Quran, of the prophet and his companions and the language of the Arab nation. Unlike Arabic, English was satanic, the language of infidels, not tolerated by *Mullahs*, religious clerics or by extremist villagers who were isolated from the rest of the world and kept in a box under the Taliban influence.

Dear Teacher, brother, lifesaver, and great friend,

September 11, 2001, changed the world and the language of the infidels became the most popular in a country governed by extremists and fundamentalists. But then disdain for English again doubled in 2001 when the U.S.-led coalition forces started invading Afghanistan in order to topple the Taliban's brutal regime, a regime that has no legitimacy among its own people. The Taliban did not understand the principles, ethics, doctrines, values and beliefs of their own religion. They harmed, harassed and even killed their own people in the name of religion, Sharia-law, Salafism, Wahhabism, Khalqi and etc..... I was a country boy who never heard those names or titles, but I witnessed the brutality, ruthlessness, and heartlessness of the Taliban against innocent men, women and children.

---

[1] Pashto/Pashtu/Pakhto is part of the Indo-European language family and is spoken by the majority of Pashtuns in Afghanistan.
[2] Dari (Afghan Farsi or Persian) is another official language of Afghanistan.

I had to attend lessons and preaching with Zarbaz, the *Mullah*, full of propaganda against American soldiers every day. "Don't shake hands or talk to Americans," Zarbaz said. I witnessed and even became the victim of the hatred towards Americans by our *Mullah*. It was terrifying, but I had to do it because it was compulsory. "God punish those who have business, aid or shake hands with Americans," Zarbaz insisted. I didn't know the difference between what Islam really teaches and what our *Mullah* taught because I was too young. I believed in him and everything that he said. However, I did learn as I grew up and experienced the world that I never knew existed. I was not the only kid who became the victim of the false and baseless teachings. There were far more who joined extremists to kill and harm their own people, but I chose the path that my parents always wished and hoped for me and my seven siblings. I could be a lucky person, or somehow miracle saved me, because I could have been one of them who would never follow their dreams or not even have survived.

When I decided to learn English, you were the only one who could speak, read, and write the language, but you refused to help. I wanted to learn the English language so badly even though I didn't know much about it. I knew that it was a devil language, that whoever spoken would perish and burn in the hellfire a thousand times stronger than the fire we make in our houses. I was scared to death and never wanted to be burned; I imagined the scorpions, snakes, dragons that the *Mullah* taught live in the hellfire. I was bitten once by a scorpion and suffered the pain, nausea, difficulties of breathing, vomiting, headache and eyes that felt like burning in the fire. I didn't want to be bitten by scorpion again, but I had dreams to follow, a career to pursue. I wanted to make my parents proud and to prove wrong those who always thought that I couldn't do it because I was from a very poor family.

It might sound stupid to you, but it's the picture of the community where I was born and raised. It has been a very long time since I left, but I always pray and hope for the best for everyone that is in the position that my family was. I cried very hard and hated my life when you told my oldest brother that you were not going to help me. Did you know that you were the only option? The only one who could speak, read and write English in the entire town? We looked hard to find someone else, but we failed. There was not any language institute or courses where I could pursue my dream, one that was rarely possible in a village and country that had been isolated from the rest of the world for decades. I thought that you didn't accept me because I was poorer than others, I didn't have proper clothes, shoes or money to pay the tuition, books, etc. I didn't know that you had your own problems. I asked the question, "How did people decide not to help others when they could?" "Why does money decide for people and not humanity, pride, honor, and dignity?" I learned that I was wrong about you and you were not the person I thought. You were a great teacher, mentor, friend and brother to me.

When I met you, Hamza, I realized that I was a bit closer to the dreams that my parents dreamed of for me. I was young, self-doubting and a kid with nothing, a kid who had no money to buy books, notebooks, pens or pencils. Life was never easy, but I remember my momma would say, "No matter how hard and how high the mountain is, there is always path."

Although I didn't know anything about English, you shared everything you had, including old English newspapers that you had kept for years. I wished I could read those newspapers, but I couldn't because I had to start with the English alphabet. I was very excited to learn how to spell my own name. I don't think we talked about my father's past; he once taught history and religion at school, but it was before I was born. He could read the English alphabet, but that was all he could teach me. He always talked about foreign languages and their cruciality, "The more language, you learn, the more friends you make," he always insisted. It was his motivation, love, support, enthusiasm, eagerness and passion that gave me the appetite, optimism, confidence, and sureness that I could do it.

Now I know that the one way to learn another language is to understand the culture, traditions, history, and values. I couldn't know this then because we had no electricity, TVs, internet or social media to connect us to the world that we didn't know existed. Back then, we were trapped in a box locked by religious extremism that kept us apart from the rest of the world. Even though my family and many others in town wanted to break the lock and raise their voices against injustice, inequality and inequity, they simply could not do it because they could be punished or killed.

I almost forgot to tell you, Hamza, that you are my hero and life-saver. I could never thank you enough for everything you have done. Even after years of working, learning and living in the U.S., I still don't know the right words of gratitude for you and your family. May Allah bless you and keep you safe and healthy.

Foreword

In a distant land, there have been American forces engaging with the people of Afghanistan for decades. In small villages across the country, Americans built wells, schools and tried to improve the quality of life. From district centers to provincial capitals and in Kabul, the United States advises Afghan leadership on various government matters and National Defense. At times, all too often, engagement included bullets, rockets, and grenades with the Taliban and other enemy forces throughout the country. None of these millions of engagements is possible without the help and bravery of interpreters like John Safi. There is no chance of success without our Afghan brothers and sisters.

When people ask me what the war was like in Afghanistan, I have a hard time explaining the last 20 years. In my experience, there are few Americans who understand Afghanistan and its nuances. There are even fewer who have experienced the raw realities of war so intimately as Johnny Boy has.

Afghanistan is much more than a conflict with the Taliban. Afghanistan has beautiful mountains and valleys that make Lake Tahoe blush. Afghanistan has people within those mountains who have been fighting conflicts and working to survive for decades. The Afghan people will accept you into their home and give you their last meal whether you speak Pashto, Dari, or English. The people will take up arms against evil when given the resources and hope. The Afghan people hold a special place in my heart. Every American should strive to better understand the conflict and people within its borders.

I was honored to spend most of my adult life taking part in such engagements across Afghanistan and attempting to understand the nuances and people within. During my double-digit deployments, I experienced intense firefights as an Army Ranger from Nangahar to Helmand and everywhere in between. When my warfighting days ended, I used my combat experience as I attempted to create space for peace as I met and negotiated with the same Taliban leaders whom I had fought in my younger days. As a result, I have spent time with a few dozen interpreters and cultural advisors throughout my time in Afghanistan. I shared many close calls with those interpreters, with bullets whizzing by our heads as we ducked behind cover. Other times, I know I would have failed the mission without my interpreter, who was my ears and voice whether we were on a dangerous operation or in a tough negotiation. The bond shared with an interpreter in dangerous situations is developed through a shared understanding of, and purpose to fulfill, the mission. Many more stories exist like Safi's and the American people need to understand their sacrifice.

During my time in Afghanistan, rotation after rotation, I would pack up my rifle and go home. I would get to enjoy good meals and let the wine and whiskey flow amongst friends and family. Our partners, the interpreters, and cultural advisors, continued the fight. They picked-up with the next group of American men and women and put their heart and soul into a whole new set of relationships. While I feared losing brothers and sisters in arms in my platoon, our partners also feared the loss of brothers in arms, again and again, and again with a new set of young men and women. The sacrifice, courage, and dedication to American forces by those who had never set foot on American soil are humbling and inspiring.

This story gives an insight that is rare and raw. John conveys the complex challenges given to American forces during some of the most brutal years and most demanding areas. His ability to relay this is unparalleled.

In addition, John's stories give an original and rare insight into the Taliban propaganda machine from a small village in Kunar to the battlefields across Afghanistan.

The stories you are about to enjoy cannot be found splashed across the front page of newspapers. These stories share the nuanced approach American forces had to take when deep in "Taliban country." Building relationships with villagers and connecting on a human level while simultaneously not knowing when the next fight would come or who to trust. John shares a genuine love and comradery with his American brothers that shines throughout the book.

There are those people in life that when you first meet them, and hear their story you feel connected and humbled, and you admire and appreciate them. When I met John, this is how I felt, and how I hope you feel after reading his story.

> Timothy R. Torres, U.S. Army Ranger
> '21 Tillman Scholar
> Founder "A Voice for Two Nations"

Acknowledgments

Ma, you know how much I love you and how much I owe you thanks and appreciation. This book could not have been written without your constant encouragement, strong belief in me, great understanding, and the lessons that you taught me. There was not a single word that I wrote without thinking of you, and sometimes I cried. Before I went to bed every night, I took a second to think, "I really am that person!" and then got up the next morning and wrote more. I was born to a very poor family, a family that nobody trusted because we were simply poor, but you and Dadda never let us down. Your life is a living history of the ongoing conflict and bloodshed in the country for more than five decades. I can't imagine, and will never have to, how hard and difficult it was, but I tried to do my best to pour it onto paper and to bet it sounds a lot like this.

I apologize that I was not there for you when you went through the deprivation, difficulties, and tough times in life, but you always said that life has ups and downs and we have to deal with it. I cannot agree with you more, Momma. You are my rock, and I owe you my whole life.

It's hard and inevitable that I won't be able to name everyone who absolutely deserves mention; if you are one of those not mentioned, I sincerely apologize, but I promise that I am working on another book that will have the list that you will find yourself there. When I put a period to the last paragraph of 130K words, I thought I was done, but I didn't realize that a very important and hard part of my writing was still needed. The part of editing, a very important journey, which could not have been possible with the selfless support, effort, and time of Melanie Benson, a former Assistant Director for the Duke University Program in American Grand Strategy. When I first heard that she was going to edit my writing, I broke into tears. They were not the tears of sadness and trauma caused by the war; they were the tears of happiness. You are a phenomenal editor, a kind and beautiful soul who created this book from scratch. You are a magician and couldn't imagine how happy and thrilled I was when Jason Howk told me about you. That you helped me out of kindness, like Jason, was incredible.

Jason Criss Howk! Thank you for everything you did. You never gave up on my constant emails and questions. You are a friend, coach, mentor, leader, amazing writer [Leaders Always Go a Little Further] and a brother to me. I will never, ever forget this, not even for a moment. You made this dream possible.

I'd like to thank and appreciate a former Assistant Secretary of Defense and combat Marine, *New York Times* bestselling author Bing West for his encouragement, strong support, and hospitality whenever I visited him. Bing West authored more than six books and his seventh and final book about wars in Iraq and Afghanistan is *The Last Platoon* as well as *New York Times* bestseller, *Call Sign Chaos* with Secretary of Defense Jim Mattis.

Thank you Lieutenant Colonel Magennis, Lieutenant Colonel Bankston, Command Sergeant Major Kevin Devine, Major Kerr, Major Gasperini, Sergeant First Class Flanagan, Captain Suarez , Captain Blume, Captain Renken, Staff Sergeant Benson, Captain Grosz, Captain Billig, First Sergeant Bolin, Captain Michael, Captain Adam, Sergeant First Class Eaton, Staff Sergeant Anderson, Captain Gross, Sergeant Stahle, and everyone else from 1st Platoon, C CO, 1-32 IN, 2nd Platoon, Battle Company, 173rd Airborne, [2-503D] and 2/327th No Slack, 101st Airborne.

Thank you to Laura Fister for reading and first editing my writing as well as being positive and encouraging. Thank you to Mary Hughes, Kris Power and the rest of the instructors from school who always encouraged and inspired me. Thank you to Michelle Benson, Katie Flanagan, Connie Gobin, Tabitha Devine, Dawn Brower, Marilee MG, Stephanie Devine, Amanda Rice, Elizabeth, Heather Anderson, Jenny Jordon, Jennie Mann, Mandy, Anthony Devine, Kylie Devine, Brittani Bauer, Zoe Hansen Kersey, Keith Kersey, Wendy Oliver, Chris Camacho, LaNeisha Emerson, and Kaitlyn Seaton.

Get the Terp Up Here!

27

And thank you to my brothers and best friends for life, Derrick Devine, Sam B. Hurd, Saleem, Nauzad, Yousaf, Fayaz, Aziz, Salim shah, Salih, Haqmal, Mursalin, my little buddy, Jackson Devine and Ajmal [Pre medical student].

Kevin Devine and Pat Flanagan, it is really hard to think of words to show appreciation and thanks to you guys, but I couldn't find any that would be strong enough to show my appreciation and fully recognize your services for both nations. I wouldn't be here today without your support, which means you saved my life. People ask me if I have a family in the states, and before I answer them, you, Kevin and Pat, come to my mind every time. I am absolutely proud to call you brothers.

I love you all!

At the very end, once again, thank you to my beautiful and kind parents, especially, my Momma. I am very sorry for being so naughty and a troublemaker, because I have to admit that I was not an easy kid to raise, but you were also a drama queen [kidding]. I am very blessed and grateful that I have both of you still living, kicking, and watching your feisty and naughty son pursuing a dream to become a medical doctor. It's your dream as well as mine because you always jumped the gun and called me a doctor while I had many years to go, even before I got my GED.

Nasirullah "John" Safi

Oregon, America

Ch 1: Secret English Lessons

My hometown was ruled by religious extremists, rather than by the government.

When American soldiers began arriving in town and at my school with supplies and humanitarian aid for families that were in desperate need, it was a golden opportunity for the *Mullahs* to spread their anti-American propaganda. "Americans are pigs and monkeys," Zarbaz would say during his daily lessons and teachings, spreading hatred toward Americans. I had never seen pigs and didn't know that a pig was an animal, but the word in Arabic, *Khanzeer*, meant "bad person".

"These are the signs of the end of the world," Qari Sami said during a Friday prayer. *Mullahs* were trying to scare people, and because of their teachings, some families refused to take anything from the American Provincial Reconstruction

Teams (PRT) while other villagers burned whatever they received.

Yet despite what *Mullahs* and other religious extremists told the public, many families received support from the Americans. PRTs became very popular, and many people who couldn't read and write in our own language (Pashto) became familiar with the term because it was widely heard and spoken among locals. We did not know what "PRT" stood for, but we knew that they provided us with assistance including construction projects that made big changes to the entire town. Many villagers were grateful, and we could not believe what our religious teachers had told us about them. Americans were not bad people. In fact, they were much nicer and more helpful than they were previously described by the *Mullahs*.

Even though animosity and anti-American propaganda were part of the daily teachings of many *Mullahs* at Madrasas and mosques, I began going to school to make my parents proud by becoming either a doctor or an engineer. My dad did not get along very well with Zarbaz, which I did not understand at first, but the reasons were crystal clear later on that he didn't like Zarbaz's teachings but couldn't oppose him. Zarbaz had deep roots and influence with people who believed in him and followed whatever he said and did. Since I was a kid, I believed everything he said, and I was scared that if I didn't listen, I might become a pig or monkey. As Zarbaz taught," Allah turned humans into animals when they refused to obey his teaching, principles and path."

I had to go to the Madrasa for some quiet of time because I had no other option for education. My father had taught history classes before I was born, but now he was home taking care of the farms for other people. It was not our farmland, but my parents had to take care of it in order to survive and feed the family of ten.

Everything changed when I encountered American soldiers at our school with school supplies, but I was still scared, "Don't shake hands with Americans or Allah will punish you in the hellfire," I remembered.

"The soldiers who came to my school were not pigs or monkeys. They were just like us but whiter," I told my father.

He laughed and replied, "Now, you know why I don't like, Zarbaz. He is a liar and very good at talking even with very little knowledge of Islam."

"Then why did you let me study with him?"

My father looked frustrated, but he always encouraged me and my siblings to challenge him with good questions because he liked the tough questions. "We could get in big trouble if I refused to send you study with him," he responded.

"The white-men had uniforms with weapons unlike AK47s," I told him. I recognized AK47s because almost everyone had at least one at their houses and fired them during wedding parties and in celebration of male births in town.

"I don't know about their weapons, but they must be American. With them, the Afghans who cover their faces were the translators," he assumed.

While we were talking, my oldest sister brought in green tea, and I thought our conversation was over, but it got even better when she jumped in. She was such a chatterbox and a favorite of everyone in the family because she was always helpful.

"What you two are talking about?" she asked my father.

"Nothing really, your brother saw Americans in his school today and was telling me about them."

She looked at me and said, "What about them?"

"Oh, they were not monkeys; they were just like us," I responded.

Both my dad and sister laughed. "Who said that they are monkeys?"

"Zarbaz and the Qari always talk about them this way."

"No, silly, did anybody talk to them?" she asked.

"Yes, there were two men, both with covered faces, translating into Pashto."

She looked at my father and questioned, "Why did they cover their faces?"

"To keep their identity hidden from the Taliban and people like Zarbaz. The Mujahidin did the same thing; they went after families of the government officials and ruthlessly killed and tortured the prisoners."

Even though, my father was not part of the communist government, he witnessed the atrocities carried out both by the communist government and the Mujahidin as well as the Taliban in the '70s, '80s, and '90s.

That day, I would have never thought that I would become an interpreter, working for the Americans one day, covering my own face to keep my identity protected and hidden from the Taliban.

"Don't receive their aid. It's from hell, and God will burn those in the Hellfire who receive it," the Islamic study teacher, Zabihullah, said during our Islamic study class. I had never seen him stay in the class or even in school when American soldiers were present. "The English language is the language of hell," he mentioned multiple times. "Arabic is the language of heaven."

Still, I continued to push to follow my dream of learning English. I was young and did not think much of risk, as long as I was following my dream and the lessons my parents taught me and my siblings. Otherwise, I would never understand the world and think freely and openly about outside of Afghanistan.

It became more difficult when English classes were thrown out of the school curriculum. There had been two English classes every week taught by a teacher who was also an assistant doctor. Unfortunately, he had to stop working in our school after receiving death threats. I was not lucky enough to study with him because his class was for high schoolers and I was still in elementary school. Without an English teacher at school, I started homeschooling with my father. He did not understand much English, but he could read and write the basics like the alphabet and names for some things.

My homeschooling was going well, but to stay out of trouble, we needed to be very careful and secretive. As the situation got worse, those who had any ties with the government or any other organizations being targeted by the religious extremists were attacked for being spies for American troops, but in reality, they were just teachers and farmers. The entire town was in fear of the Taliban and their brutality.

With every new word, I felt like I could speak the whole language, but with the basic phrases and grammar my father could teach me, I was not even close. I would have to find somebody with more English skills and knowledge.

My homeschooling ended while I was looking for someone else to teach me, but it took longer than I was expecting. My father taught me all he knew, but there was nobody in the village that I knew who could speak English and would agree to teach because everyone was scared to death by the Taliban. My oldest brother who always inspired and helped me, knew how badly I wanted to learn English, so he also looked for a teacher. As the popular English phrase goes, "teamwork makes the dream work," and I got the news around my 13th birthday. We do not celebrate birthdays, but I got the present that I was waiting for. My brother had talked to a man named Hamza from a nearby village. Hamza learned most of his English by working closely with American advisors back in the 1980s while they were supporting the Mujahidin against the Russian invasion of Afghanistan. Hamza was a farmer and a well-respected man in the village because of his service against the Russians. At first, he was not interested in teaching me because he did not want to lose his reputation or get into trouble. However, after many trips back and forth to his house and farms, he agreed to give me lessons if I would not tell anybody about him and the classes. I was super excited and could not wait to begin the English lessons that I had been fighting for.

There was always a challenge after challenge, but one way or another, I had to deal with it. I would now need to pay for the tuition, books, and other English related materials, of which I had none. There was also no way to find those books in our village. My parents had suffered far worse than I could imagine, and they were my role models, people that never felt broken, lost, defeated, or hopeless, even though they were the poorest in the entire town.

"I won't be around to see you fulfill your dreams," my mom always said. She suffered from various illnesses, including arthritis and cardiovascular diseases. She was a very strong woman and the one that the entire family counted on; she was the backbone of the family whom we couldn't afford to lose. She would make us all cry whenever she would mention that she wouldn't be around to see her kids growing and pursuing their dreams, goals and a life that they deserved.

Although I was not old enough to work, my family could not afford to take care of the expenses, so I had to figure something out to pursue my dreams. Since my new English teacher, Hamza, was a farmer, I thought he might need help with his farm. This was the only thing I could come up with, so I asked him if he was willing to teach in exchange for my help with his land rather than asking for money. I was not sure this would work, but it seemed a wonderful idea to him as his kids were too young to give him a hand. About 12% of Afghan land is arable and approximately 6% currently is cultivated. Farms in Afghanistan are different than in the U.S.; most Afghan farmers use bulls, shovels, and other tools to prepare their land, which grows about 95% of the needed wheat, rice and corn. I felt proud that I was about to do something that I had never done and would make my parents proud.

I couldn't wait to start and take English classes with Hamza, but I still had to go to school in the morning. My school was not far from Hamza's farm, but he couldn't set up a particular time to meet up because he was a farmer as well as a family bread-maker who had many other things that needed to be taken care of. Sometimes it would take me hours to catch him after school, waiting on his farm in the afternoon where I would spend a few hours working before our English classes. He had English books, old newspapers, and even magazines that he acquired throughout the years. He was such a wonderful, smart, kind and big-hearted man, and he appreciated the way I showed my trust and hard work. Even though I was young, he knew I was not going to betray his family and put their lives at risk.

"Safi, I am risking my life for you, because I know your father; he is a great man," he said one day.
"Thank you, we always talk about you at home," I responded.
He smiled at me and said, "Hopefully good talk."
"My mom is praying for you all the time," I added.
"That's what I need; we all need prayers. Tell her to pray for my father, he is not feeling well."
Hamza had cows, bulls, sheep, chickens, ducks and goats. It was fun working around the animals most of the time, but it was a pain when they were not in a good mood, running off because the farm had no fence. It was an absolute headache for both of us.

"Safi! Did you see the white and reddish-colored goat?" Hamza asked one day. Hamza had dyed his favorite goat with henna to be red, a common practice.

I was supposed to keep an eye on it, but somehow, I got sidetracked by the other animals and had no clue where his favorite goat had gone. It was the goat that he used for milk, but it was a troublemaker.

"She was just here," I responded.

"I hope she didn't go to the neighbor's property."

I felt very scared, and my body started shaking at his mention of the neighbor's property. His neighbor was not a good person. Hamza always trying to avoid him because he didn't get along with him very well, and they always fought and argued over nothing. I feared if something happened between them then I won't be able to take English with Hamza. I prayed that his favorite, naughty goat didn't end up in the neighbor's property. Luckily, we both found the goat on the neighbor's property, but he was not home. Otherwise, it would have been another day of conflict, argument and cursing. There was not a single day went by without some trouble, or suffering whether because of the animals or neighborhood fighting.

I never realized how stressed and anxious my parents were when I couldn't make it home on time due to a big load of work at the farm, and I had no phone to contact my family and give them a heads up in case I was late.

There was always something to do, but the full enthusiasm and encouragement of my family and the hard work and effort of my English teacher helped me to achieve my goal. Everything was paying off, and I was able to speak some

English, but I still had a long way to go. The more words I learned, the more I was interested in learning as much as I could in a very short period of time. I never knew when Hamza would change his mind or when something bad might happen so that I would not be able to take English with him. I knew that Hamza would never say "no" unless he found himself and his family in greater risk and danger from the Taliban.

That day arrived after about six months when a bunch of bad guys got killed during a night raid carried out both by Afghans and Americans in the Badil Valley, less than five miles away from my village. Badil is a remote valley of Tsawki district and was a hotbed and safe haven for many insurgents. It was Friday night around 1 a.m. Under a full moon, there were helicopters and jet aircraft flying over the entire valley. Although helicopters flew over our towns every day to supply American soldiers, it was unusual to watch helicopters with aircraft over the valley for hours. We didn't know what was going on, but my father thought that it wasn't normal. Even though it was early in the morning, we were scared and didn't sleep.

"Don't light it!" my father yelled at my mom.

She was going to light the candle because it was dark in the house. While my mom was talking to my dad, we heard a big boom and lightning came out of the valley. The helicopters fired at the nearby mountains across from the village, about 10 miles away from where we lived. I had gone to those mountains many times to collect firewood for the family. I knew where the helicopters fired; there were bunkers and caves that shepherds used for their animals. Once, I had used them for hide and seek games with other kids from the village while we were collecting firewood.

I went back to sleep after the helicopters were gone, but my father headed to the mosque for morning prayer as usual. When I woke up, my father was already back home and talking to my mom about people that were killed. While we were having breakfast, the loud speakers of the mosque went off for funeral ceremonies that were going to be held in the valley for the five insurgent that had been killed.

I didn't know what was going to happen to my English classes with Hamza. When I went to see him on Saturday for a new lesson and conversation, he was so scared and felt threatened that he didn't even want to see me. I couldn't blame him, but I was very disappointed. I left for home with the knowledge from his lessons over the past months. Hamza was a great man, brother and mentor to me.

Ch 2: September 11, 2001

"God gives sovereignty to whom he wants, and he takes sovereignty away from whom he wants. He honors whom he wills and humbles whom he wills." –The Quran

The old radio that my father had was the only source to learn, hear and understand what was going in the country and around the world. He loved his radio and treated it like one of his family members, keeping it clean and well-maintained. It was made in Japan, a model that lasted forever. The radio was already older than me when my father bought it from a villager. My mom always made sure to hide the radio from the rest of us while my father was gone because he would have been upset and angry if someone would have broken it.

My father, with his old Japanese radio, listened to BBC Pashtu broadcasts from Britain. He really liked the BBC and listened to it as much as he could afford to pay for the batteries. He listened to the news every morning and while he was listening, nobody could ever say a word because he was getting so into the news that you would think he was meditating. He loved to share good news with the rest of the family, friends and even villagers, but there was nothing good to share on September 11, 2001 with the heartbreaking and overwhelming news that the U.S. just lost 3,000 innocent men and women.

Even though many people in my village had no access to daily news reports or newspapers, everyone heard about the September 11, attack on the U.S. *Mullahs* became the reporters, apologists and propagandists of the attack. They used mosques and madrasas to preach that what happened in the U.S. was fair punishment from Allah on the *Kufar*, the infidels that deserved it. The man behind the attack was a Saudi-born, wealthy Arab, Osama Bin Laden, an honored guest of the Taliban regime. I was too young to understand what was going on, but 'Death to America and 'Long live Osama Bin Laden' with the Taliban white-flag was seen everywhere in town, at madrasas, schools, mosques, markets, stores, on cars and even on houses. Bin Laden became a hero, beloved by everyone. His name was chanted and praised by the Mullahs, local residents, students, teachers and of course the Taliban. Everyone, whether you liked them or not, started supporting and assisting the Taliban because they manipulated into believing in the jihad against the *Kafir*. I heard the word 'jihad' in the mosques and madrasas more than I could express here.

Nearly everyone celebrated what was called the "Jihad against Jews and Christians". People did whatever the Mullahs asked them to do; they celebrated "victory" by distributing sweets and candies. "Kill the *Yahood* and *Nusara*," became the shared call. All the while we didn't really know how to acknowledge the deep sorrow, pain and devastation brought to this part of the world.

Even though the Taliban had never taken the official responsibility, nor had they admitted that Osama Bin Laden and his operatives were behind the despicable and vile attack, the celebrations, charities and parties were held across the country by the Taliban themselves, their sympathizers, and Mullahs. Bin Laden, who was operating out of Afghanistan and who had fought the Russians alongside the Mujahidin in the 1980s, became hero, champion, victor and vanquisher for Muslims around the world after the September 11th attack.

***

I had noticed many airplanes in the sky above our town many times before the September 11th attack; they were easy to identify and flew high in the sky during winter, creating huge smoky clouds as tracks behind them.

"Dad, why is it making clouds," I asked one day while we were both sitting outside in the sun because the house was cold.

"Oh, it's the exhaust system like cars," he responded.

After the failure of the Taliban to hand over Osama Bin Laden and his Al-Qaida operatives to the United States in 2001, the sounds of those airplanes were never the same; they no longer flew during the day so I could watch the dense white smoke. They mostly flew at night with big sounds covering the entire region. It was the U.S.- led military strikes launched on Afghanistan. Yet, we didn't think that the Taliban regime was going to collapse after many years of brutalization and cruelty against their own citizens. Both physical and psychological fear remained among the people, but hard days and punishment were ahead for the Taliban. Mullahs turned the entire town into a "guest house" for foreign militants coming from Pakistan to fight the Americans.

I ended up staying home from school after the bombings, even though there was not a single school targeted during the entire operation. Still, I liked to go to the local market with my dad; it was just a few miles away from the house. He didn't like to go to the bazaar unless he needed something and that wasn't very often. My oldest brother usually did the shopping, but one day my dad asked," Do you wanna go to the store with me?"

"Of course," I responded.

"Ok, but I can't get you anything today," he said.

"I have my own money."

"Oh really, how much do you have?" he asked again smiling.

"10 rupees,[3]" I answered, "but Mom has my money." My mom always kept my money because she was the trusted family banker who would give you "interest" if she had it.

"Okay, get your money so we can head out," he said.

It was a beautiful sunny day that seemed pretty normal on the way to the market, but all that changed when we reached the bazaar.

A local Taliban commander, Mulawi Waliullah, who fought the Taliban from the beginning of the regime, and his fighters had taken over the entire town, urging people to join

---

[3] 10 Pakistani Rupees were probably equal to about 10 cents (USD), but it was a lot to me. Pakistani currency has been used in the country's provinces that are close the Durand line with Pakistan for years even though the government tried to ban its use. However, because many people who live along the Durand line travel back and forth to Pakistan without visa or other paperwork the currency has remained.

them in jihad because they were about to leave to fight the Americans. He and his fighters were equipped with RPGS, AK47s and machine guns, while walking around with speakers and chanting, "Death to the Americans, and long live Osama and Mullah Mohammad Omer." It was exciting for everyone except for my father because he had experienced many governments and suffered enough. It felt like everyone wanted to join them to get to heaven, get *Hoora* -the 70 virgins, milk, honey, all sorts of fruits and vegetables, meat and so on that they were taught and preached by the Mullahs" I was too young to realize that it was nothing but a struggle to keep the power for the brutal regime.

"Don't get fooled and trapped in their hooks! They are very smart when it comes to manipulating and brainwashing people," my father told me. "He was very brutal when he was the chief."

My dad was absolutely right. We couldn't trust them because they were going to do anything and everything for their own advantage and personal interest. I also learned that Waliullah had beaten many people in town and occupied their property, farms and even houses when he was the so-called Taliban chief in town.

His brutality came to an end right after Waliullah left on the 'Jihad' that he had promoted, and he never returned home. There was a rumor that he lost his life fighting the Northern Alliance forces. Yet, the propaganda against the Americans never stopped.

Students from nearby Madrasa were asked to protest in the support of the Taliban and Osama Bin Laden. As I returned to school, I saw my classmates, friends and teachers along with other protesters chanting and yelling who carried the slogan of "Death to America." My father and my brothers weren't there, otherwise I would have gotten in trouble because my dad never let us to become part or watch such things. But we kids did things despite the permission of our parents. Even though, I wasn't part of it, I still could get in trouble.

However, the protests didn't last long as the Taliban's supreme leader, Mullah Omar and his fighters lost control over 90% of the country in less than a month. Mullah Omar was the Taliban's supreme leader and commander in chief, who lost one of his eyes fighting the Russian soldiers in the '80s. He was named after *Dajjal* by many people due to his heinous and horrific crimes against the nation in the '90s.

"*Dajjal* will be a person with one eye, who will seek to convert people away from their faith, the true faith and beliefs and lead them to the devils and satanic beliefs. He will fight Jesus Christ and save the world at *Mahshar*, judgement day," my mullah taught.

Mullah Omar was not *Dajjal*, but the similarities whether his physical appearance or cruelty against the innocent men, women and children from different tribes in the country were apparent. He was the one behind every possible punishment, killing and destruction in the country while taking away equal rights, social justice, freedom of speech, freedom of living, human welfare and other universal principles from the nation that suffered for decades.

In October, 2001 became the year of change, freedom, justice, equal rights, democracy and prosperity for Afghans that had lived under constant torture and harassment for six consecutive years. The news that we hoped for and dreamt of came when the U.S. military intervened in Afghanistan through air and ground forces with the support of Northern Alliance and Uzbek militia force, commanded by General Dostum, to fight against the Taliban, Al-Qaida affiliates and those responsible for the September 11 attack. The beginning of the mission became clear when an aircraft targeted the Taliban's radio communication centers one night.

"Wake up, wake up!" my mom yelled at everybody. She thought it was an earthquake.

"It's not an earthquake," my father responded while my mom kept praying.

We made it out of the room to an opening in the house, but within seconds there was more shaking and a huge explosion. "It sounds like a bombardment," my father added. We were still out in the opening, shaking our cloths and praying. 'Shaking cloths' was a ritual during earthquakes; I don't know if it had any religious basis, but it was cultural practice.

My father grabbed his news radio to find out what exactly was going on. This had never happened before in my lifetime, but of course both my parents had experienced and survived airstrikes and bombardments. My father couldn't find anything on the radio, but he assumed that it sounded like an airstrike hit the Taliban's targets in Asadabad, Kunar, Afghanistan.

"Let's go back in, it's cold outside," my mom said. However, even though it was cold and late at night, we decided to stay outside, awake, rather than going back to the room. Whenever there was an earthquake at night, we preferred to stay out in the open because our house was old, made of stones and mud instead of cement. It could collapse at any moment, but we couldn't afford to fix it to turn it into a sustainable and reliable house.

"It's okay, we can stay out here for a little while and it's not too cold," my father responded. He thought that there was going to be more airstrikes and bombing because he was reminded of the Russian military's bombings and airstrikes in the '80s.

"Okay, I will start making tea then," my mom suggested.

"Don't make a fire outside," my father scolded.

"Okay, I wasn't going to," she said, but my father was only making sure that there was no light or fire out in the open because the Russian military targeted civilians while they were simply cooking or making fire to stay warm. We lived in a country without electricity, and wood fires were the only source of surviving during the winter.

It was a scary night; a night that brought my parents back to the '80s and '90s, when thousands of civilians including women, men and children were killed, tortured, immigrated, and disappeared. It was an airstrike that left everyone speechless the next morning.

I could tell that my father was anxious to find out what had occurred right after the strikes. "What is wrong with the radio? Don't tell me that you guys used it yesterday while I was gone," he looked at us angerly.

"I didn't use it," I responded.

"Nobody used it; I had it locked in the box," my mom assured him.

"Okay, but why is it not working?"

"I don't know," my mom responded.

Even though we were all scared to death, awake all night and tired, my father and oldest brother left for a village mosque for morning prayer as well as to find out what happened.

"Do you remember the big antennas that were installed on the hilltop?" he asked my mom after he returned from the mosque around 7:00 A.M.

"What antennas?"

"The ones right next to the village," my father replied.

"Oh, you mean the antennas by the public hospital?" My mom questioned.

"Not those antennas; I am talking about the ones up on the hilltop, used for radio communication. They are gone, completely gone," my father told her.

"Oh no, what about people living there?" My mom said with sadness in her voice.

"As far I know from people at the mosque, there were zero civilian casualties," my dad responded. "But the whole building surrounding the antennas was turned into a firepit. I heard that the windows, doors and some walls have fallen, but without any serious injuries to villagers," my dad explained.

My mom felt relieved and happy after she received that good news. The incident took her back to her childhood and young adulthood that had been spent in war, daily fighting and rocket attacks that caused bloodshed and where she lost her friends.

For the Taliban, the bombing was an excuse to convince people that Americans are evil. They did their best to lead people to assume that Americans killed innocents. Therefore, everyone should join them for jihad against the Americans. But, *Shariat Ghag* radio, the Taliban's propaganda machine, was hit badly and completely destroyed so that they could no longer easily promote hatred and anti-American propaganda. Instead, locals who had strong ties and friendships with the Taliban became propagandists, apologists, recruiters and justifiers of their inhuman acts and daily crimes. The Taliban religious police, who used to implement and enforce Sharia Law, became the main recruiter for the Taliban to enlist young people for their jihad. Mosques turned into recruiting centers across the country, even our mosque, where some villagers got caught in the Taliban's trap and never returned home.

When my father heard about other villagers, he was scared for us, that we his children might be manipulated by the mullahs and the Taliban religious police. He even talked to my mom about keeping her eyes on us to make sure that we didn't end up joining them. The mullahs and the Taliban religious police were masters at recruiting youngsters who had no clue about jihad whatsoever.

"Don't ever go to the bazaar by yourself. You need to tell me, your oldest brother or mom," my dad said after he found out that I went to the bazaar to see the Pakistani fighters who just arrived to fund, aid and assist the Taliban at the battle against the Americans. As I grew up, I learned that the Pakistanis were a main partner to the Taliban in establishing the Islamic Emirate of Afghanistan in 1996. Pakistani leadership, including former President Pervez Musharraf,

Get the Terp Up Here!

50

admitted during later interviews that, "the Taliban were his people, created, financed and aided by the Pakistani establishments since the beginning."

The Americans had also already landed in Afghanistan to fight alongside the Northern Alliance and General Dostum's militia forces against the Taliban. Even though Pakistan promised to ally with the U.S. military and the international alliance against the Taliban during Operation Enduring Freedom in Afghanistan, it continued to support and assist the Taliban. Hundreds of men equipped with AK-47s, hand-grenades, old-English rifles, rocket propelled grenades (RPGs), machine guns (PKM), swords, axes and knives arrived in our town. All donned a white headband with the slogan "Death to Americans".

Even thought my siblings and I were not supposed to go to the bazaar, I snuck out and joined other kids from the village to see the men from Pakistan. It was their first day and first stop before the long journey ahead of them. When I made it to the bazaar, it was over-crowded with vehicles parked everywhere and *Naats* [religious music] was playing loudly. There were new people that I had never seen it before and it was unclear if they would stay or leave. It was a small town; we had no restaurants, cafeterias or hotels so the Taliban religious police forced people around the villages to provide, food, water, blankets, cold weather provisions and a place to stay for the Pakistani fighters. The villagers and fighters didn't speak the same language; it seemed that the fighters were from Pakistani tribal areas and Punjab because they spoke Punjabi and Urdu.

I returned home after a few hours, very scared and anxious because I hadn't forgotten that my father told me not to leave the house. My father wanted the best for his family so he would get angry knowing that I hadn't obeyed. While at the bazaar, I had looked around the whole while, praying that I didn't see my father or my oldest brothers or I could get in trouble right there. And thankfully, none of them were home when I got back; they were still at the farm.

"Where did you go?" my mom asked.

"Playing games with Soorgul and Noorullah."

"Okay, but remember what you father said," she added.

"I do," I told her.

"What is going on at the mosque?" she asked.

"What mosque?"

"The summer mosque?" she questioned.

"There are a lot of people with knives, swords and weapons," I responded.

While I was talking to her, we heard someone knock on the door. "Go, see who is out there," my mom told me. As soon as I opened the front door, a small wooden door that could be broken easily, I was confronted by a man with black turban, long beard, a *dooray* rubber stick and AK-47, accompanied by our mullah.

"Where is your father?" they asked.

"He is not home."

Although he wasn't home, I thought they were here to arrest him. He had been arrested and jailed multiple times before.

"Let him know that I was here, and have him come to the mosque as soon as possible," the mullah said, and they left for another house.

"Go get your father," my mother told me. She had heard everything.

"Where is he?"

"He might be at the farm or the winter mosque," she responded.

We had two mosques for the village, a smaller mosque in the woods used during hot weather because it was shaded by trees, and the bigger mosque in the village known as the winter mosque.

My mom and I didn't know what was going on, but I had to go get him. I left the house, but after walking about 5 minutes, I saw him on way back home.

"*Daada!*" I called to him, "The Mullah with another guy was at the house looking for you."

"I know, I just saw him," he responded.

"They are not going to arrest you again?" I questioned him and he laughed and said, "No, not this time, but we have to make a lot of food."

"Why? It's not *Akhtar* yet," I stated.

"Every villager has to make food for the Taliban fighters that came from Pakistan," he said.

When we made it home, my mom was still anxious to find out what was going on. My parents couldn't figure out how to feed and provide blankets and winter supplies for the Taliban reinforcements, when they couldn't even feed their own family. Even though, they had to do what the Mullah and the Taliban commanded, my parents didn't provide anything.

We didn't have enough food at the house for ourselves. But By 7 P.M., my dad and oldest brother, Ahmad and I left to go to the mosque for evening prayer without food.

When we arrived at the mosque, other villagers were already waiting there with their meals, but some villagers were still arriving. "Salaam-alai-kum," my dad said to everyone at the mosque, peace be upon you.

The Pakistani-Taliban were sitting there, weapons right next to them, looking pretty silly but scary at the same time, I thought. The 20 or so men who stayed in our village were a mix of Pashtu, Punjabi and Urdu speakers. Not everyone could understand them, but my oldest brother, Ahmad, who used to work in Karachi, Pakistan could communicate. They ended up staying overnight at the village, keeping us all awake as they preached and prayed through the loud-speakers all night long, talking about battles that happened at the time of the Prophet. They didn't realize that they were going to encounter a different type of war, one against their terror. I found out that 1/3 of them were teenagers who had no clue where they were heading or what to expect.

The next morning after breakfast, again prepared by the villagers, the Taliban re-enforcements left my village to fight the Americans, the Northern Alliance and General Dostum's militia forces in northern Afghanistan. But before they left the village, the Taliban religious police and the mullah asked villagers to raise money to help the Pakistanis in their jihad. There were no rich families in the village, so they did not receive what they hoped. They left and never returned. There was news later that many of them were killed, captured, or jailed.

Ch 3: The Rise of the Taliban

"Allah will not change the condition of people until they make the effort to change it themselves first." --The Quran

Afghanistan had been in war, experiencing bloodshed and daily fighting for the last five decades. Generation after generation has witnessed and suffered horrible and heinous crimes, abuse, injustice, inequality and inequity.

"You are lucky that you didn't see what we saw," my mom always said. It made her emotional whenever she talked about it. Her eyes would become full of tears and looked like a garden pond, speaking to her innocence, suffering, heartbreak, and pain that words could never describe.

"*Maa*, I am very sorry that I wasn't there for you, to tell you that you were not alone. I wished I was born so I could talk to you, assure you, hug you and wipe off your tears. I would have told you that you were my role model, hero, rock, world, heaven and angel," I wanted to tell her. My mom always thought of us as the "moon and stars," the purest love that could never change. I owe her my entire life and she will always be the pride of the family and the life-changer of me and my seven siblings. She is wonderful, strong, committed, patient, tolerant even in conflicts, war and never-ending chaos.

It's true that I was not born in the '80s, but her daily stories and memories have been life lessons that I couldn't learn in school or anywhere else in the world. Because of that, I was glad to be a big part of her life during the Taliban's brutal regime that harassed my family for just being who they were.

I always share my mom's stories about the Russian with Westerners who want to know what life looked like during the invasion, civil war and under the Taliban. Her stories are wonderful; I love the way she explains things, her resiliency, ability to cope and optimism. Allah, in his divine power, gave her the strength to cope with crisis, chaos, challenges, and catastrophe both mentally and emotionally.

My dad would also share his experiences. "We felt lucky at the end of every day because it was chaos, bloodshed and atrocities throughout a country that needed to be changed. Change would be an urgent survival tool, tactic and way of life for the well-being and dignity of the people after the Russian withdrawal."

When the Russians left, the Mujahidin took over. The people believed them to be the translators of the dreams that everyone had for a better future and the guardian angels for their safety, but the Mujahidin turned the country into a battle zone, a nightmare and a ghost country in which many of its citizens got killed, tortured and lived with an uncertain tomorrow. This way of life continued under the Taliban's regime. They were a regime that didn't believe in human rights, self-determination, women's rights, equality, equity, respect and dignity for a people that already suffered so much. War is ugly and it's even uglier when you hear about it from witnesses like my parents who were the victims and the survivors.

"We got caught in the middle of a fight between the Taliban and the Mujahidin (Northern Alliance) force led by a local commander, Jandad Khan. We experienced our own death; we thought that we wouldn't make our way out, but Allah is great, and he saved us and we are thankful to him," my parents would recount.

Afghans hoped for a better future after the Taliban came to power in the 1990s. *Talib* means "student" in Arabic, and in Afghanistan, it refers to someone studying the Quran, Hadith and the related subjects, transcripts, principles and commands. When I was studied the Quran and the basics of Islam such as how to pray, communicate with elders, and so-on, first at the mosque in my village, and later at the madrasa, I was a *talib*.

This understanding of *talib* led many Afghans not to question the Taliban's rule. However, the Taliban manipulated the word, and they were fighters and murderers that tortured the innocent population, not obeying their own religion and its principles. As the Quran teaches, "the murder of one innocent life equates to the murder of the whole of mankind." Similarly, the saving of one life, one human equates to the saving of the whole of mankind."

I was playing with other kids when the Taliban entered our town and captured the district center from Jandad Khan, a local Mujahidin commander. It was the early afternoon when a rumor started circling that the Taliban were on their way to the district center from Jalalabad. Having no defense to fight the Taliban, Jandad Khan and his fighters ended up fleeing to Badil Valley, a nearby remote valley, in two pick-up trucks instead of facing the enemy force.

My mom rushed and grabbed my arm; even though there was no fighting yet, the rest of the villagers were shocked and scared. Those who experienced and lived through the Russians, the Mujahidin and the civil war like my parents and older siblings could predict the coming chaos. Unlike the civil war, the first couple of days passed by without conflict, but days, weeks, months and even years were ahead of us, and we couldn't tell what could happen. The initial fear and anxiety turned into anticipation when mullahs and locals from surrounding villages led appreciation ceremonies to welcome the Taliban, "our guardian angels." They received a very warm welcome and support from villagers who hoped for a prosperous, secure and bright tomorrow for themselves and their kids.

My father joined the others obligated to go meet the Taliban when they arrived at the district. He found that some of the Taliban did not even speak our language because they were from areas in Pakistan that spoke Punjabi and Urdu. He also started doubting that they would be able to capture city after city without any military training, background and familiarity with weapons. This first visit changed his mind about the Taliban, but he still hoped for a better future because he had no other option like the rest of the villagers. "You do or die," was the only option for many people. However, villagers who were former military officers and government officials during Dr. Najib's government knew that these Taliban operations required much more money than the support from the madrasas; the Taliban couldn't do it without both financial and military aid and assistance from Pakistan. Indeed, they came from Pakistan where thousands of madrasas operated under Pakistan's government.

"They are Pakistanis; you can tell from their broken accent, and some of them can't even speak Pashtu," my father said to my oldest brother Ahmad.

"Yes, I heard them speaking Urdu, and I even tried dialogue with them but seemed like that they were in hurry," Ahmad responded.

As a kid, you always get excited to encounter new things, situations and people. I was one of those kids who got over-excited to see the Taliban at the bazaar.

My father knew that I was going to sneak out of the house, so he had to make sure I had someone around in case there was a fight or a rocket attack, because you never knew. There were still more Taliban fighters coming to capture and occupy the rest of the province and its remote valleys. They had a long journey into very tough terrain along the Hindu Kush mountains, district centers, the capitol itself and other counties, waiting to be searched, cleared and occupied from the Mujahidin.

"I know that you are going to see them, but stay with Ajmal," my parents said. Ajmal is my second-oldest brother, who was a bit nicer and forgiving if I would make mistakes or caused trouble.

I ended up going with Ajmal and some other kids-- Soorgul, Noorullah, Zahidullah and so-on, to see where the Taliban was staying in town, about a 5-mile walk.

"That's them, right there!? Soorgul said.

"Where?" Noorullah asked him.

"The cars by the bridge," Soorgul responded.

"Oh, I see, there are so many vehicles," Zahidullah said. Zahidullah was a year or two older than I was but a very nice kid.

There were about 20 pickup trucks parked with more about to pull in; armed fighters rode on each pickup truck with AK-47, PKM, RPG, DShK heavy machine guns (*Dish-Ka* in soldier slang), ZPU, 82mm and some other weapons. Unlike the Taliban I had seen earlier with long beards, hair and turbans, the new fighters were different, some of them had no beard at all.

We stayed there for a little bit, watching the convoy of vehicles, and one of the Taliban fighters even gave us old, stinky socks while he put new ones on. I had never had socks, so I couldn't tell how disgusting they were. "Pray for us, pray, pray!" The Taliban fighters urged while they were taking off.

After that, it felt like it was a momentary gleam of light for the Taliban fighters to capture my town, province and almost 90 percent of the country. There was nothing, I mean, no government, institution, or military establishment to fight back or resist. It became a piece of cake when almost the entire territory fell into the Taliban's control; the Northern Alliance led small attempts at resistance, but there was no big fight.

At the beginning of the Taliban regime, the people were happy because it was secure and peaceful. There was no daily fighting, physical and mental abuse and harassment like that suffered under the Mujahidin and Russian-backed government in '80s. We couldn't know, however, what would happen after a few months of their regime. The Taliban, who were supposed to be guardian angels and protectors, turned out to be devils for a nation that had supported them. The religion, faith and belief that both sides shared and practiced for hundreds of years happened would soon be "modernized" to what the Taliban called "Wahhabism" in my town.

Wahhabism was an extreme faith and a new movement that was funded by an Arab Sheikh Muhammad Ibn Abdul Wahab. Sharia law was part of it, strictly enforced by the Taliban, who were mostly illiterate Pashtuns from southern Afghanistan.

Salafism, another form of Sunni-Islam was the main practice for the majority in my town, but it began dying and losing its followers right after the Taliban took over. It was a scary time, but there were some people like my father who weren't going to give up their old faith that had been practiced for centuries. As a result, he was kicked out of the mosque by a new mullah, Mussa Khan, a recent graduate of one of the madrasas in Pakistan. Mussa Khan was an extremist and a strong supporter of the Taliban.

The country started falling into chaos with every day passed. The Taliban destroyed many historic places such as Buddha in Bamyan province, shrines of saints, building and artifacts that described and interpreted our country's heritage, which had nothing to do with Islam whatsoever. The Taliban also began imposing their regime against the will and dignity of the people. Those who were not in agreement got tortured, sent to prison or even murdered. My father was one of the prisoners, jailed multiple times for no reason.

There was no place for women's education, and they could no longer leave the house without male escort and burqa. The Taliban became notorious for violence, sexism, inequality and inequity against women. "I am sorry but you can't go to school. I heard that Mussa Khan said that women had to stay home because women's education has no place in Islam," my father told my oldest sister. "I will do my best to help you all homeschool," my father said, but he was upset but couldn't do more. She was shocked after she heard this. "Okay" was all that she could respond after a few seconds, and you could tell that she was about to cry. My sister had dreamt of becoming a nurse but the was dream swept away as another victim of the Taliban's rule.

The *Amr Bil Maruf* and *Nahi Anil Munkar* religious police were brutal extremists who harassed men, women and children, prohibited music except *Naat*, their own music, tortured men for not wearing turbans or shaving their beards, forbade celebration of *Nawruz*, our new year that they considered an 'ancient pagan holiday'. The religious police forced people to pray, regardless of if they had prayed already. Sunni Muslims pray five times a day, but many were told to pray more if they were caught outside the mosque during the Taliban's regime. Some people decided to leave Afghanistan, but those who had no plans to leave the country, like my father, just kept praying for the collapse of the Taliban's brutal regime that was nothing but a dark chapter or fear, horror and daily tragedy.

Every empire eventually falls, and that's exactly what happened after five brutal years. In 2001, the Taliban's regime collapsed over the course of ten days. They would go from controlling nearly 90 percent of the country to nearly nothing, and many fighters including Pakistanis and Arabs who had been supported the Taliban for years were either injured or killed by the U.S.-led coalition force and local militia after the September 11th attacks.

Ch 4: The Turban Incident

"Hey, you! Where is your turban?!"

I was sitting in the far back of the classroom, huddled and praying, "Allah, *help me, Allah, help me.*" Even though it was not cold, my body began shaking and felt like I was getting hypothermia.

"I warned you that you all must have turbans by now," Ibrahim screamed. "Where is your turban? I don't want to hear any excuse." He looked at me like he was about to beat me with the wooden stick that he carried with him in the class. I couldn't talk and kept squeezing myself, expecting lashes to land on my back, arms and even head from the wooden stick because physical beatings were a daily reality for my classmates and me.

"My dad, my dad--" I was trying to respond to him.

"What about your dad?" he yelled at me.

"He is getting it today," I replied.

"Okay, good, I am not going to kick you out of my class today, but you better have your turban during my class." Everyone felt relief that we didn't get corporal punishment that day, I knew that I needed to get a turban to remain out of trouble.

Wearing a turban has been a big part of Afghan culture and tradition, but before the rise of the Taliban, if you were young or someone that could not afford to purchase one, it was okay. Nobody would ever bother you or ask questions. And today, it is choice whether or not to wear one. However, under the Taliban's regime, wearing a turban was mandatory for students attending madrasa or school as the Taliban wore turbans themselves as part of the government uniform. Many *Taliban* religious students found themselves in a hopeless situation. Many families like mine couldn't afford turbans as we struggled with basic needs of for our daily survival but we also couldn't afford the physical and mental punishment of the ruthless regime of the Taliban.

"Dad does not have money to buy turbans for us," my brother Sahil said. "He is still trying to pay off the money he owes to the shop." Sahil is my third-oldest brother; he is only a year older than me, and we were partners in crime, troublemakers and best friends but also competitors and rivals sometimes.

"Okay, I am going to ask *Abai*," I responded while knowing that my mom also wouldn't have the money.

"I will do something," Sahil said, but he didn't tell me what he was going to do.

We had already been kicked out of the school once, and our father went to jail for a couple of days after a local mullah, Gul Nabi, made multiple complaints against him not sending us to a madrasa or attending the mosque daily himself. These were all baseless accusations because the mullah just didn't like my father. My father was tortured by the Taliban's religious police who kept him in a small, rusty and muddy room that was underneath the guard tower in the district center. He was not even allowed to receive visitors, not that my mom would let us to see him because she was scared that we would end up going to jail too.

He got out, but it didn't mean that he was a liberated man, free to live a life without fear, harassment, and anxiety. He could go back in at any moment because of false charges. Many innocent villagers became victim to daily punishments and revenge from the religious police on behalf of mullahs and other villagers who were either the Taliban or strong supporters. If mullahs didn't like someone, all they needed to do was file a written or verbal complaint against them, and they would be taken care of by the Taliban because there was no civil, criminal, or any other court of law that could decide the matters. The accused were assumed guilty, arrested and suffered physical beatings before being dragged to jail like an animal.

Because we couldn't afford turbans, my brother and I ended up going to a different madrasa about five miles farther than the one in town to make sure that my father didn't go back to jail. The new madrasa was very popular and run by Mullah Dr. Talib. He had great influence within the Taliban, but happened to be stricter when it came to turbans. We thought he could help us because my entire family was broke, and was going through some tough financial times. We were not the only family in town with these problems, at least two families out of three had financial problems.

"How is the new madrasa?" my father asked us.

"It's okay; some kids don't have turbans," Sahil responded.

Get the Terp Up Here!

69

"How is Dr. Talib? Is he nicer than the other teachers?" my dad asked.

"He was very nice when you came with us on the first day," Sahil said with a big laugh.

"*Dadda*, if he is a doctor, why is he teaching at madrasa?" I jumped into their conversation.

"I don't know, and I don't think he is a doctor," my father told me. "I will find out for you?"

"I am trying to borrow some money, but it's very hard nowadays," my father added.

My father was a very trusted, intelligent and noble-hearted man, it was not a matter of honesty, and kindness, rather it was a matter of money that pretty much every villager did not have. So the clock was ticking, and I was still waiting on my brother, Sahil to figure out a solution like he said he would.

"We are going to steal it," Sahil said to me.

"What do you mean, we are going to steal it?" I asked him.

"Don't tell *dadda* or *abai*, but I noticed that there are trucks driving through the town that had the same materials hanging from them."

"Okay, but they are not turbans," I responded.

"I know, but we can make turbans out of them," he said.

I was curious how he would make turbans out of the pieces of cloth that were dangling off the trucks coming from Pakistan, but I just went with him this time without even thinking. He always talked me into things, even though he got me in trouble with my parents while he always got away with it.

We had to wait because we never knew when those trucks would arrive at our town, but we lived very close to town and we could see the trucks from our house. We also decided to spend more time in town without letting our parents know. They would never ever let us steal something even though my father had jailed, physically beaten and harassed by the Taliban.

Days passed, but we couldn't find the trucks that we were looking for. Finally, after a couple of weeks, a few trucks came, customized and decorated with paintings, beautiful calligraphy, ornamental décor, wooden carving on the truck doors, metal and plastic chains, pieces of jewelry as well as cotton and wool made materials that looked like turbans.

"This is it; it's the truck with the wool that I can turn it into turbans," Sahil said. The trucks were parked right by the district center, a location where the Taliban operated.

"We can't do it here, too many people, the Taliban and the store owners," Sahil said.

"I am scared, *dadda* is going to kill us if he finds out," I responded.

"Don't worry, I got this," Sahil said.

I was surprised by the way he reassured me and showed his self-confidence. You would think that he had stolen through his childhood, but he hadn't because we were scared to death of our father. He had no mercy or sympathy when it came to stealing.

"Let's wait for the trucks to leave the district, town and crowd," Sahil added.

We were about to do something that could lead us to lose our hands based on the principles of Sharia and that would cause shame and humiliation for the family. We knew that we were lying to our parents, risking their distrust, but we didn't think like adults. Sahil and I were about to take actions that could get us in a terrible situation and have consequences for my father, who could go back to prison and serve an even longer time.

It was a dirt road with thousands of holes and speed bumps, caused by rain, floods and trucks coming from Pakistan and Jalalabad. Trucks couldn't drive faster than 10 miles per hour. We were both young and great runners so we would be able to catch the trucks. That gave us an upper hand and opportunity to break into the trucks and get the turbans.

However, the trucks that we were waiting on left the district at night so we couldn't catch them. We also could no longer go to town every day to wait for more trucks to arrive because my father needed help at the farm.

It was not our farm and land; it belonged to one of the other villagers. For caring for it, my father received a portion of wheat, corn and rice that was harvested. Years ago, my parents had also been able to buy a cow that became the main provider for the family for milk, yogurt and butter. The cow was absolutely loved by everyone in the family, but we didn't know that my father had decided to get rid of her so he could get turbans and whatever else that we needed for madrasa.

"Don't sell her," I pleaded.

"I will get another one, once we make some money," my father responded.

"Can we just borrow some money from Ayaz *kaka*?" Sahil asked.

"I did ask your uncle this morning, and he refused to lend any money even though I told him that how badly we need it," my father responded.

We were all sad when my dad finally sold the cow to a local butcher. The butcher tried to give us some meat for free after he killed her, but my dad refused to take it. We didn't receive a lot of money, but my dad was able to pay his loan, bought us turbans and did other shopping for the family.

We finally rejoined the rest of the kids, and continued to study religious books with Dr. Talib.

Ch 5: My Father and the Taliban's Jail

Although the air was cold, the radiant sun felt great during the winter days.

"Grab the carpet and let your mom know to make some tea," my dad said while he was holding his small toolbox, heading outside from the house.

"Let your father know that we are out of green tea, but I will make black tea," my mom said.

I headed back out to help my father with the carpet, but he already gotten it. It was a small plastic carpet and one-third of it was gone, but it was still better than sitting on gravel. My father was now busy setting up his watch repair kit that had very tiny tools.

I chatted with my father while he fixed his old wrist watch under the winter sun. "I bet your mom got busy, but the tea must be ready by now. Do you want to go check on her and bring the tea with you?" He asked.

He was right, my mom always got sidetracked. She was a mom of five kids, four boys and one girl that meant lots of housework. She could get lucky some days if one of my siblings would help her, but that didn't happen very often.

"She was washing our clothes and waiting on me to get the tea," I told my dad.

"It's fine, fill half of the cup for me," my dad said.

"It's hot."

"Be careful, use my *saadar*," he responded. It was a big scarf that people use in Afghanistan like a robe in winter.

"*Dadda, Dadda, Dadda!*" We both looked around to find my brother Sahil because we knew it was him calling. My dad leapt to his feet, ready for trouble. Sahil was running to the house, but when he saw us, he headed to us yelling, "Taliban, Taliban!"

"What happened? What's going on?" my father kept asking him. But all Sahil could say was, "Taliban, Taliban."

"They are in the village," Sahil finally responded.

"Okay, calm down. They are probably there looking for someone," my father replied.

The Taliban religious police would never come to the village if there was no arrest or issue. They could be looking for anyone in the village, but it became obvious that we should worry when we saw them walking over to our house.

"Get everything in the box and bring it in," my father said before he went to the house to speak with my mom. I was crying, unlike Sahil, but I could tell that he was scared to death because my father was going to jail again for the reasons that we would never understand. We started putting all tools back in the repair kit when a man with a long beard and a turban reached us and demanded, "Call your father; we just saw him go in." The man had a different accent but spoke Pashtu. He had a mustache and beard that covered his whole face. The man was not by himself; he had a whole company of people, including the mullah from our mosque.

"Don't worry, I will be back," my father said when we encountered him at the door. "Let your mom know that the repair kit needs to be locked up. I have small pieces in it that I don't want to lose."

It was a bad day, a day that I cried my eyes out for my dad. They took my father without crime or fault on the day that we all enjoyed the winter sun right outside of our house.

"He didn't do anything, he is coming back home," my mom said.

But it didn't help me nor my siblings, we were so upset, heartbroken, and confused.

"Why am I going with you?" I heard my dad ask one of the Taliban, but they didn't respond. Instead, they beat him constantly with wooden sticks and rubber strips; they kicked and slapped him while we watching him from the house. They called him a communist, *Khalqi*, *Parchami* and so-on, names used for people who supported Russian-backed government in the '80s. My mom tried to keep us inside the house, but I was still able to see him from the side of my mom where she thought that I couldn't see my dad. She did her best to hold me in her arms and cover my view, but I could hear every scream from my father.

My father never found out why he had been arrested, and he never talked about what he suffered while he was in the district jail. All he told us was that he was in a tiny room, underneath the guard tower.

"Could you sleep?" I asked him after he got out.

"Not really, it was pretty small, and the room was wet and never cleaned," he responded.

I bet that living in such a room was a huge physical and psychological punishment, but the Taliban did not believe in any rights that could protect prisoners. My dad was a mess after serving his time in the world's toughest, worst, dirty and brutal jail. It was only a few weeks for him, but it would seem that he spent the rest of his life in jail because he became seriously ill. The effects never ended; he was arrested for living a life of freedom and was tortured, like many other villagers, just for living their daily lives with their family and friends.

It wasn't the last time he got arrested. Later, he got locked up with my brother after they defended themselves during a fistfight with someone closely related to a local mullah. My father was also asked to reaffirm the five pillars of Islam by the Taliban's religious police who thought themselves the true teachers of Islam.

Ch 6: Our New Home

In 2001, I travelled to Jalalabad with my sick mom. Jalalabad City was not the same city that my parents had talked about. In 2001, Hazrat Ali, former Mujahidin, with his fighters were pushing towards the city while some Taliban and Al-Qaida operatives were still holding the city. We expected that we might get caught in the fight between the Taliban and militia forces because there were already Mujahidin checkpoints along the highway where they were looking for Taliban and Al-Qaida operatives that were on the run.

"Where are you coming from?" a man with an RPG on his shoulder asked our driver. Our driver looked scared, and I could see his face began changing color, "Kunar," he said.

"What part of Kunar?" the Mujahidin fighter asked.

"Chaghasraya [Asadabad]," he responded.

"Who is in the burqa?"

"I believe his wife," the driver said and pointed to a man next to a woman in burqa.

"Yes, she is my wife," the passenger responded.

My mom didn't have a burqa, but she covered her face with a *saadar*.

"Okay, have a safe journey," the Mujahidin said.

The militias were making sure that the Taliban and Al-Qaida affiliates were not sneaking through the checkpoints by wearing burqas.

A few days after our arrival, my brother decided to go to downtown Jalalabad to find a walk-in clinic where we could take my mom. Jalalabad City was still partially under the control of the Taliban so most places, including businesses and even *Sehat Ama* public hospitals were closed, and the whole city looked quite dead.

"Is your brother back yet?" my mom asked.

"Not yet, *Abai*," I responded. I knew that she was worried about my brother and didn't want him to go to downtown Jalalabad in the first place.

"I am praying that he is okay. It was bad when we came to the city couple of days ago," my mom said.

"He is going to be fine; he is a grown man," my aunt responded to her.

"I know he is going to be fine, but it was crazy along the highway and even in the city when we came," I added.

"We love you, Shereen Gul, and Ahmad, we love you even more," my aunt said.

"He is a great man, my baby," my mom smiled.

While they were talking, I began playing *toop danda*, a game like baseball with my cousins outside of the house. "*Lala, Lala,*" I shouted when I saw my oldest brother walking to the house. He looked terrified and panicked.

"What is going on? Are you okay?" my mom asked him.

"I almost got hit by two pickups with Arabs that had PKM machine guns, AK47s, grenades, RPGs and Dish-Ka on the top of their trucks, driving in Chawki Mukhaberat," my brother responded.

"What were they doing there?" my uncle asked him.

"I don't know, but I saw that one truck picked up some groceries while the other one parked there watching everyone," Ahmad responded. I could tell that he was still scared. "They didn't care that they almost hit anyone close by when they took off," he added.

"My sister is feeling much better now, and I think we need to stay home for now; don't go downtown," my uncle said. "I heard, Hazrat Ali's *Shaari* militias are going to steal and loot everything they can right after they capture the city," he added. He was right; as soon as the Mujahidin fighters entered the city, they celebrated their victory by stealing and looting people's property, shops and even houses.

As the entire city fell into the hands of former the Mujahidin fighters, various commanders controlled different parts of the city. Those commanders had a long history of the disputes and hostility that could lead them into another battle in the city. By then, the Taliban and Al-Qaida were pretty much gone and consolidated in Torah Borah. Torah Borah, "the Black Caves," is part of the Spin Ghar, an area of white mountains, always covered with snow, about 20 miles from Jalalabad City and approximately 30 miles west of Khyber Pass and 6 miles to the north of federally administered tribal areas, which had been a very famous complex built for the Mujahidin back in the '80s when they fought against the Russians. Torah

Borah consisted of many different sized caves where Al-Qaida members were believed to be hidden including their leader, Osama bin Laden in 2001.

After my uncle told the family to stay home, we decided to spend as much time as we could in the house, but the assaults of the militia forces weren't limited to the city. They ended up patrolling neighborhoods with no official uniforms and with AK47s, PKMs and RPGs on every street and corner of the city. "Do not open the door to anyone," my uncle said.

"Can we play outside?" Ihsan, my cousin, asked his mom.

"I don't know. You should have asked your dad this morning," she responded.

"He was gone when I woke up this morning," Ihsan said.

"Okay, but if he gets back and you guys were still out there, he is going to get angry," she said.

"Okay, can we play here in the house then?" Ihsan asked her.

"Yes, but no *toop danda*. We still haven't fixed the window glass that you guys broke the other day. I lied to your father because he wanted to know what happened," my aunt told him.

Ihsan looked at me and said, "let's wait for my dad to come back."

In the evening, my uncle arrived home with groceries and firewood. Ihsan and I helped him take them into the house, and after we got done, we both asked him, "can we go outside and play?"

"Yes, but be careful. There are a lot of vehicles driving out there," he said.

While we were playing, there were many pickup trucks, full of fighters, driving back and forth on the highway, but we didn't know what was going on. It was getting late and dark, but we were continued playing until my aunt shouted at us, "this is it, boys, it's getting late. Come in; I am locking the gate."

We went home for dinner, but couldn't talk because everyone was listening to the news on the radio when we arrived. "There is fighting going on in Torah Borah," my uncle said. They were still listening to the news and having green tea when I fell asleep.

I woke to a huge explosion that shook the entire house.

"*Ya, Allah Khair, Ya Allah Khair,*" my mom was praying while holding me in her arms.

"Shereen Gul! It's bombardment!" My uncle called. While he was talking to my mom, there was another explosion that was even bigger the last. Within minutes, we also heard the sound of aircraft flying over the city.

"It's almost morning pray time," my uncle said. It didn't look like he or my brother would get sleep that night.

"Ahmad and I am going to the mosque," my uncle added.

"Okay, be careful! Those aircraft are still flying over there," my mom told him.

"The jets are flying over Torah Borah. There is a big operation backed by U.S. air and ground forces along with Afghans going on right now," my uncle said.

When they returned from the mosque, my brother asked, "did you see the soldiers in the pickup trucks?"

"Yes, they are Hazrat Ali's men," my uncle responded.

The fighting didn't stop for almost two weeks, and when it did, the world's top terrorist and mastermind behind the 9/11 attack, Osama Bin Laden remained alive and hidden.

2007

My childhood friend, Wahid, and his family were mercilessly murdered by the Taliban while they were asleep in their house at the end of 2006, a little while after the US-Afghan operation against the insurgents in Badil Valley. The Taliban not only shot Wahid in the head, chest and heart, but they also stabbed him.

I couldn't believe that Wahid was gone; we grew up together and had been friends since childhood, but terrorists took him and his family. Wahid saw and suffered so much since he was born. He lost his father during the Soviet invasion along with other family members. I remember him saying that he was going to be an engineer so that he could take care of his mom, younger sister, uncle and grandma, but his dream was buried in blood, all over in his room, door and windows. How in the world could someone do that? Did they have a heart? Did they have no mercy, humanity or sympathy? There were many questions after Wahid's death, but I never found the answers.

Get the Terp Up Here!

84

I wished that Wahid could feel everyone's pain and heartbreak after he got killed. I and the rest of the kids-- Bashir, Haroon, Baseer, Iftikhar, Idress and Yosaf missed him every day and still do. I knew that he was high up watching us, but it was the saddest and darkest day for everyone at the village and a new beginning for me and my family.

"Jalalabad is a nice city with more schools and English courses," my dad told me. I had been to Jalalabad multiple times when I was a kid, but we would soon find out it was a different city than in 2001.

"We can't live here anymore, the Taliban just killed an entire family," my mom explained.

"It was a tragedy and no parents or relatives are going to see their beloved ones die," my dad responded. "Oh, I just sent a letter to, Mustafa, your uncle, to ask if he could help us find a house close to his family," my dad further added.

"I was going to ask you that," my mom replied.

"I knew you were going to," my dad said smiling.

By 2007, with the threats increasing, my family decided it was time to leave my birth village, Tsawki, in Kunar Province and relocate to the city in Jalalabad. We would not receive threatening letters from the Mullah, and we would be away from the violence. We could blend in there. But leaving was way harder than we thought. We didn't know if we could ever come back to visit or live in Tsawki. It was unbelievably hard because I missed my friends and the place where I was born and grew up with many memories of milestones.

In the country, you live. You build a house. You feed your family. You gather wood nearby to heat your home. It's a simple life, one of basic survival. Life in the city was completely different for us. There was rent, and other bills to pay. We were a country family, not at all prepared for life in the city. It was very complicated in the beginning.

When we arrived at Jalalabad city it was much safer but not as cheap as my hometown, but at least we could survive with no more death threats from the Taliban.

Despite the fighting, I was excited to go back to school and continue and resume my English courses, but I forgot that tuition and everything else that my family needed to survive would not be free like my hometown. I couldn't afford tuition and neither could my family. I kept self-studying to make sure I didn't forget what I had learned during my six months of lessons with Hamza. I remembered the lesson that my parents taught me and my siblings, that "life has ups and downs, but there is always a solution with patience, tolerance and stamina."

That's exactly what happened when life unexpectedly turned around. I managed to go to a very good government school in 2007. Later that year, I was able to get into free English and computer programs provided by a non-governmental organization (NGO), known as Mediothek that was supported by the Germans. In addition, my school in Jalalabad was a couple of miles from Forward Operating Base Fenty, a U.S. military installation, where I could practice English with American soldiers without being at risk whenever they stopped by my new school. Life sorted itself out and got easier; my brothers got jobs and my family began getting on its feet. While I missed my friends back in my hometown, I was glad that I could fulfill my dream of becoming bilingual and obtain what I was struggling and fighting for so long.

Ch 7: Brave by Default

Summer in Jalalabad boasts daily temperatures above 120 degrees. So I, like most American kids, was in my three months of summer vacation from school. Kids who could afford to take summer classes did so in order to prepare for the next year, but those classes were private, requiring tuition. Since we could not afford that, I would have to find work.

My uncle knew a lot of people in the transportation department of the government and heard of an opening for a computer operator. I didn't know much about computers, but even knowing how to type was more than most government officials knew.

"There is a job vacancy for someone knows a little bit computer," my uncle told my mom.

"What is computer?" My mom asked.

"I don't know much about computers, but I know it types writing," my uncle told her.

"Okay, but I don't know if he can do it," my mom said pointing at my father.

"I am not talking about him, I am talking about Nasir, my uncle responded. He looked at me and said, "If you want the job, I can help you get it because I know everybody there."

"Yes, yes, I do want it," I told him, "but what about school?"

"They only need you for a couple hours a day even after school," he replied.

"Okay, I want it."

Technology of most kinds is new and largely unknown to the people of Afghanistan. The work of the government was done by hand on paper. The U.S. government and NATO partners had provided millions of dollars for computers and other technological advances to help modernize Afghanistan's government processes, but there were still only a few offices with computers in them. Much of the equipment was lost, stolen or sold on the black market. Other equipment would sit in offices, unused, for years becoming filled with dirt and serving no useful purpose except as homes for mice and insects.

I found myself in just such a place, but I was happy to have work to help pay for English and computer classes. The office looked like a dumpster. There were bags and huge piles of handwritten documents all around. You could hear animals scurrying across the floor in and out of the piles. I was young and had never stayed overnight without my family, but I was asked to do night shifts at least three nights a week. When I shared my concerns about the night shifts with my family, they agreed that I should quit working there immediately. It wasn't appropriate for me to be away overnight in the company of adult men. Even if nothing bad happened to me, I would be viewed badly for doing so in a society where people can be judged as a criminal based on gossip alone. My new job lasted less than a week. I never went back.

It took quite a bit of time for our family to stand on its own. My father was old by Afghan standards. At home in Kunar Province, he was still able to work on others' lands. In Jalalabad, there were lots of young men looking for work and woefully few jobs to be filled. As per our culture, the responsibility for our family was left in the hands of my oldest brothers. One of my brothers opened a tea house in the city where I worked part-time for him, delivering tea to stores and shops in the city. This was a challenging job because of the cultural history of *chai boys* and *Bacha Bazi* related to pedophilia and tea sales. "*Salaam,* how are you, cutie boy?" was something I heard whenever I had to deliver or bring tea to stores and businesses around town. "I will pay if you just stay here with me," one of the shopkeepers always offered.   We did not make a lot of money in order to support a family of ten so my second oldest brother, Ajmal, also searched for a job.

Ajmal had already finished high school and wanted to be a teacher, but pursuing his dream wasn't an option given our urgent need for money. It was easier and quicker for him to help provide for the family by becoming a truck driver. He was stationed in Jalalabad and delivered supplies like food, water, wire, wood and heavy tools to American soldiers in Laghman, Kunar, and Nuristan Provinces. It was a well-paying job, and he was happy to help his family, but the risk was way greater than he initially imagined. He knew the danger of the job that could possibly kill him but he has chosen to do it for his family.

It is not uncommon in Afghan culture for family members to support each other in their work. Having quit my job and while still looking for a new one, I decided to help my brother with his. I couldn't drive, but at least I'd be able to help him with his loads. My brother got a call from his manager the night before, informing him that he'd be transferring water and Meals Ready to Eat (MREs) from Jalalabad Airfield (JAF, Forward Operating Base Fenty) and Asadabad (ABAD, FOB Wright) for the soldiers at Combat Outpost Korengal (KOP).

Korengal Valley is located in northeastern Afghanistan. Referred to as "the Valley of Death" by American soldiers, it is the area where most of the fighting and casualties in the war against terror have occurred. Aside from the deaths of coalition forces and members of the Afghan National Army, many locals were captured and executed by insurgents because of their work for the local government and American soldiers. Others were maimed and sent back to their villages as a warning to others. If these marked men were caught a second time, they would be executed.

My brother understood the danger of tomorrow's work. I did not. More than anything, I was excited to go back to my birth province. I missed my home and the other kids like crazy. Even if I could not go and visit the village where I was raised, at least I'd be able to see it by driving by.

It was important for us to be on time as there was only one escort available each day to protect the Afghan locals who worked for the American soldiers. My brother's goal was to make it to Forward Operating Base (FOB) Fenty in Jalalabad city by 9:00 A.M. to get our loads. Arriving later meant that we couldn't get on post and had to wait until the next day.

We got on post after having ourselves and our truck searched and got loaded by about 11:00 A.M. Our truck, and more than ten others, were loaded and finally ready to leave for Kunar Province. Only a few of the trucks were going to Korengal Valley. Ours was one of them.

"We did it, we did it," Ajmal said, cheering up and celebrating with his friends who were the other truck drivers. But we had a long journey a head of us. A journey that could cost us our lives or leave us with serious injuries and disabilities.

Attacks on supply convoys via ambush or improvised explosive devices (IEDs) were common. The trip between FOB Fenty and FOB Wright would have taken an hour or two on any other road, but not this one. This road felt like it had a million holes. Parts of it had been destroyed by natural disasters, other parts by Taliban mines and IEDs. We passed several places where insurgents were known to hit American and Afghan forces. We weren't sure if it was luck or if the American soldiers had kept us safe that day, but we were grateful to finally arrive safely, more than five hours later, at FOB Wright. After a day of fear and rough riding, everyone needed a break, including the trucks.

"Everybody here?!" An Afghan interpreter shouted after we parked.

"Tell them we are gonna get you when we leave," an American soldier said. "Hold on-- tell them, DO NOT leave without us," he further added. He was a white soldier, maybe in his late 20s, with a rifle hanging by his side, but I couldn't tell his rank.

"Okay sir, okay," the drivers responded.

"*Turjaman sahib*, can you ask him when we will leave?" One of the drivers asked the interpreter.

"I don't know, but we will come get you," the soldier replied.

We awoke from our rest at about 3:00 A.M. We had another twenty or so miles in our journey, through a very hostile area known to be Taliban-dominated and a hotbed of insurgent activity. Before we left, we were briefed to avoid using headlights as much as we could.

"Tell them no headlights," a soldier said, not the same soldier we talked to earlier.

"Okay," the drivers responded. Many of the drivers had learned the 'thumbs up' sign. They used it for every answer even if they didn't know the question.

The Taliban usually chose to attack during daylight, but they could easily target whatever they could see. It was a full moon, and we could see the road clearly even without headlights or night vision goggles.

Although there was road clearance team ahead of our convoy, tasked with disposing of any explosives we might encounter along the road, most everyone was expecting an ambush. At about 4:00 A.M., the lead truck was hit by an IED. Our convoy stopped so the damaged vehicle could be removed, stuck on the road in the middle of nowhere. It seemed to take forever. The drivers talked among themselves, anxious to move again before daylight in hopes of avoiding more attacks.

I remember looking around, noting the farm land alongside the Pech River, admiring the nearby valleys, which were beautiful but known to be deadly. There were two more similar attacks on the road that night. We finally arrived at Combat Outpost Michigan, which guarded the entrance to the Korengal Valley, about 1:00 P.M. the next afternoon.

An American soldier with his interpreter gave us our instructions. "This is it, the Americans don't drive into the valley," he said.

"*Turjaman sahib*, tell him it's dangerous," the drivers said to the interpreter after he translated.

"I know; there are going to be aircraft watching the trucks," he replied. "Tell them to be safe out there," the American soldier added and left with his interpreter.

Five trucks, including ours, were to drive into Korengal without an American escort. The soldier explained that we'd be on our own, but that there were Apache helicopters and jets that would be flying through the valley that day. This was good news. Taliban insurgents were afraid of helicopters. They were less likely to be active while helicopters were in the air.

I listened to the other drivers talking while my brother inspected our truck and made the last of our preparations. An old man in his 60s told of his last trip into Korengal, "There was a convoy of eight trucks headed to the Outpost with helicopters flying over the entire way. One of the trucks broke down, and the driver had to stop to fix it." The old man laughed and said how lucky the driver was that he did not get killed and the truck burned.

Another driver said that he wouldn't take such a risk if he had any other way to make money. Another responded that it wasn't possible to make as much money as they were without doing this job. Yet another spoke of his sadness in seeing little kids working to support their families, saying that he would never allow his kids or wife to ask other people for money.

One of the drivers asked if anyone had any Taliban music they could play along the way. None of the drivers liked the music, but they often played it in hopes it would help garner sympathy if they were stopped. Like my brother, these proud men were doing what they had to do in order to support their families. They were brave by default. Everyone wanted to share their stories and tell what they were planning to do after the trip, but it was getting late in the day, and my brother told everyone, "it's time to go; it's better to leave."

The road was rough dirt with many holes and rocks. Aside from the threat of an insurgent attack, even a small driving mistake could lead to death. It was when we started out along this road that my brother began to explain to me what might happen to us. The Taliban often sets up illegal checkpoints along the short road between Combat Outposts Michigan and Korengal. He told me about his two friends that were captured and had their ears and nose cut off for working with the Americans.

When I asked why he had not explained this to me before now, he said it was because he didn't want me to be afraid. It was much too late for that. My brother was already married. It wouldn't matter so much for him if he lost his nose and ears, but I was young. All I could think was that no one would marry me. I decided in that moment that I would kill myself if it happened to me and told him so. I listened intently to my brother. I was very sad and frightened but also excited to hear his stories. He'd never talked to me about such things before and had never shared any of this with our family. He told me not to worry. If something goes wrong, we would not stop, even if they began shooting at us. We agreed it would be better to die while running away than to be captured and cut into pieces.

The sky was clear and there was no sign of rain, but we could still hear big booms coming from the valley ahead. These were not the sounds of thunderstorms but of bombardment. The American soldier who had sent us on our way couldn't tell us, but we later learned there was a huge operation involving American and Afghan troops going on that day.

A few hours later, our convoy arrived safely at the Korengal Outpost. We all wanted to take the loads off our trucks and get them delivered as quickly as possible so we could drive back while the helicopters were still flying. An American soldier and his interpreter informed us that unfortunately, nearly everyone at the Outpost was supporting the ongoing operation, and we'd have to stay overnight.

We were all exhausted, but there was little sleep to be had with the sounds of helicopters and jets above. I was finally able to rest for a while after the bombardment finally stopped, but my brother and his fellow drivers were awake all night.

I was awakened in the morning not by my brother, but by the sounds of the mullah preaching, as they usually do after the morning prayer. The helicopters were gone. No more booms in the distance. Now it was a matter of waiting for someone to walk out the front gate and tell us to get the loads off the trucks. That news came a few hours later from a black soldier carrying a rifle and an interpreter carrying a case of water and cookies. The soldier greeted us with a few Pashto words before his interpreter took over, apologized for our wait and then gave us instructions for unloading.

By early afternoon, all of the trucks were empty and it was time to head back to Jalalabad. A few of the laborers from Korengal Outpost had decided to ride back with the convoy. They were headed back to the city to visit family for the upcoming Eid al-Fitr, a three-day holiday that is the Muslim equivalent of Christmas. The booms in the distance were now silent, replaced by the funeral calls for insurgents killed during the operation, which could be heard for miles. We couldn't wait to get out of this place. Our truck was in the lead along the zig-zagging road. There were lots of rocks and curves and blind spots, and little room for error. After a little while, we found ourselves ahead of the rest of the group.

About two miles into the trip, we saw a Taliban checkpoint ahead of us. My brother pretended to stop. "Don't look," he said. He slowed down the truck and shouted that he was trying to pull over, but he did not. Instead, as he had previously promised, he kept going. We heard more than a hundred rounds fired. They crashed into the truck.

"Are you okay, are you okay?!" he kept asking, but I couldn't talk. It sounded like the mountains around us were crashing into the metal roof. My brother was hit in the left leg by one of the bullets, but fortunately he was still able to drive.

"Give me my scarf," he instructed.

"Where is it?"

"Must be in the box," he replied while driving. I didn't know he was shot.

"What do you need it for?" I asked

"Nothing, I just needed it," he replied

We arrived safely at Combat Outpost Michigan a while later, alone but alive. We later learned that the other trucks, with their drivers and passengers, had been captured after we escaped. The Taliban, angry and hungry for revenge after the bombardment, brutally beheaded them the same day. The bodies of the dead were hung from the trees to warn others of the peril that awaited anyone who decided to work for the Americans or Afghan government.

Ch 8: A Dream Revisited

The weather was cold, and it was even getting colder. I still had many years to go before I graduated from high school, and I had the dream to one day become a medical doctor. My mom had jumped the gun and had already started calling me a doctor whenever I came home from school.

"My doctor son," she always said.

"*Abai*, I am not a doctor yet," I replied.

"I thought you are going to be a doctor," my mom said.

"Yes, but I have to finish school and then university."

"What is a university?" She asked.

"It's in Jalalabad," I replied.

"She wants to know what *is* university," my sister clarified.

"Oh! It's another school, but I don't know anything about it," I told my mom.

"You need to ask your father. He knows about the school," my mom instructed.

My mom just liked doctors and would love to have one in the family. She believed that doctors are really hard workers and had the commitment to help sick people when needed. One of my distant uncles, Sarajulhaq, was a good doctor who helped my parents on my occasions while they had no money to pay for their check-ups and medicine. My mom is not an educated woman, so she thought that finishing high school makes you a medical doctor. I wanted to become a doctor to fulfill her dream, but at that time, things began getting worse when the Taliban began targeting civilians.

My family decided to move to a safer place where we kids would be able to attend school and pursue the goals my parents had for us. Despite the challenges, my parents were happy about the decision they made. It was a tough adjustment to a new life in the city, but the first thing my father did was to find a school.

The closest school was Nangarhar High School, which was very popular in the city and was secure so that I did not have to worry about rockets or being attacked by the Taliban or other terrorists. It was a school focused on discipline regarding uniforms, books, attendance and other rules compared to other schools in the city. It was also not easy for someone like me to get into this school in the first place because you had to have some sort of relationship within the local government or ties with teachers to get you in. I had no ties, relationships, or money to bribe someone but I had to do my best; as the saying goes "hard work pays off." I did have great grades that could help, but after a whole week of trips back-and-forth every day, begging the principal and teachers to accept me, they still insisted that they did not have room for more student. Really, it was just an excuse to receive more bribes.

"I can't do it," Qahar, the principal, said on the first day.

"My son is very intelligent and well-disciplined," my father added.

"I can tell, he looks pretty smart, but we have no room for more students," Qahar insisted.

"Can you do something about it? I can't afford to have him go to another school; they are very far from where I live," my dad asked.

"I wish I could help," Qahar said before leaving the meeting.

My dad looked at me and said," Let's go, I will talk to your uncle." I knew my family was struggling so much at that time. We had only a little bit of money to survive, but my father and oldest brother managed by borrowing money from my uncle who was already living the "good life" in Jalalabad.

"Let's go," Ahmad said.

"Where are you taking him?" my mom asked him.

"We are going back to school. I talked to one of the teachers. He is from Kunar as well," Ahmad told her.

"What is his name?" I asked.

"Selab."

"Is he from Tsawki?" my mom asked.

"No, he is from Nari," Ahmad replied. Nari was another town about 60 miles away from our hometown of Tsawki.

Back at the school Selab told us, "I don't have to do this for you guys, but I make very little money each month." Then he added,

"I talked to the principal and he is fine with the arrangement."

"Thank you so much," we replied gratefully.

I did not know that my oldest brother had made a deal with Selab who was willing to help in exchange for money. My brother never mentioned to me until after I started attending, and he never talked to my parents about it because they would have never let him do it.

Nangarhar High School was a very good school, but it was a little far from our house, so I had to wake up early every morning to walk to the school. I had to walk to school every day because there was no bus service. While I didn't care about walking, I was worried that I would be late. It was fun walking when the weather was warm and sunny but no fun in winter when it was really cold. I had no proper clothes to wear, and sometimes when it was very windy, it would hit me in the face, making it feel like I was losing my whole face. I liked the summer and wished it always summer that at least I didn't have to buy clothes to stay warm.

My new school was a lot different from the old one in the village. It had rules that needed to be strictly followed, otherwise students could get in trouble. I began my school with great excitement, but I had no clue that the principal was very strict and serious about school uniforms. The first few weeks were nothing but just a living hell. He checked classes every morning to make sure students had proper uniforms. While he was checking those classes, he always had a wooden stick with him to punish those who did not have uniforms. I was not the only student who could not afford to buy them, and that gave me some confidence that I was not alone.

Even though there was not a single day that went by without punishment for a couple of weeks, I never wanted to tell my parents because I knew they had no money to get uniform and the school supplies for me. My excitement for school turned into boredom, and I would stay home sick or come up with an excuse to avoid those punishments. I never talked to my parents about them, but the marks on my hands from the principal's wooden stick spoke for themselves. While I helped my oldest brother one day with moving stuff around the house. He looked at me and asked, "What is going on? Did you pick a fight with someone in the school?"

"Nothing."

"Don't lie to me," he persisted.

"I am not lying."

"What are those marks then?" he asked and you could tell that he was becoming angry because he thought that I had been fighting at school.

"Why didn't you tell me this before?" he yelled at me when I finally confessed.

"I was going to."

"What do you mean, you were going to?" he shouted, and it felt like he was about to slap me in the face. I was scared and speechless, but I should have told him sooner so that he could help me figure something out. I knew he would do anything to help me avoid further harassment.

When we were done moving stuff around the house and he said, "I will be back soon," but he did not say where he was going.

At the end of the day, he came back with a uniform that he bought it at the thrift shop. I could not be happier.

"Don't hide or lie about things," he said.

"I didn't lie, but I was scared."

"It's okay, but if you ever need anything, ask me, not Dadda."

My parents still found out about it later, and they were not pleased with me. My father even yelled at me for not letting him know what was going on.

"Who did this to you?" my father asked.

"The principal, Qahar."

"Was it just you or whoever had no uniforms?" he asked.

"Those who had no uniforms," I replied.

My father calmed down after I said that I wasn't the only one because he thought that the principal had a grudge against us.

I had the next day off of school because it was Friday, but I wore my uniform to school on Saturday. Even though my uniform was old, I liked it. It did not matter to me whether it was old or new. All I cared about was to stay out of trouble, and it really worked because the principal never punished me again. I was grateful for everything my family had done for me, and now I went to school every day full of joy.

I was even more excited for school when there was an English language class. Even though it was only twice a week, those became my most favorite days. I always wanted to pick up where I started studying English, and I found that classes twice per week was not enough to help me understand what the American soldiers who came to our school were saying. I wanted to take conversation classes too, but that required additional money. My brother Ajmal agreed to help pay my tuition.

"I will start paying for your classes, but where do you want to take those classes? he asked.

"There are a lot of English courses in downtown Jalalabad," I responded.

"I know that, but it has to be a little bit closer to the house," he said.

"There are classes right next to my school."

"Okay, ask your classmates how much they pay."

I had been waiting for this miracle to happen for so long and resurrected my dream, bringing the hope and desire that I always had back to life. I could also practice by speaking with soldiers at school without the risk of getting killed by the Taliban. While the new school was much different, the teachers and some students were much more open-minded, there were still some students influenced by religious clerics and some teachers that had extremist thoughts. "I heard that some students in my class are talking to American soldiers. If I ever find out who, I will never let them pass my class," one teacher threatened everyone in the class. I was one of those students that he talked about, and even though I was very good at his class, he could fail whoever he wanted. He was just trying to find an excuse to punish me, because he didn't like the questions I asked him every time he tried to manipulate us. He was always spreading extremist ideas such as talking about American soldiers and the government of Afghanistan as a 'puppet government'.

After my brother promised to pay the tuition, I registered for more English classes. Within 6-7 months, I improved, but I was still struggling with understanding the accents and dialects of the American soldiers. There was also a 6-month long computer program in my school, provided and supported by the German government, but it was for students who could pass the English test. I took the test, got a great score and was able to attend the class for free. I couldn't be happier than this.

"I did it! I got into the free computer course," I announced when I got home.

"How did you get in?" my sister asked.

"I passed the English language test."

"Good, how many students?" my sister asked.

"I don't know but there were a lot of students."

I couldn't wait to let my father know but he was in the mosque. I knew he was going to be proud and excited about the accomplishment.

My English continued to get much better, and I was able to speak with American soldiers who were part of the Provincial Reconstruction Team (PRT) patrolling around the city and visiting schools. The PRT was very popular for reconstruction work in the city; they built schools, clinics, and other infrastructure. Locals whether or not they could read and write to understand the term "provincial reconstruction team," understood the work and missions they carried out through the city by providing humanitarian aid (HA) and other developmental projects.

The day that changed my life forever happened during a normal high school-day in 2008. I arrived at school around 7:00 A.M. because I had to be at school no later than 7:30 A.M. every morning. There was a boy scout team sitting at the entrance gate and, if you were late, they would catch you and take you to the principal. It was a beautiful sunny day. The school was not overcrowded because American soldiers and military trucks sat at the front of the gate, securing the whole parameter.

"Where are you going?" Afghan police who were there with them asked.

"I am going to school."

"You go to school here?" he questioned me.

"Yes. Can I talk to them?" I asked the policeman, gesturing toward the American soldiers.

"I don't know, you should ask their interpreter," the policeman responded.

"Where is he? I don't see him."

The policeman laughed and said, "Are you blind? He is right there, sitting in the chair in front of the store." The interpreter did not look like he was an Afghan because he had on the same uniform, helmet, body armor, boots and glasses as the other soldiers.

I skipped school that day and practiced English for hours and hours with the soldiers. At the end of the day when I had to go back home, I was offered work with the American soldiers as an interpreter. I wasn't sure if I could it because my English reading, writing, and listening were not strong enough to understand everything that I had heard while I was talking to the soldiers. Still, it was a great day and I could not believe that the soldiers thought that my English was strong enough to be a military interpreter. I went home with that piece of very exciting news.

"How was school?" my mom asked.

"It was good," I lied.

I didn't want to let my parents that I had skipped school and then received a job offer from American soldiers.

My parents would never let me take the job. My mom had already began calling me "her son, the doctor".

However, I wanted to tell me brothers about my English skills and the offer. Ajmal, who was still a truck driver and was still paying my tuition, worked with both American soldiers and interpreters on a daily basis while delivering supplies for the American troops in Eastern Afghanistan.

"I talked with soldiers," I told him.

"What soldiers?" both Ahmad and Ajmal asked.

"*Amerikyan*," I replied. "They were at my school and they said that I can work for them."

"What?! —" Ajmal cut me off.

"Yes, I could talk to them, but it was hard to understand them sometimes."

"That's great, but where can you work for them?" Ajmal asked.

"I don't know."

"Did you tell *Dadda*?" Ahmad asked.

"Not yet, I told them I was at school."

"What do you mean? You didn't go to school," Ahmad questioned.

"No, I didn't. I skipped it to practice my English. "I continued, "I can't tell *Abai* and *Dadda* about the job."

"You need to finish high school first," Ahmad told me.

"I can still finish if I get the job."

"Okay, I will talk to our parents and will convince them once you get the job," Ajmal agreed. At the time, none of us knew that you had to be at least 18 years old to secure the job.

I had millions of thoughts and wishes for my family if I were to get the job. My father would be able to pay off his loans from my uncle and the other people back in the village. We were getting on our own feet slowly, but we still struggled to afford things such as rent, food, clothes and other necessities now that we lived in the city where everything had to be bought. I had a dream that my parents would have their own house one day and the life that they truly deserved after all the atrocities and hardship that they had experienced and all of the hard work they had done. They wanted to have their own house. My mom had already started saving a little money to purchase a home, but it could take more than a decade.

In August 2008, I heard one of my classmates talking about working for the American soldiers at FOB Fenty, where Missional Essential Personnel (MEP) hired local interpreters.

"The test was tough," Bahram, my classmate, said.

"How did you do?"

"I don't know. There were 100 questions," he responded.

"Do you have to go back?" I asked him.

"Yes, they are going to call me," he replied.

"Okay, how often they hire interpreters?" I questioned. "Can I go with you?"

"I think they hire every day; you just need to go there and tell them that you want to be an interpreter," Bahram responded.

I decided to go to Forward Operating Base (FOB) Fenty (also known as Jalalabad Airfield (JAF)), where the attraction-selection-attrition process for interpreters took place. I had never been to FOB Fenty [on post], but it was very close to our house. I always watched the helicopters and big aircraft fly in and out, day and night. I had never imagined that one day I would fly in one of those helicopters. But in fact, within a year, I became part of air assault missions and operations conducted by both Chinook and Black Hawk helicopters.

I waited for my brothers to get home so I could let them know that I was going to Jalalabad Airfield (JAF). Ajmal came home early but was very tired, and Ahmad was still working downtown.

"I heard from a classmate that the Americans hire people at the airfield," I told Ajmal.

"Did he go there too?" Ajmal asked.

"Yes, he did and waiting for them to call."

"Okay, let me talk to Ahmad; he will be here soon," Ajmal said.

"Do you think he is going to let me go?" I asked.

"Yes, we talked about the job," Ajmal responded.

Later that night my brothers discussed it and agreed to let me go to the airfield the next morning.

I woke up early for morning prayer, breakfast and school as usual, but I never let my parents know that I was going to an American military base for a job. I wanted to make sure that I didn't get there late because I remembered my classmates said that you needed to be there as early as you can in the morning.

"Aren't you early for school?" my dad asked.

"I have to go early for my computer class today."

Before I left the house, my mom shouted, "where is my kiss?"

Get the Terp Up Here!

She always kissed me on the cheek or head before I went to school so she kissed me on the head and said," Have a great day and stay out of trouble."

"Always, *Abai*," I smiled at her.

"My boy," she said.

Ch 9: A Popular Birthday

"Mom, Dad, when is my birthday?"

I know that birthdays are not a serious thing in Afghanistan, unlike the United States and other parts of the world, but why didn't you at least record it so that I could tell people and celebrate it, like my friends do? Have you noticed that I haven't asked you for a while? I didn't care like the rest of my friends in the village, and I never would have thought that I would ever leave my hometown. I was a country boy, living with my family in a very small town surrounded by high mountains, with a small portion of farm land near the Kunar River that fed from the melting glaciers, snow and natural springs of the Hindu Kush and Pamir Mountains. Who would have thought that I would come to the United States of America, the land of opportunity?

I can't blame my mom for something that she couldn't write down because I know that she couldn't read and write. It's not her fault at all, but I wish that she would have asked my dad to write it down. Dad is an educated person who went to university, so why didn't he do it? It's true that pretty much everyone in our hometown doesn't know their date of birth. Because of this, January 1st is not only celebrated as the new year, but it's also a special day for thousands of Afghans who like to celebrate the day as their birthday.

In fact, many of those holidays and observance were banned under the Taliban's regime and Sharia Law. There were people who got punished, fined, beaten and locked up in prisons for remembering and celebrating our holidays that have been observed for centuries. "Birthday celebrations and many others holidays are considered pagan, or of Jewish and Christian tradition and values. Muslims shouldn't be observing them, and if they do, Allah will punish them with his heaviest punishment in the hell fire," our religious studies teacher Qari Zabihullah taught us. While growing up, I never understood why, under the Taliban's regime, most holidays were strictly forbidden. We kids remained excited to celebrate the holidays that remained as a way to escape the violence and bloodshed. Until after September 11th, I had never celebrated Nowruz, our new year or farmer's day (March 21st). After 9/11, other holidays also became widely observed again by a population that would have never imagined celebrating these special days under the Taliban's rule.

"There was no hospital nor a clinic in the entire town," my mom always said. I can't imagine now that there was no hospital and that all births took place at home without help provided by a nurse or skilled birth trainers. Many families who couldn't afford to go to hospitals in the big cities ended up losing their lives.

"You were lucky to survive and not get killed; because of the heavy fighting, the rounds were flying like rain when you were born," my mom would tell me. "There was no help whatsoever; everything was pretty destroyed." I loved to hear her stories of fighting, hardship, and suffering that she experienced. It sounded heartbreaking and devastating after the country experienced a bloody Russian invasion and later the civil war. I didn't blame her or my father for not recording my date of birth and neither because they were fighting for their survival while the local government, civilian service, education system, social services, and military institutions were all dysfunctional and destroyed. "Nobody cared much to think of birthdays, making it to the next day was a miracle," my father said once while talking about the Russian invasion and the civil war. "I would have loved to write it down for all of my kids, and have a registrant's date of birth, but all we cared about was survival." I liked to talk with my father who loved to tell stories to his kids.

"I probably have a record somewhere in the paperwork, but it has been a very long time, and not sure if I can find it," my father answered after one of the many times I asked about a record of my birthday. "At one point, we lost everything that we had when our house burned down while we were visiting your uncle, Ghulam Rasool," my father stated.

Again and again, I wasn't able to find answer that I sought from both my parents, siblings, uncles, cousins and nephews that they are older than me. I never searched too seriously as I understood from the mullahs' teaching that it was a tradition of "pagans, Jews and Christians". On other hand, I wished that I knew my date of birth after I applied for the interpreting/translating job for U.S. military because it was the first question that I encountered. It wasn't until after several attempts that I would end up securing the job.

"What is your date of birth? Must be January 1st?" the American civilian processing my paperwork at the badge office asked me. I didn't understand; he hadn't even looked at my *tazkera* yet because it was still in file with other papers. How did he know my "birthday"?

"Yes, it is," I responded.

He smiled and said, "I have interviewed many Afghans that were born on January 1st." I couldn't understand, so his Afghan interpreter jumped in to help. The American looked like that he was in his late 50s, and I could tell that he had been in the country for many years because of the way he understood Afghan culture and tradition. "There were some Afghans who would just shrug and others that would tell me their full story," he added. He looked at his interpreter and asked, "Do you remember that gentleman who owns the shop started telling us about Russian when I asked him about his age?" "Yes, I do," his Afghan-American interpreter responded with a big laugh.

"Safi, right, it's your last name?" his interpreter asked.
"Yes, sir."

"Would you like to change your birthday here? It's totally up to you," he explained.

I was shaky at this point, thinking that I might fail the interview because in the end, they were the ones decided whether I could get the job or not.

"I don't know, is it going to be okay if I do?" I asked him. We ended up speaking Pashtu, my mother tongue. I could tell that he was from Kandahar or southern Afghanistan due to his accent and dialect.

"You are fine, if you don't want to change it, it's okay," he further said. He then had to translate what we just talked about because his boss wanted to know what we had discussed.

"There is no birthday on your *tazkera* and the ID card I am going to make one so you can have one," he explained.

"Safi, think of an easy day and month so that you can remember," his interpreter suggested.

I didn't know what day and month I should choose. The date that I chose would be my birthday for the rest of my life.

"What about March 3? My nephew was born on March 3," the American said.

"Sounds good," I replied.

Before he translated, he started singing, "happy *new* birthday, Safi." We all laughed, I had never celebrated a birthday and didn't know how.

"Have fun with your new birthday," the American said after he printed out my ID. Since then, March 3 became my official birthday.

Ch 10: Becoming an Interpreter

The airfield wasn't too far from where my family lived, but I had to walk and wanted to make sure I got there on time for the 8:00 A.M. selection. "On time" is something that Afghans never took it seriously, but now I know that it is important in Western culture. I thought I would be the only person there for an interview, but I found myself with more than 10 people standing in line to become interpreters. In fact, the others were older and bigger than me. I still didn't know that age mattered and could disqualify me for the job.

Mostly everyone standing and waiting in the line tried to get out of the rain underneath a small shelter of Afghan security guards [ASG]. I ended up staying out in the rain until two well-dressed men arrived around 9:00 A.M. I didn't think that they would the people to pick us for interviews because they were not soldiers. They were civilians with no weapons, uniforms, helmets, body armor and military boots.

"*Salaam*, my name is Karim," The Afghan-American interpreter greeted us, "Sorry, you guys had to wait in rain, but we will make this quick."

I was soaked but also excited and nervous. I couldn't wait to return home with a piece of surprise news. As Karim promised, the process moved quickly; guys ahead of me got picked for the job, but I was still waiting to be called. The closer I got to being called for an interview, the shakier I got. Finally, I heard Karim say, "next person please," and it was my turn. I tried to calm down and show confidence that I could do the job.

"*Salaam*, let me see you *tazkera*," Karim asked.

I had my *tazkera* ready to go and handed it to him.

He looked at me, smiled, and said, "You are not 18 yet."

"Okay," I replied. I didn't know why that mattered.

"You must be 18 or older to work as an interpreter."

I was speechless as he handed back my *tazkera*. "A few more years," he added. "Come back when you turn 18, I will hire you," he shouted as I walked away.

I headed back home with a piece of sad news while it was pouring. I was soaked by the time I got home and arrived much earlier than on a normal school day. Neither of my parents were home. I just couldn't believe what had happened. I even hated myself for being young and unable to get the job that could change our lives forever, at least financially.

My brothers were gone for the rest of the day, but my parents returned home around lunch.

"You came home early today. How was the school?" my mom asked.

"It was raining all morning and the principal decided to let us go home because we don't have classroom, so we have to sit out in the open," I replied.

"I thought that they are building more classes," my dad said

"Yes, but they haven't started work on it," I responded.

"Where is, *Lala*?" I asked my dad, hoping to find my oldest brother.

"I don't know. He said that he had to take care of something this morning," my dad responded. "Why? What's up?" my dad questioned.

"Nothing, I was just curious," I replied.

After a while, both my brothers Ahmad and Ajmal came home, and you could tell that they were excited to find out my news.

"How did it go?" Ajmal asked

"Not good. I didn't get it."

"Why? What happened?" he asked.

"The MEP said that I am too young," I responded.

"I knew it; I haven't seen or spoken with any interpreters that are as young as you," Ajmal said.

"No worries, focus on school," Ahmad replied.

"What is going on?" my mom asked because she heard us talking.

"Oh, nothing, we are just talking about his school," Ajmal said.

"We should tell them, he didn't get it anyway," Ahmad said. "They are going to find out one way or another."

Ahmad told my mom that I tried to work for the Americans but that I didn't get the job. She wasn't happy and even cursed me for not letting her know.

"I am glad that you didn't get it," she replied with a big smile. "If your father finds out, he is going to be angry."

My father didn't find out for a couple of days.

"You are lucky that they didn't tell me," my dad laughed, and spoke, "Remember next time you wanna do something, you have to let me know," he added.

"I was scared," I responded

"I know, but I am glad that you let your brothers know," he said.

Even though I didn't get the job, I never gave up. I was happy with the little bit of struggle and work I had done to be a translator. At the end of 2008, just a couple of months later, two of my classmates ended up working as interpreters for the Americans. I decided to go back and tried again, with friends on the other side I figured I might have a better chance.

All I cared about was getting the job, surprising my brothers and changing our lives.

I went back to Fob Fenty in November 2008. It happened to be the luckiest day, and I got picked during the first interview. There were more steps ahead, and I was nervous.

"Safi?" an Afghan-American interpreter said. It wasn't Karim who could possibly recognize my face.

"Yes, here," I responded.

There were about 15 guys who were chosen for further process, and I was one of them. "You guys are coming with me," the MEP interpreter said, and we followed him to the second ECP where American soldiers were sitting. "Okay, they are going to do to the biometric here before we go on the post for other stuff," the MEP said. I had no clue what biometric screening looked like, nor I had ever heard of it.

The biometrics and questions with the soldiers didn't take long, and we got done around noon. I thought we were done after the biometrics, but it turned out that we still needed to pass the examination, background check, and medical tests.

"We are just going to take care of the paper test, and we will see how much time we have after," a MEP representative said.
"There are 100 questions with multiple choices, make sure you guys read each question carefully before answering them."

"Hold on, don't look at them, put it on the table," he yelled at one of the new recruits, who grabbed his paper test to read it.

"I am sorry," the new recruit replied.

"It's okay and don't worry, it's a very easy test."

I couldn't wait to put my brain into use and test my English language skills.

"Time starts now," the MEP told the group.

"Time?" I asked.

"Yes, you only have 90 minutes to answer the questions."

The test was tough, but I managed to answer questions to the best of my knowledge even though I didn't know most of them.

"Alright, time is up," the MEP interpreter called, "I will let you know who passed the test after they are corrected."

"How did you do?" one of the recruits asked me.

"I don't know, it was tough."

"I couldn't understand some of the questions," the new recruit added.

"Neither could I."

"I went for the longest answer," he said.

"Let's pray that we all are going to pass it," I said.

While we were chatting about the test, an American civilian came out with his interpreter and said, "Congratulations, you all passed the test, and we will see you tomorrow at 9:00 A.M. for the medical tests and some other paperwork."

I couldn't be happier and excited when I heard that I passed.

I went back home with big news to let my brothers know that I got the job. They were both home when I arrived at the end of the day.

"I did it!" I shouted to my brother.

"Calm down, what did you do?" Ajmal asked.

"I got the job!"

"What job?" he asked.

"To be an interpreter."

"I am going back tomorrow to sign some more paperwork."

"I will go with you," he said.

"Okay, but you can't get on the post."

"I know, but I need to see some drivers there while they are waiting to be loaded-up," he added.

I went back to FOB Fenty the next morning, still with my parents not knowing about the job and thinking that I was leaving for school.

"Let me know if you have any questions," the interpreter instructed as he handed me the agreement paperwork. "Then sign at the end of each sheet," he said.

"What is emergency contact?" I asked him.

"Well, an emergency contact means that if something happens, in case someone dies or injured, we are to reach that person," he replied.

It was probably the question that struck me hardest and scared the hell out of me. "Can I put my brother's name?" I asked him.

"Yes, but make sure you put his phone number there," he replied.

Ajmal was the only person in the family who had a cell phone. He had gotten it for work, but it became the family phone. Ajmal became my emergency contact in case I died or was seriously injured.

"Whenever you are done, make sure we get you the paper for opening up a bank account," the MEP said. I had no clue what a bank account was, but would soon have one in order to work as an interpreter.

Before I headed back home, the interpreter said, "You are done for now, but make sure to answer the phone when we call you,"

"Okay, but do you know when?" I asked him

"I don't know but could be a week or two, we never know," he responded.

"Okay, thank you." I headed back home after a long day, thinking about what would happen to my mom if I died, got injured, or was kidnapped by the Taliban. At the same time, I was also excited to get my first paycheck and give it to my parents.

I let my brother know that he was going to receive a phone call, and I bugged him every day, but after nearly two weeks he still hadn't heard.

Finally, he got the call. "Somebody called and said that you have to be at Fenty by 9:00 A.M. tomorrow," he said.

"Did you ask who was he?" Ahmad asked Ajmal.

"No, I didn't, but he introduced himself from the interpreters' company," he responded. "Oh, he said that you need to get hygiene supplies — toothpaste, toothbrush, clothes, blanket and whatever else you need before you report," Ajmal directed me.

I never had toothpaste or toothbrush before because we always used *miswaak*, a traditional and natural alternative to the toothbrush widely used in Muslim countries. I could get some of the stuff, but I couldn't figure out how to take clothes and blanket from home because my parents still did not know about the job. Both Ajmal and Ahmad were very helpful, and we managed to get whatever I needed for work.

Finally, on January 19, 2009, I got my work assignment for Combat Outpost Monti. I left the next day without letting my parents know. It was a great feeling to return to my birth province, but the risk and danger I would face were greater than I could imagine. It was a long trip, full of risk from the Taliban's illegal checkpoints where they searched for people who worked for the Afghan government and Americans. While I hadn't start working for the Americans yet, I had to have a piece of paper on me that showed that I was going to work for the Americans upon my arrival at Monti. The journey was not as easy as I had thought. I could be kidnapped, injured or killed on my way to Combat Outpost Monti, but I was excited to start my job.

Ch 11: Welcome to Combat Outpost Monti

1st Battalion, 32nd Infantry, 10th Mountain Division (Light)
2009

At the beginning of my employment with the U.S. government I was assigned to Charlie Company, 1st Battalion, 32nd Infantry, 10th Mountain Division located at Combat Outpost Monti, Asmar District of Kunar Province as a linguist. Despite the title, I immediately became more than just an interpreter.

I fought alongside U.S. soldiers in countless engagements with the enemy. In late 2009, while conducting a dismounted patrol in the Barge-Matal District, I was struck by shrapnel when an insurgent fired an RPG during a fight. Every day I look at the scar on my right arm, which serves as a permanent reminder of that day. At the time, the district was completely overrun by Taliban insurgents. I was part of an operation that took more than one month to successfully clear the area of insurgents. Due to the complexity of the mission, we heavily lacked re-supplies. There were no showers, we only ate only Meal Ready to Eat (MRE) per day, and I had no ability to communicate with my family. Because my family had not heard from me from over a month, they assumed I was dead. My mother held a memorial ceremony in my remembrance and my family and friends attended. They were shocked beyond belief when I finally walked through the front door of my home.

Photo from the mission in Barge-Matal. We each averaged 1-2 hours of sleep per night. Our beds were most often large rocks.

Despite my wounds and my family's pain, I diligently supported the mission because I was part of the team, and they had also become another part of my family. Every single person I fought alongside of I think of as a brother.

During my time with Charlie Company 1-32 Infantry, I endured countless dangerous situations, which could have left me seriously wounded or killed. Some of my brothers were not as lucky as many of these missions experienced heavy casualties. Several of these operations have been documented by American uniformed and civilian journalists including in the book *The Wrong War in Afghanistan by* Bing West, a former Assistant Secretary of Defense and U.S. Marine. I am mentioned in the book because I translated for him for a few weeks while he was visiting Combat Outpost Monti.

Some members of 1st Platoon, Charlie Company, 1-32 Infantry with Former Assistant Secretary of Defense Bing West. I'm second from the left. Dangam District, Kunar Province.

Barge-Matal Nuristan

***

"I made it, I made it," I said when I called Ajmal a few hours after arriving to let him know that I was at Monti. It had been a rough, risky and scary journey that could have left me injured or dead. I was thrilled to be at the outpost, but I still had a lot to do in order to keep my job because it required good English language skills and understanding that I needed to work on. Unlike living with my family and going to school every day, life was different working as an interpreter for the American soldiers. There was a lot to learn besides the English language. I struggled to learn "the military life," a life that many civilians don't know and don't want to know.

"Get in the truck," PFC Solis, one of our gunners said.

"I am trying to," I replied, but after 5 seconds he realized that I didn't know how to open a Humvee door.

"Someone open the door for him," PFC Solis laughed.

I finally got into the Humvee truck, but this was just one example of the daily challenges and struggles of fitting in that left me full of anxiety and fear that I had to deal with for weeks and even a few months. I had never been away from home and felt homesick already, I missed my mom, siblings and even some friends from school.

"Are you okay?" Irfan, the senior interpreter at Monti, asked.

"I am tired. I just got back from the mission," I replied.

"Okay, go get your dinner at the chow hall."

"I'm going to, but can I use your phone?" I asked him.

"Sure, what do you need it for?" he replied.

"I would like to call home."

I didn't have a cell phone and wouldn't have money to purchase one until I got my first paycheck.

"*Salaam*, how are *Abai* and *Dadda* doing?" I asked Ajmal when he answered.

"We are good, and how are you?"

"I am doing good."

"--Safi, don't mention anything about work," Irfan reminded.

"Okay," I nodded my head.

"How is the *Turjumani* [interpretation] work?" Ajmal asked.

"Good. Hey, how is *Abai*? Did you tell them?"

"They are good, and yes, Lala talked to them," he replied.

"I am sure they both parents are sad and pissed."

"They were, but I have been telling them that I talk to you every day," Ajmal responded.

"This isn't my phone, but I am getting one soon."

"Great, do you wanna talk to *Abai?*"

"Yes, but I have to go soon." I wanted to talk to her as long as I could, but I knew she was going to cry on the phone.

"*Abai! Abai!* Where is *Abai?*" Ajmal shouted to the others at home.

"What's up?" I heard my mom reply.

"Nasir is on the phone."

My mom took the phone but couldn't talk and kept crying and crying, "Where are you?" she finally asked.

"I am in Kunar province. I am doing great."

"How are you? How is *Dadda?*"

"We are good. He was very angry at you when we found out that you were gone, but he is good now," my mom said.

"I am getting paid soon," I said.

"We don't need your money," she scolded me. I was talking to her when Irfan waved at me and said," Are you done? I am waiting to call home."

"*Abai,* I have to go, but I will talk to you later. I am getting a phone soon," I said.

"Okay, take very great care of yourself, and we are all praying for you."

I didn't want to stop talking or hang up, but I had to give Irfan back his phone.

I was worried about my English language skills, both listening and speaking, and I got even more worried when I saw that a bunch of interpreters were sent back to Mission Essential Personnel [MEP] due to poor language skills as well as a lack of knowledge of the surrounding areas. I could be one of those sent back, but even if I didn't have strong English language skills, I still had great knowledge of the surrounding districts and their dialects because I was born and raised in the same province. I knew the values, culture, and traditions that everybody practiced here. Kunar is a mountainous region and a province of the country where people had a bit of a different accent and used slang that was typically restricted to a particular context or groups of people. The Taliban used this slang as codewords to attack both Afghan and American soldiers. Knowing this slang made me particularly valuable.

Even as I struggled to improve my English language skills, I never complained or refused a single mission, and I even went on extras. I made some great friends that I felt honored and proud to call brothers, mentors and English teachers. Sergeant First Class [SFC] Kevin Devine, a Native American and Massachusetts born-and-raised, was a platoon sergeant who would become my English instructor, job saver, boss, brother and friend for life. He taught me a new English words, slang, military terms, dialects, and accents that I could have never learned at English courses. However, SFC Devine's sense of humor also got me in trouble a few times with some of the slang he taught me!

Ch 12: "What if we call you John?"

I was doing everything possible to avoid getting fired at work. Although I never complained about what I was doing, it was dangerous and sometimes a life and death situation. But I had dreams, and one of those dreams was to buy a house for my family and to help my father pay off his loans. When I arrived, there was a small Army unit of three platoons and a headquarter company [Charlie Company, 1-32] operating out of Combat Outpost Monti. Their objective was to secure and assist the population of Asmar, Dangam and Shigal districts, including the highways, which the Americans had named after the U.S. cities like San Diego. Charlie Company 1-32 was not alone, there was also a very small ANA unit of 10-15 men along with their U.S. Marine advisors [ETT] stationed at Monti. One of those advisors was the Medal of Honor recipient Sergeant Dakota Meyer. Nobody then could predict that SGT Meyer would one day receive the nation's highest medal of honor. He was quite smart and social with Afghan National Army soldiers and a great friend with 1st platoon, led and commanded by LT Kerr. Dakota loved to join the "killing squad" --LT Kerr, SFC Devine, SGT Hall, SGT Anderson, March and so on-- for a workout at COP Monti. SGT Meyer and his team joined us for many patrols and missions against the Taliban, Hezb-e-Islami fighters and other insurgents in the Hindu Kush mountains. Indeed, SGT Meyer was quite an impressive soldier, fighter, leader, and friend.

You had to be assigned to a particular team, unit or platoon at Monti to work with as an interpreter, but while waiting for my assignment, I was working with everybody to improve my English. I even went out on patrols more than once a day voluntarily.

One day, I was watching *Black Hawk Down* at the MWR, when Irfan walked in.

"Safi, let's go, you are going to meet your boss."

I jumped up from the couch, "Okay!"

"You are going to be working with Hemat, another senior interpreter," Irfan added.

"Which platoon?" I asked.

"I don't know, but we are going to find out," he replied.

"I think Hemat works with 1st platoon," I said.

We went to 1st platoon's barracks, called B-Huts, but didn't go inside. Irfan knocked on the door and said, "I will talk to them." A man with his M4 walked out of the building and asked, "what's up?"

"We are here to see LT Kerr," Irfan replied.

"Okay, hold on a second," the soldier said.

I still didn't understand ranks, even though they all wore ranks and name tabs. The soldier went back in, but after less than two minutes, two big men with their M4s came out of the barracks and asked, "What's up Irfan?"

"Not much, sir. Did Forcy talk to you?" Irfan asked him.

"About what?" LT Kerr asked. "Oh, you mean about the *terp*," LT Kerr added.

"Yes, sir. Nasirullah Safi is going to be working for you," Irfan responded.

"What? How do you say your name?" SFC Devine asked turning to me.

"Nasirullah Safi," I responded.

Devine looked at Kerr and said, "Hell no; we need to change your name."

I was confused and didn't understand how Devine was going to change my name. "Okay, sir," I said smiling at them.

Irfan and I headed back to our barracks, but I looked at him on the way and asked, "how are they going to change my name?"

He laughed and responded, "I think they were joking."

"Are you sure?" I asked him.

"I think so, but if not, they will probably call you an English name," Irfan responded.

"What do you mean by an English name? Do they have to change it on my birth certificate?" I questioned him.

"No, they just pick an easy name; they did it for one of my friends," Irfan said.

"What did they call him?" I asked.

"Mike."

I ended up working and hanging out with soldiers from 1st platoon to improve my language skills and to pick up their accents, but they still struggled to remember my name.

LT Kerr was the platoon leader for 1st platoon, and SFC Devine was his platoon sergeant. LT Kerr was a muscular, tall man who had a very strong accent that I couldn't fully understand for a while. Kevin Devine was not as taller as Kerr, but was bigger than him and was much easier for me to understand. Devine had been on many tours to Afghanistan (including one to the Pech valley, just about 40 miles to the west of COP Monti) and Iraq, making him pretty damn smart about local culture, traditions and the tough terrain of the Hindu Kush Mountains of Kunar province.

"What did you say your name was? Devine asked.

"Nas—Nasi--," Kerr was trying to respond.

"Nasirullah," I pronounced.

"Say it slowly." I did and they both tried again, "Nazirallah."

"Pretty close," I told them.

"Well, it's damn hard. What about John? Can we call you John?" Devine asked.

"Yes, I like it," I responded.

Since then, my name has been John, and I kind of like it.

Ch 13: Learning the Lingo

I was thrilled when SFC Devine said, "We will help you improve your English." During our tour, Devine, a great soldier, became more than my English teacher; he was also a mentor, brother, best friend, role model and hero. It was such an honor to support and assist him and the rest of the platoon in hundreds of daily patrols, missions, operations, meetings, shuras and key leader engagements both with local elders and Afghan Government officials in the course of 12 months.

"Thank you, sir."

"Let me know if you ever need anything like books or a notebook." Devine added.

"Okay, sir."

Even though, you don't call or address noncommissioned officer [NCO], "sir", I addressed every soldier as "sir" because I couldn't tell the difference.

"Don't call me sir," Devine said. I thought he was mad at me or that I had done something wrong. "It's today's lesson-- you don't call an NCO "sir"," he said with a laugh.

"Okay, what do you call them?"

"Sergeant, or their names," he responded.

"Okay."

I was able to learn new words, both military and civilian, in a very short time, but some accents were still difficult for me to understand. Jacob Kerr, who was from upstate New York, was still hard for me to understand. On the contrary, Kevin Devine, who was born and raised in Martha's Vineyard, Massachusetts had the easiest accent to understand. I worked to improve my language skills not only to ensure my job was safe, but I also didn't want to get into trouble while translating for local elders and government officials on a daily basis.

I liked COP Monti because I knew a lot about local culture, tradition and values, and I wanted to do good work there. Monti was in tough and dangerous terrain deep in the Hindu Kush mountains of Kunar province, about 20 miles from the Khyber Pakhtoon Khawa, the tribal areas and a hotbed of the Taliban insurgents. English slang and military words were not going to be good enough; I also needed to learn more about running key leader engagements [KLE] and other meetings that discussed security, construction, and other developmental projects. To learn, I wanted to join other senior interpreters who had a long and concrete experiences of doing such tasks and duties.

"Can I join you for a couple of meetings?" I asked both Irfan and Wahid.

"I don't know; let me ask If I can bring you with me," Irfan responded.

"Okay, I really need to understand and learn how to run a meeting."

"One way to learn and improve English is to speak with the soldiers. I know it's hard to understand everything they say, but it's pretty normal for new interpreters like you," Wahid added.

"Okay," I responded, but I knew I was a little shy. "I can understand most of the things they say now."

"I know, I heard that you are getting better," Wahid encouraged. "Keep up the hard work and you will do great."

If you couldn't find me at my barracks, I was hanging out with platoon medic, Tomeo, and the rest of the soldiers to improve my English and pick up new words while out on missions, daily patrols, or operations with them.

"You are never in your barracks. Where are you staying?" Irfan asked.

"I am still staying in my barracks, but I always go over to the platoon's barracks."

Irfan looked at me and said, "What are you doing there? You don't like to hang out with us?"

"Learning new words and slang," I told him. "I've learned a lot."

"That's great," Irfan said smiling.

The effort I put in was put to the test when Hemat, my work partner, decided to go home on leave and let me take care of the business. I wasn't sure if I could do it, but I had to even though I felt like that I wasn't fully ready.

"You got this," Hemat said.

"I got it. I will do my best," I assured him, realizing that now was the time I would need to go out of my comfort zone.

First platoon was assigned to secure the Dangam district, which was surrounded by the high Hindu Kush mountains, cliffs, hills, and slopes to the southeast of Bajur Agency of the federally administered tribal areas [FATA] of Pakistan. It was once known as the hotbed and safe haven for the Taliban, Haqqani [HQ] and Al-Qaida [AQ] operatives. The Taliban's fighters could easily infiltrate Dangam to attack the Afghan forces if there was no American presence. First platoon [1-32] would be the first American troops to operate deep in Dangam Valley against the Taliban and other terrorists. This would be a nightmare for the Taliban who were accustomed to operating freely. First platoon would restrict the Taliban's operations in a way that the local government and police couldn't.

I was sitting with the other interpreters, watching television when SPC Carlson shouted, "John, we are going on patrol." We left for the Dangam Valley, which should have been a short trip, but we ended driving to the very end of the valley where the main road narrowed and our vehicles couldn't drive through any farther.

"It's beautiful out here. Are you from here, John?" SPC Curtlee asked me.

"Not from here."

"You said you are from Kunar," he replied.

"Kunar is a big state, right John?" SPC Cepeda jumped in.

"Yes, and I am from Tsawki," I responded.

"Where is that?" SPC Cepeda asked.

"It's closer to Asadabad," I responded. "The capital city."

"Okay, I am just teasing you John, but it's really beautiful out here," SPC Cepeda concluded.

We didn't stop at the district center that day because the patrol was about reconnaissance and understanding of the area of operation [AO]. We returned to Monti without getting shot at, and wouldn't go back out for the next two days. Instead, we hosted the district governor, Shah Mahmood, the police chief, Shahzada, and local tribal elders both from Mushwani and Salarzai Tribes at Monti for meetings to discuss issues and challenges that they faced since the locals had been kept isolated, manipulated and brainwashed by the Taliban against American soldiers.

"The Americans are very nice; I found them very helpful," a local elder said after the meeting while I was escorting them off the base.

"Did you see that guy who looked like an Afghan?" another elder asked.

"Was he an Afghan?" the elder looked at me and asked.

"Which one?"

"The one sitting next to you," he said.

"The taller guy?" I asked, referring to Kerr.

"Not him, not that white guy, I am talking about the big, short guy," the elder said.

"Oh, no, he is not an Afghan," I replied, realizing that they were referring to SFC Devine who was native American, but looked like an Afghan.

"Can he speak Pashto?" another elder jumped in.

"Ha-ha, not a whole a lot but some Pashtu," I replied.

"Did you teach him, *Turjuman Saab*?" he asked me.

"I did a little bit."

"He should learn it because he looks like an Afghan," the elder said, and they all laughed.

First platoon was like a family, everyone respected and risked their life for one another on a daily basis. SFC Devine, "Daddy D" and LT Kerr were great leaders who absolutely loved their soldiers and would do anything to make them safe, happy, entertained during our deployment. I kept learning new words and slang with SFC Devine, but I never used them before looking them up in the dictionary because the guys were pretty excited to play tricks on me with "special" words.

Ch 14: Dangam Valley

2009

After President Obama issued an order to send 30,000 additional troops to Afghanistan to train and advise the Afghan forces and to fight the Taliban, Al-Qaida and other terrorists, 1st platoon [1-32] Charlie Company was tasked to set up a firebase, a small outpost also known as a patrol base, in Dangam, less than 10 km away from Bajour, a hotbed and safe haven, for the Taliban, Haqqani Network (HQN), Al-Qaida (AQ), Tahreek-e-Talibani- Pakistan (TTP) and other militants. It was going to be the first U.S. observation post (OP), firebase and patrol base built deep in Dangam valley in the Hindu Kush Mountains.

The Dangam Valley was not too far from Combat Outpost Monti, but the narrow and winding dirt road was never been safe from the Taliban's improvised explosive devices [IEDs] and ambushes. It was easy for the Taliban insurgents to infiltrate Dangam Valley from Bajour because of the proximity. First platoon [1-32], led by LT Jacob Kerr and his brave soldiers, took huge risks to assist and support the people of Dangam Valley who had been harmed by the Taliban for years. It was a great feeling for 1st platoon [1-32] to visit a village deep in the Hindu Kush mountains that never visited by the Americans before. "Hell yeah, we are the first Americans here," I heard, SPC March, the radio operator yell, on our way into the valley.

"John, ask them if they are serious about building an observation post up there," the district governor, Shah Mahmood, directed me to ask LT Kerr and SFC Devine.

"Yes, we are going to build it, but it's gonna take a little while," LT Kerr responded.

"They don't have to do that. I have spare rooms here at the district center that they can use," the district governor responded.

"John, thank him for the offer, but I already talked to my boss," LT Kerr replied.

"This is your home," Shah Mahmood replied in English.

"He can speak pretty good English," LT Kerr replied.

"Much better than you, Johnny boy," SFC Devine added with a big laugh.

"What did he say?" the district governor asked, curious to know.

"Oh, he said that you speak better than I do."

He smiled and said, "Not at all; I could speak very good English before when American came to visit from Asadabad once in a while."

"How often had the Americans come to visit?" SFC Devine asked.

"Not very frequently," the district governor responded.

"We are going to be here all the time," LT Kerr said.

"Welcome, Welcome," the district governor again replied in English.

"What about the Taliban?" SFC Devine asked.

"Both Afghan and Pakistani Taliban attacked the district center four months ago and tried to take over the district, but they never succeeded."

"Was everybody okay?"

"Unfortunately, we lost one of great policemen and three others were wounded, but their injuries were sustainable."

"I am sorry to hear that. The Taliban will never take over the district now," LT Kerr assured him. "I wanna talk to the local elders about some projects, but I have another meeting now," he continued.

"John, tell him that it was nice to meet him," SFC Devine said.

"Nice meeting you too," the district governor replied.

First platoon [1-32] was able to visit nearly the entire Dangam Valley, a valley that was abandoned and kept isolated from the rest of the country both by the Afghan government and American troops. Most of the platoon was familiar with local culture and tradition, and most of the senior NCOs had served at least one tour to Afghanistan before. They knew so much about Afghanistan that it made my job a lot easier.

Jacob Kerr was a graduate of West Point Military Academy and a young lieutenant, but he was supported by experienced warriors and brave fighters that knew the country. First platoon [1-32] earned an esteemed name and reputation in the valley, and everyone knew LT Kerr and SFC Devine.

"These are the first Americans in our village," a local elder said during our visit to his village

"Seriously?!" LT Kerr was surprised to hear it.

"Yes, not even the Russians came to our village in the'80s," the elder added.

"We feel like we are forgotten here," a teacher from Baidad school said. "We don't have enough supplies for our school while other schools in Asmar (closer to Monti) have everything they need," the teacher explained.

"John, ask him if they ever talk to the district governor," LT Kerr instructed.

"Yes, we have talked to him many times, but he always says that he doesn't have the budget."

"Okay, I will see what I can do."

"Thank you so much, everyone will highly appreciate that," the teacher responded with a huge smile.

After these meetings, 1st platoon [1-32] was busy as hell for the first couple of months of 2009. The platoon conducted mounted and dismounted daily patrols and missions deep in the valley. Some of the villages were located so deep into the valley that there were no roads, but 1st platoon managed to walk to reach them, even though the risk of ambushes was doubled and tripled.

"John, tell LT Kerr that it's very dangerous to walk and climb up to those villages. There are local Taliban," the police chief warned.

"That's what we are trained for," LT Kerr responded.

"I have never seen anybody like him," The police chief commented.

"John, what did he say?" LT Kerr asked.

"Oh, he said that he had never seen anybody like you."

"What does that mean?"

"He means that you are brave."

"Ha-ha, thank you," LT Kerr gestured to the police chief.

"What about me?!" SFC Devine joked.

LT Kerr looked at him and said, "You are a scary bitch." "--Don't translate that," LT Kerr added to me.

"I don't think we have a word for 'bitch' in Pashto," I laughed. "Do we have a word for 'bitch' in Pashtu?" I translated for the police chief.

"I don't think so," he responded, "why?"

"Oh, they were just joking," I replied.

"Okay, but he is very brave," the police chief insisted.

"What did he say?" LT Kerr asked.

"He said that you are a scary bitch."

Everyone laughed. "You are fucking full of it. You just said that you don't have that word in Pashtu," LT Kerr responded.

"I created one for you, sir."

"Whatever, *kuni*."

I was glad that the police chief didn't understand the word *kuni* because it's a Pashtu word that means "fagot".

"You are an asshole, sir, and even the police chief can understand that." SFC Devine, SPC March and other soldiers in the office were laughing so hard.

"John, ask the police chief what he thinks about the danger from the Taliban now that we are here," SFC Devine said getting back to business.

"The dreams and desires that the Taliban have held for years to take over the district is gone now," the police chief responded. "They heard that you guys are here and visited almost every village in the valley, even those never visited before."

"Good, we are waiting," LT Kerr replied.

The police chief smiled and added, "I heard that the local Taliban are trying to get reinforcements from Bajour to attack you guys."

"What? John, ask him how he knows," LT Kerr said.

"It's a very small valley; we hear things from locals and some of the policemen have families who live deep in the valley."

"Okay, we are gonna fucking kill them," LT Kerr replied. "John, you guys should talk to the National Directorate Security [NDS] chief; he probably knows about it," the police chief told us.

"Yeah, we are heading to his office," LT Kerr responded.

"Okay, thank you. We got to keep going," SFC Devine added.

LT Jacob Kerr, SFC Devine and the rest of the platoon [1-32] established an incredible bond of friendship with both government officials and locals who had previously been brain-washed and manipulated against the Americans. Many of those people were from the Salarzai, Mamond and Mushwani tribes who lived on both sides of the Durand Line.

The Mushwani had a long history of hostility and fighting against the Taliban and supported the Afghan government and the Americans. However, it was believed that the majority of local Taliban, their supporters and sympathizers were from the Salarzai tribe. LT Kerr, SFC Devine and the rest of 1st platoon [1-32] disproved that belief by establishing an unbreakable partnership with both Salarzai and Mushwani tribes. The tribes often invited us for meals and tea parties at their houses.

First platoon [1-32] visited Dangam almost every day for daily meetings with local government officials -- the district governor, police chief, National Directorate of Security (NDS) chief and local tribal elders-- to discuss various topics including security and development projects like micro-hydro power for electricity, potable water [pipe scheme system] and supplying the needed materials for schools. As a result, the Taliban lost the majority of their supporters in the valley, and now they turned their focus to doing whatever they could to destroy the strong relationship that 1st platoon [1-32] had established among the local populations.

"I can't believe it. Now, everyone talks about you guys!" the district governor told us during one visit.

"Are they saying good things?" LT Kerr asked.

The district governor, Shah Mahmood, laughed and responded, "Always good." He added, "John, tell LT Kerr that you all are very good at gaining the hearts and minds of the people here."

"Anything about an attack?" LT Kerr asked.

"I hope it's a rumor, but I spoke with Habib and he thinks that Taliban plans to carry out a massive attack."

"Where?"

"Wherever they can but possibly here in Dangam," the district governor replied.

"Where is Habib?" LT Kerr asked.

"He must be in his office," the district governor told us.

"Okay, thank you. I am gonna go talk to him, but if you hear anything please let us know," LT Kerr said, ready to go see Habib.

"*Salaam, Sangah-Sanga-e*," SFC Devine greeted Habib in Pashtu.

Habib laughed and said, "he speaks very good Pashtu. Did you teach him?"

"Yes," I laughed.

"What did he say?" SFC Devine asked.

"He asked if I taught you those words."

"Hell no!" SFC Devine said shaking his head. "Nah, I'm just kidding."

"What kind of tea— green or milk?" Habib asked, welcoming us into his office.

"John, tell him *Shudu* chai," SFC Devine said.

"Well, he heard you say it so I don't have to translate that."

He laughed, "I am taking your job!"

"John, ask him what he thinks about a Taliban attack." LT Kerr cut into the conversation to get to business.

"I was going to call you if you guys didn't come today. I heard that the Taliban, mostly the Pakistanis, have planned an attack," Habib responded.

"You mean an attack on the district center?"

"I don't know; it could be in the district center, an ambush along the road or and IED."

"John, ask him how did he get this information," SFC Devine requested. A lot of the time, this kind of intelligence wasn't accurate and needed further analysis because both the source and the reliability of the intelligence were unknown.

"One of my sources told me," Habib responded. "I will let you know if I hear anything else, but let's have tea now."

While 1st platoon [1-32] expanded its area of operation (AO) and gained much local support, the Taliban regrouped to attack in order to disrupt the mission, the reconstruction projects and our daily patrols in Dangam district. Intelligence flooded in. I carried an Icom scanner that intercepted the Taliban's conversation and helped us to monitor and listen to the Taliban's and other insurgent communications about attacks. Even though the Taliban sometimes used coded language, I did my best to understand and help the local policemen in the district.

"John, tell LT Kerr that it's pretty clear that the Taliban plan to attack, but they are scared since you guys come out here more often," Habib, the NDS Chief, told me.

"I know, my guys are ready."

"Where are they hiding? Let's go get them!" SGT Hall added. SGT Hall was one of the most experienced soldiers that 1st platoon [1-32] had. He had finished a tour to the most dangerous and deadly "Valleys of Death," Korengal, Shuryak, and Pech River Valley in 2006.

"They probably used improvised explosive devices [IEDs] along the road," Habib added.

"What about ambush?"

"It's possible."

"Ask him, John, where he thinks that they will ambush us," SFC Devine jumped in.

"Anywhere between Asmar and Dangam because of the mountains," Habib replied. "Most likely in the Cheshan mountains."

"The Taliban always fire rockets and mortars at Monti from there," LT Kerr agreed.

"Yes, my source has been working on it, but I am gonna need some help," Habib said. "I need to give my source some cash."

"Okay, I will ask my boss," LT Kerr told him.

"He should talk to Larry and the Human Collection Team or the U.S. intelligence team at Monti," SFC Devine added.

"The number I have for them doesn't work sometimes," Habib responded.

"John, make sure he has your number too," SFC Devine added.

Habib laughed and said, "I could never lose your number, John."

"He likes you, Johnny," SGT Hall joked.

My radio scanner picked up the Taliban's coded conversations day and night. Soon, I learned most of their slang and code words. Because I was born and raised in the same province as the insurgents, I already knew most of the slang, but the code words took a little while to figure out.

"Do you have enough cows?" one of the Taliban fighters,
Abu Zubair, asked over the radio.
"Not enough, but we are getting more tomorrow."
"I need the exact number," Abu Zubair insisted.
"I am not sure, but probably couple thousands."
"Okay, but Mullah Saab the exact number."

The Taliban militants used "cows" for PKM rounds. Hand radios were mostly used by the Taliban deep in the valley for communication because there was no cell phone service, but the Icom scanner that I carried played an incredible and preventive role during our daily patrols and missions because it intercepted most of the intelligence about enemy movement. Further, many locals that had felt betrayed by the government became open sources of intelligence [OSINT] for 1st platoon because of the relationships we built.

The Taliban had not attacked us yet, but we knew it could happen at any moment. It was still early, cold and chilly outside while the surrounding Hindu Kush mountains were covered with heavy snow that you could see for miles.

"John, tell LT Kerr that the trails and walking paths up on the mountains from Bajour are covered by snow," Habib told me. "The Taliban can't use them right now. They are waiting for the snow to disappear."

"When will it disappear?" SFC Devine questioned.

"Soon because the sun is strong."

Even though it was cold and still snowy on the mountains, the Taliban insurgents fired rockets and mortars at Combat Outpost Monti at least 2-3 times a week, but most of those rockets ended up landing in residential areas, schools and mosques in the town right by the outpost.

"The Taliban fired those rockets from Cheshan and that's right where Saabandi is," Habib told LT Kerr. LT Kerr pulled his map out and asked Habib about the village and Cheshan mountain.

"We need to find those motherfuckers," LT Kerr said.

"John, don't translate 'motherfucker'," SFC Devine jumped right before I could translate.

"Does Habib know that one of the Taliban's rockets killed a four-year-old girl and her mom last week?" LT Kerr asked.

"Yes, I know the family," Habib responded.

"John, tell him, we went to the house yesterday."

This was a heartbreaking tragedy that happened in February 2009. It was just one example of the Taliban's brutality and heinous attacks against civilians; the Taliban always used civilians as human shields to protect themselves. In March 2009, we received contact from some local houses deep in the Dangam Valley, and we learned that the Taliban took everyone hostage to use their houses for the attack against us, but 1st platoon [1-32] never fired back--

"There are kids in the house!" SPC Carlson yelled during an attack.

"Don't shoot!" SFC Devine responded.

"Sir, Sir, there is a guy shooting at us from the house in the valley," SPC March radioed.

"Are you sure? Ask SPC Carlson if he is positive," LT Kerr responded.

"Yes, he is, but he is saying that there is a civilian in the house."

"Don't shoot at the house," LT Kerr insisted while SFC Devine was on the radio talking back with Combat Outpost Monti.

We found out that the locals never wanted to let the Taliban use their houses nor did they want to provide food.

"The Taliban came like a thief and stole our property, houses and food to attack you," a local elder told us.

"I know. I told my guys to avoid civilian casualties as much as they could because it's the difference between us and the fucking Taliban," LT Kerr responded.

"We know and thank you. The Taliban killed a girl and her mother last month in a rocket attack because they don't care about civilians."

"We went to the family and assisted them as much as we could-- John, tell him, that we are here to help, but if the fucking Taliban attacks, we are soldiers and we fight back."

"*Turjuman Saab*, tell him that I understand. I have been fighting the Taliban along with my entire Mushawani tribe for years now," the elder responded.

Ch 15: Settling into Observation Post Castle War Frog

Observation Post Castle War Frog was one of the posts located on a hilltop in Dangam Valley, surrounded by the Hindu Kush Mountains flush with shrubs, honeysuckle, gooseberry bushes, pines and holly trees. The outpost had a couple of houses made of rocks and mud on its lower side but not much else. There was also no road to the observation post, and everything including water, food and other supplies were transported and delivered by donkeys through a zigzag of rocky trails. SFC Devine looked at LT Kerr, "Sir, we need to do something about this place."

It was only about 10 miles from Combat Outpost Monti, but 1st platoon [1-32] conducted most of its daily patrols, missions and ambushes against the Taliban from Castle War Frog rather than Monti. It was a great location to watch over the district center, the town and the area southeast of the valley for enemy maneuvers, but it was also an open target, surrounded by a mountain peak that could be easily used against us. First platoon [1-32] preferred to stay overnight most of its deployment at the observation post [OP] along with the local police and, some days with the Marine embedded training team, in order to avoid traveling back and forth to

Monti because there was a huge threat that the Taliban could use Improvised Explosive Devices [IEDs] and ambushes along the road between Monti and Dangam Valley.

"How do you like it here?" I asked LT Kerr.

"I fucking love it; it's great-- no meetings, no boss, nothing."

"--Johnny boy, it's more freedom here than Monti," SFC Devine said cutting LT Kerr off.

"What do you mean more freedom? We don't have MWR, computers, TV or a telephone."

"That's what I am talking about, Johnny boy!"

When 1st platoon [1-32] arrived in 2009, there were no buildings or resources for the policemen on the hilltop except a tiny room that looked like a cave and was made of rocks with thousands of holes through the walls. The Afghan policemen were very friendly, hospitable and sociable with 1st platoon [1-32] and created a great friendship and brotherhood with every soldier at Castle War Frog.

"John, find out where the police commander is," LT Kerr instructed when we arrived at Castle War Frog.

"He went to the police department, but I can call him on the radio," a policeman responded.

"It's okay, we are gonna be here for a little while. Is he is coming back?"

"Yes, he is probably on his way back now."

"Ask him if I can go to their room," SFC Devine requested.

"Yes, but *Turjuman Saab*, tell them that it's a very small room," Abasin, the policeman, warned.

"No worries, we can see it-- ha-ha," SFC Devine started to laugh as he watched LT Kerr need to duck to enter the room.

"Ha-ha, I am a tall man," LT Kerr replied.

From inside the room, you could hear the breeze outside and could even feel it through the holes that weren't blocked by newspapers, plastic bags and empty bottles in order to keep the room warm at night.

"Where are the lights at?" LT Kerr asked.

"We don't have lights or electricity," Abasin replied. "We use that lamp right there."

"What is that?!" LT Kerr asked surprised.

"It's a lantern," I replied. "It's pretty easy to work. You put the gasoline in the small tank at the very bottom and that's it."

"How the heck do you know that?" SFC Devine asked.

"My family has been using it since I was born."

Abasin was very polite, smart, friendly and social with everyone from 1st platoon [1-32]. He was always there if we needed anything, but unfortunately, he was killed on way to his home in 2014, while I was working in Jalalabad. That day, I received a random call —

"Is this John?" the caller asked.

"Yes, who is this?

"I am Abasin's father." I heard him start to cry, "Abasin died." He couldn't talk, but he managed to say that his son was killed by the Taliban. "He was coming home to visit his kids and wife, but the Taliban ambushed and killed him."

"I am so sorry, that's so sad. I wish I had his number so I could have kept in contact with him."

"He was always talking about you," his father said. "He was a great soldier."

***

First platoon [1-32] turned the observation post into a heaven for the policemen. We brought HESCOs, sandbags, plywood, c-wires, and other tools and equipment to help build the post, but there was still an urgent need to build a road in order to get everything to Castle War Frog.

"John, ask the police chief if he can get these things to the observation post," LT Kerr instructed.

"I don't know, it's a lot of stuff, but I will figure something out," the police chief responded and then continued, "John, tell him that I can use a donkey but the old road is not drivable." The road had been destroyed by rain and flooding, but after surveying it, SFC Devine and LT Kerr decided that 1st platoon could fix it. It turned out to be an easy fix and 1st platoon [1-32] was able to complete it within weeks, despite the major threats of a Taliban attack.

At the post, the policemen couldn't be more thrilled after 1st platoon [1-32] began filling HESCOs and sandbags day and night because spring was just at the corner. With the change of season, the Taliban would start their fighting and operations against the Americans and Afghan forces. My Icom scanner intercepted more insurgent conversation in Pashtu, Urdu and sometimes Arabic. It was crystal clear that the Taliban and their foreign backers and supporters were going to carry out an attack against 1st platoon [1-32] in Dangam Valley.

"Sir, I have been hearing weird conversations between the Taliban," I told LT Kerr.

"What do you mean 'weird conversation'?"

"They use coding and slang about the attack. The Taliban use 'axes' for rocket-propelled grenades [RPG rounds] and 'cows' for PKM rounds."

"Well, keep us updated."

Ch 16: My First Injury

"We need a medic over here!" I heard someone say, but I wasn't sure who.

We never thought that the Taliban would attack at night since they never had night vision goggles, but we were wrong.

We spent much of the day at the district center conducting daily meetings and shuras with the district governor, police chief, NDS chief and some local tribal elders. It was a pretty damn busy day and went by without an attack, but it seemed unusual because the local town was not as busy as it used to be and everything closed early, unlike before.

"What is going on, Johnny boy, did you scare everybody?" SFC Devine joked.

"Ha-ha, I think he did!" LT Kerr jumped in.

"I don't know. It's just not normal," I replied.

"Did you hear anything on the Icom scanner?"

"No, but it was off while we were in the meeting."

"What do you think, John?" LT Kerr asked me.

"I don't know, but I think we might get shot at it."

We headed back to the OP and planned to spend overnight with the policemen. Right after we arrived, I saw Abasin running to me and shouting, "John, I need to talk to you." I thought that there must be something he heard on their radios, but it turned out that he made a chicken and rice dinner for everybody.

Since we spent most of our time at the observation post, 1st platoon [1-32] and the Afghan National Police began to share meals, and we would have at least one Afghan meal a day; 1st platoon loved it.

"This is yummy. John, tell him thank you," SFC Devine said while he was eating.

"It's really good; how does he make it?" SSG Benson asked.

"Can't tell you, it's a secret menu!"

"Secret my ass."

After the meal, SFC Devine, SGT Hall and SGT Benson stayed with the policemen while LT Kerr attended his meeting via radio in his small camping tent outside, about 20 feet away from us. The policemen always felt secure and safe while we were there with them at the OP. SFC Devine shook everybody's hands and left around 9 P.M., but I stayed with policemen, listening to the radio scanner. A couple of the policemen lit a joint. I didn't smoke, but the smoke hung in the air.

"Can I open the door?" I asked them.

"No, not at night. The Taliban would be able to see and identify our location."

"--Excuse me, John," Hamidullah said while he was leaving the room to use the bathroom. It was a small room so if you wanted to leave, you had to maneuver around the others. He had barely left when he came back and said, "there are some flashlights deep in the valley!"

"John, sit down; he is just high," Abasin laughed it off.

"I am serious, let's go check it out!" Hamidullah insisted.

We ended up going outside and found out that Hamidullah was right when we saw unusual flashlights along the ridgeline.

"I gotta go let LT Kerr and SFC Devine know!"

"Okay, I will call another observation post across the district and ask them if they saw or heard anything," Abasin said.

"The policemen saw some flashlights along the ridgeline," I exclaimed when I saw LT Kerr.

"Okay, what ridgeline?"

"The one back there, between Dangam and Bajawar."

"Let me know if you hear anything on the radio."

While I was talking to LT Kerr, Hamidullah came over and shared an update.

"Hey, we just talked the other observation post and they said that it could be a patient."

"What does he mean by 'patient'?"

"It must be someone sick that locals are bringing to the hospital. They always do that because there is no road for the ambulance so the villagers need to carry the patient to the taxi stop or the hospital."

It was almost 10 P.M. when I headed back to go to bed, but before I did, my radio picked up the Taliban's communications.

"Where are they? Are they still here or gone?" A Taliban militant with the call-sign *Fedai* asked. Unlike before, he didn't mention "Americans" or "infidels", but of course they were talking about us. *"They were still at the district when I left,"* the call-sign *Abu-Zaed* replied. I was waiting on the Taliban to say more, but the conversation suddenly stopped and the scanner starts making a buzzing sound until it picked up the Taliban's music again.

I went outside to ask Hamiduallah and the other policemen on guard duty if they heard the conversation.

"We didn't hear it, but we saw more flashlights in the Saabandi village," Hamidullah responded. "But they have disappeared now."

Around 11:30 P.M., the lights disappeared, and we thought that the patient had made it to the doctor's house or got into a taxi. We didn't know that the Taliban were deep in the valley, surrounded by mountains, hills and trees so that we couldn't see them anymore.

"Ok, let me know if you hear or see anything, but now I am going to sleep."

I was out like a light, but I woke up to a big explosion, boom and detonation. "We are under attack; we are under attack!" I heard all around me. "Get cover! Get cover! Where is it coming from?!" someone was shouting.

"The ridgeline, the ridgeline!" someone responded as another rocket-propelled grenade [RPG] hit the observation post.

"John, tell them that the other OP will hit the Taliban with Dish-Ka!" Muhammad shouted. First platoon [1-32] and the policemen's response and defense were much quicker than the Taliban anticipated. It was a huge slap across the faces of the Taliban.

"Where is John?" SFC Devine shouted.

"I am here, SGT," I shouted back

"You, okay?"

"Yes, I am."

"What about the police?"

I was running back and forth to communicate between the policemen and 1st platoon [1-32] to make sure that there were no friendly accidents taking place because the Afghan policemen did not carry night vision goggles

"John, have Muhmmad call the district and let them know that we are going fire mortars," LT Kerr shouted.

"Got it, sir!"

I was talking to Muhammad when I heard someone say, "John, grab this; I am getting more ammo."

"I can't see it, where is it?" I asked.

"It's fucking on the wall!"

I started touching the wall to find the gun, "fuuuuuuuck!!" I screamed. I had burned my hands so badly that I couldn't talk for a bit.

While Muhammad and Abasin were trying to find out what happened, I heard someone call, "we need a medic here; John got shot!"

"I didn't get shot but I burned my hands," I shouted.

"How the fuck did you burn your hands, you idiot?"

"I grabbed the machine gun from its barrel and it was extremely hot."

"Do you even fucking know that it gets hot after hundreds of rounds of fire?" SFC Devine asked. "God damn it, how are you feeling right now?

"They are burning like a hell."

"You fucking pussy," SGT Hall said.

"Where is fucking Tomeo?" SFC Devine asked.

"He is still with SPC Tibbs, but almost done," SGT Benson said. "Tibbs got shot in the leg, but he is doing good."

"John's right, they are hurt bad, but I will take care of him" SPC Tomeo assessed when he arrived. "I am going to put some lotion and bandages, but they are still gonna burn for a while" SPC Tomeo said.

SPC Tomeo did whatever he could to help but I had to deal with pain and sharp burning while listening to the radio scanner and translating both for 1st platoon and the Afghan policemen for the rest of the night.

"How are you feeling?" LT Kerr asked while he was calling for fire support from Monti and air support both from Jalalabad [JAF] and Bagram airfield [BAF].

"I am good sir."

"Can you let Muhammad know to call the police chief and let him know that we are going to conduct a fire mission from Monti soon?"

"Yes," I replied and left to speak with Muhammad.

"John, tell LT Kerr that the Taliban are still there, collecting their casualties," the police chief said on the radio.

I went back to speak with LT Kerr when I heard Muhammad radio, "John, *Qumandaan Saab* wants to talk to you."

"Ask LT Kerr if he can get an air support," Police Chief Qumandaan asked. "The Taliban are in the run right now."

"John, tell the police chief that the Apache helicopters are watching a few people on the ridgeline; it looks like they are carrying something," LT Kerr responded.

"Shoot them, they are either Taliban fighters or their reinforcements," the police chief confirmed.

"That's what I thought."

"John, tell him, if they see anybody with weapons this late, shoot them because they are Taliban," The police chief instructed.

The fire mission stopped after the Apache helicopters arrived and began targeting and engaging the Taliban militants deep in the valley. The entire valley turned into hell for the Taliban when aircrafts dropped bombs that shook the entire valley like an earthquake and killed many of Taliban who were evacuating and transporting the wounded and injured fighters. The Taliban suffered massive causalities and talked about all night long and even into the next day.

"Where is Mullah Saab?" one of the Taliban fighters asked.
"I don't know; I have been trying calling him, but he is not responding."
"Pray for his safety and may Allah keep him safe."
"I hope he is safe, but I heard some friends mention that he was killed last night."
"May Allah accept his martyrdom and sacrifice."
"What did you find out about our friends?"
"Their radios didn't work, and I couldn't go there because the helicopters are still flying."
"May Allah accept their sacrifice," The Taliban added

"Where are the wasps now?" the Taliban fighter asked referring to the helicopters.
"I think, they are gone."

The Apache helicopters had scanned the entire valley but had now gone to refuel at FOB Wright near Asadabad. After about 40 minutes, the helicopters returned and continued to fly over the ridgeline and deep into the valley all night long while LT Kerr and SFC Devine were on the radio talking to people back at Combat Outpost Monti.

As a result of the attack, SPC Joshua Shane Tibbs got medevacked out of Castle War Frog because of his injuries, but I stayed with the platoon with both of my hands swathed in bandages and with millions of emotions and thoughts occupying my mind after the fight. Soon, I felt much better, but the scars remained for months; even though my family saw the marks, I never told them what happened.

Ch 17: Improvised Explosive Device (IED)

"Johnny boy, you ready?" SFC Devine asked the next morning before we headed to the district for our daily key leader engagement [KLE] and security meetings with local government officials.

"I think I am."

"How did you sleep?"

"Not very well; I felt pain all night."

"Let me see your hands, the palm-side," SFC Devine took my hands. "You are crazy, Johnny boy. Keep the bandage on."

"John, tell LT Kerr and SFC Devine that I am sorry that I wasn't there last night, but I heard you guys did a very, very good job fighting the Taliban," the district governor, Shah Mahmood, apologized.

"Thank you, the police did an amazing job last night. They fucking fought like bad asses," LT Kerr replied.

"They should get promoted," SFC Devine added.

The police chief laughed and said, "I wish they could, but they need the money more than ranks to support their families."

"How much does each policeman make?" SFC Kevin asked.

"5-6 thousand Afghani."

"What would that be in dollars?" SFC Devine asked.

"I think, one U.S. dollar is equal to 150 Afghani," I replied.

"John, I talked to Muhammad and he said somebody got wounded," the police chief asked, joining the conversation.

"Yes, one of my soldiers was shot in the leg, but he is okay. It wasn't too bad, but we had to medivac him," LT Kerr responded.

"I am sorry, but I hope he gets healed soon."

"John, tell LT Kerr and SFC Devine that it's very unusual that the Taliban attacked you guys at night," the police chief added.

"Well, the Taliban learned their lesson now," Haji Habib, the NDS chief added.

"John, ask Haji Habib if he has heard anything about the Taliban casualties?"

Haji Habib was a smart man, born and raised in Shigal District, he had been working as an intelligence officer in Dangam District for years. Dangam was a very important district geographically because it was a doorway into northern Kunar. Habib was the right partner for 1st platoon because he knew a lot about both domestic and foreign Taliban fighters who were fighting in northern Kunar province against the Americans and Afghan forces. He had great relationships with local tribal elders and government officials, which gave him an upper hand when collecting and gathering information on Taliban, Al-Qaida and other terrorists in the area. In addition to that, he was beyond easy to work with, trust and share intelligence when it came to the Taliban's fighters, ammo caches, and weapons in Dangam.

Haji Habib's office was a favorite of everyone to stop by whenever we visited Dangam district because he was always bringing something to the table whether it was food or *Shudu* chai.

"Man, I love the *Shudu* chai he makes with almonds, raisins, walnuts, and pistachios," SGT Hall announced during a visit.

SGT Benson looked at me and asked, "Can I get that glass tray that he uses for fruit?"

"Yes, put it in your pocket the next time we go to his office."

"Are you sure? He won't mind, right?"

"Hahaha, I am just fucking with you, don't do that."

"You are an asshole. I almost believed you."

"John, do you guys know how many Taliban fighters participated in the attack last night?" Habib asked continuing on with business.

"I don't know, but we got shot at from all sides," LT Kerr responded.

"Our intel says that almost one hundred local and foreign fighters carried out the attack last night," Haji Habib replied.

"How many of them did we kill?"

"More than ten, including some Arabs who planned to take over the observation post and then the district center."

"That'll never happen while I am fucking here."

"He is very good, I like him," LT Kerr praised Haji Habib later on our way back from the meeting. Indeed, Haji Habib was a professional officer who loved his country, people and job. Unfortunately, the Taliban killed him during an insider attack in 2013 when he went to see one of the local Taliban commanders. The meeting was set up to capture and later kill Habib.

After the attack on Castle War Frog, the Taliban and their sympathizers spread false and baseless news that they had killed more than twenty Americans including their interpreter. They also lost no time creating a plan of retaliation for the men that they lost during the attack on the observation post.

> *"Hamza, can you hear me, can you hear me, Hamza?" Qari, a Taliban militant kept calling on his friend on the radio.*

> *"I can hear you, but your voice is not very clear," Hamza responded.*

> *"I am here with friends and the radio doesn't work very well."*

> *"Ghat Mullah Saab wants to know how many Americans you guys killed."*

> *"Alhamdulillah, praise be to Allah, more than 20 with their infidel interpreter."*

Get the Terp Up Here!

176

*"Allah Akbar, Allah Akbar-- God is great, God is great,"
Qari started shouting, and I could even hear other Taliban
in the background chant with him.*

*"Ghat Mullah is coming to visit to offer his condolences,"
Qari said. "He will tell us the next plan."*

*"Some friends said, that we are still gonna go for the plan
that we talked about," Hamza added*

"Okay, but make sure nobody ever sees you."

This was a pretty clear sign that the Taliban was going
to plant an improvised explosive device [IEDs] along the road
San Diego, between Combat Outposts Monti and Dangam. We
traveled back and forth to the Dangam Valley at least five days
a week on San Diego when we were needed back at Monti as
the quick reaction force [QRF] for other platoons who were
conducting missions in Asmar and Shigal districts.

"John, tell LT Kerr that the Taliban might plant an
improvised IED along the road," Haji Habib warned. "It's very
hard to tell, but it could be anywhere between Asmar [Monti]
and Dangam, or it could be an ambush."

"I don't think, the Taliban would fight again," the police chief
said with a laugh. "You scared them so badly." Everyone
laughed.

"John, tell LT Kerr that we have a long narrow dirt
road with so many speed bumps and holes that I think an IED
would go off whenever I drive back and forth," the district
governor cautioned.

"This is an ambush valley, you can get ambushed anywhere in the valley," Haji Habib said. The Taliban could use the mountain valleys, big rocks, hills and trees for cover during an attack.

"There are parts of the road that look like somebody blew it up before," SFC Devine said.

"That's what I'm talking about. There are more by Baidad village," Shah Mahmood responded.

"John, ask the district governor if he has tried to do something about it," LT Kerr told me.

"I wish I could, but it would cost a lot of money," the district governor responded. "The provincial governor, Wahidi, filled his pockets with the funds and didn't care about the construction. Whatever you guys see around here or even in Asmar [Monti], the Americans have built, not the governor."

"Excuse me, I almost forgot I need to make a call really quick," Haji Habib said moving toward the door.

The police chief held his hand to his ear like he making a call and said, "Taliban, Taliban," joking about who Habib was leaving to talk to. We all laughed.

When Habib came back in, he told us, "I just talked to one of my sources, and he believes that the Taliban are preparing a suicide bomber to detonate himself either on convey or at the district center."

LT Kerr looked shocked when he heard "suicide bomber," and told SPC March, "let everybody fucking know not to let anyone close to the convoy other than the police and people that work here."

"I asked my source to follow up on it and make sure where this individual is," Haji Habib added.

"Thank you so much. We gotta keep going, but will see you soon."

***

A few months later, I was in my room, watching a movie when someone knocked on the door. I didn't answer because I thought, there it might be another interpreter messing around with me like we always did. But within seconds the banging on the door got even harder. "Stop it!" I yelled.

"John, you here? It's SGT Anderson."

"Holy crap, yes, come on in Sergeant!" I responded and got out of bed.

"Were you jerking off or something?"

"Ha-ha, no I was watching *The Notebook*."

He looked at me like he had never heard of it. "What's up?" I asked him.

"Just wanted to tell you that we leave tomorrow at 9:00 A.M." And when he turned to leave, he looked back and said, "Hey John...that's a girl movie."

"It's a good movie, though."

I finished the movie. It was a very interesting love story, and I was very emotional, but I couldn't tell anybody that it almost made me cry. Even though I couldn't understand everything they said in the movie, the characters and pictures spoke for themselves. I went to bed a bit early because I was going to have a long day the next morning with both government officials and local tribal elders to discuss security and some projects that were under construction. I usually woke up early for morning prayer and set my alarm for 8:30 A.M., but I was woken up earlier when my phone went off.

"*Salaam Alikum*, this is Commander Rahim from Afghan Border Police Kandak." Col Rahim was an Afghan Border Police commander in Asmar but lived in Dangam valley. His family was very well known, influential, and strong.

"Oh, *Salaam*, how are you, good morning," I got lost with words because I didn't remember giving him my phone number, but I was the '911' that everybody used to report suspicious and terrorist activities or to arrange meetings with 1st platoon [1-32].

"Are you still sleeping?" he laughed and asked, "Can you let LT Kerr know that I got a call from my youngest brother who said that there is a bomb."

His mention of a bomb jolted me awake. "Let me go tell LT Kerr now." I rushed into the barracks while some soldiers were still sleeping but found LT Kerr and SFC Devine both awake and packing up their backpacks.

"Sheesh! there are people sleeping," LT Kerr said when I rushed in.

"IED, sir!"

"What? Let's go outside."

"Calm down, John, "SFC Devine said.

"Tell us what's going on." LT Kerr said while I was still on the phone with Col Rahim.

"There is a bomb right before Baidad village."

"Can you ask him where exactly in Baidad village?" Both LT Kerr and SFC Devine asked.

"Let me find out and I will call you back," Col Rahim said. We didn't hear back for a while, so I began to call the commander's number but only got a busy signal.

When we finally connected, Col Rahim told us, "It's a wire-guided IED planted next to a culvert by the spring at the corner."

"What about the Taliban? Did anybody see strange people around?" SFC Devine asked.

"No, but the wire goes all the way to the mountain top. One of my villagers who happened to find it informed my family. She cut the wire because she didn't know what it was. The wire went through a trail that leads to her house."

"That's great, but make sure people stay away. We will meet you there." LT Kerr said.

The lady who cut the wire lived with her husband and six kids in a house on the slope of a mountain in Baidad village of Dangam Valley. She was carrying water from the water spring when she saw it and cut it with rocks, not knowing that it was an IED wire. We were lucky that she notified her husband and Col Rahim's family; otherwise, a tragedy could have happened.

We didn't have an Explosive Ordnance Disposal [EOD] team at Monti; the closest team was at FOB Wright in Asadabad or at FOB Joyce in Sarkani. When the EOD from FOB Wright arrived later that morning, we headed to meet Col Rahim at the spring. The Afghan Border Police had circled the IED spot was with stones and gravel. The IED was planted in the middle of the road, buried with soil and dirt, but the Taliban failed to bury and hide the rest of the wire in the rocky terrain. It was just one IED, but it took almost a whole day for the EOD team to detonate and look for other possible bombs in the area. They didn't find others.

"Back up, back up!" a SSG from the EOD shouted to everybody.

"John, let the police know that the EOD is going to detonate it," LT Kerr said.

"Johnny boy, don't forget about those kids, tell them go home," SFC Devine add.

While the EOD detonated the IED, Apache helicopters were flying over the mountains and valleys to make sure that there are no Taliban insurgents hiding for an ambush. "Yay, fuck the Taliban!" I heard the EOD guy said after they detonated and discharged.

"John, anything on the Taliban radio?" SFC Hall asked.

"Nothing, but it's not even working."

"Yeah, I am pretty sure the Duke is on in every truck." The Duke system or "Jammer" is a vehicle-mounted, very light-weight system that neutralizes remote-controlled explosives. It was an important system and played an incredible and life-saving role for troops during daily patrol and missions.

"Hurry up, John, I need you!" SGT Hall shouted from the river bed.

"Coming," I responded. It was hard to walk up and down the dry bed, but I made it, "What's up?" I asked him.

"Let's go find this mother fucker," SGT Hall said. "We are going to follow the wire."

My adrenaline kicked in. I looked back and noticed everybody was behind me while I had no weapon and the radio still wasn't working. We followed the wire all the way to the hilltop where we found a bag that the Taliban left behind, containing a motorcycle battery, chewing gum, biscuits, water, some digging tools, a knife and lots of wire and cord. Finally, the radio picked up the Taliban's conversation--

> "Akrama, Akrama, can you hear me, can you hear me?" Fatih said. "Mubariz, Mubariz?!"
> "I can hear you," Mubariz responded.
> "Did you hear anything about Omari?" Fatih asked.
> "I talked to him and he said that the battery didn't work."
> "Okay, if you talk to him, have him call me on the radio."
> "Okay, may Allah keep you safe and secure."
> "Let all friends know to take great care of themselves. Wasps are flying."
> "I talked to Yassar and he said that there is American in Baidad," Mubariz added
> "I know, be careful out there."

After the detonation of the IED, LT Kerr and SFC Devine wanted to meet the family to thank them, but they refused to meet us there because they could get compromised and possibly get murdered later. However, the husband agreed to meet us at Combat Outpost Monti the next day. When he came to the post, Company Commander Captain Bryant and the rest of the Charlie Company not only thanked him for the heroic and courageous act that saved many lives, but we also gave him a gift that could benefit the entire family.

"What do you think, what should we give the family?" SFC Devine asked.

"A goat and some cash," I replied.

"Should we give him dollars-- or what's the money here in Afghanistan?"

"Afghani, but people here use Pakistani rupees."

"We've got Afghani currency," LT Kerr said.

The man, who we learned was named Ibrahim, became a very good source. He reported any suspicious and terrorist activities in his village.

Ch 18: Shin Kowrak Ambush

April 2009

"John, you ready? We are going to FOB Joyce," SFC Devine said.

"Always, sergeant."

He looked at me and said, "I don't know about that, John."

"Yeah, neither I do, John," SGT Hall jumped in.

"I like it there; it's much better than Monti," I told them.

"Fuck no, FOB Joyce sucks; so many fucking officers that you have to salute all the time."

"I will get you an officer rank. I will ask the tailor to make one for you," I joked with SFC Devine.

He laughed and said, "Wish it was that easy."

En route to FOB Joyce we had to drive through the Shin Kowark Valley. It was one of the smallest valleys of Shigal District in Kunar Province, approximately 15 miles to the south of Combat Outpost Monti. The valley separated COP Monti, FOB Joyce, FOB Wright in Asadabad and farther north. It wasn't too far from the Bajwar and Mohmand tribal regions where the Taliban had infiltrated and used to pass through into Kunar to attack both Afghan and American troops.

"John, what's a fucking 'Shin Kowrak'?" LT Kerr asked during a patrol of the area.

"It's a fucking valley, sir."

He laughed, "I know it's a fucking valley, John, but what does it mean?"

"I don't fucking know."

"Ask the elder."

The elder smiled and said, "I have lived my entire life here but I never understood what Shin Kowrak means; I can tell that it's not a Pashtu name." This was not a strange situation. Many Afghans lived their entire lives in places with names they did not understand. Shin Kowrak was one of the valleys named by Alexander the Great who invaded what is now Afghanistan in 330 B.C.

Today, Shin Kowrak and its surrounding villages and valleys are dominated by the Hezbi-e-Islamic [HIG] fighters who have carried out attacks against both Afghan and American troops for more than a decade. Shin Kowark was very well known for ambushes back in the '80s, and abandoned Russian tanks and vehicles still remain as a symbol for HIG fighters. Shin Kowrak wasn't as bad as Daab Valley, but we always got shot at because its peaks and terrain made it easy for fighters to retreat and hide.

Gulbuddin Hekmatyar, the founder and leader of the HIG political party, had been in hiding for more than 15 years, and it was believed that he was in the Shigal District. There was intelligence that one of his high-profile commanders, Kasmir Khan, was providing Hekmatyar safe haven in Lawseen Valley, a few miles to the northwest of Shin Kowrak.

Khan was responsible for many attacks on Americans and Afghan troops in Shin Kowrak and the rest of Shigal District, Dangam, Daab Valley, Browalo Khowar, and even farther north. Shin Kowrak still remained the main target reference point [TRP] because we would get shot at more than 90% of the time. Rocket-propelled grenades [RPG], PKM machine gun, recoilless rifle [80mm] mortars, sniper, and AK47s were the weapons that HIG fighters used to attack us from both sides of the river.

In 2009, Hekmatyar was the most wanted person by both the U.S. military and Afghan government, but he had been a partner of sorts with the United States under President Ronald Reagan's administration during the war against the Russian occupation of Afghanistan in the late 1970s and 1980s. He was once an unreliable asset to the Central Intelligence Agency while they worked with the Pakistani Inter-service Intelligence [ISI] Agency against the Russians. I remember my father telling us, "Gulbuddin was a ruthless man who had no mercy for people. He killed thousands of his own people during the Russian invasion and the Afghan civil war that followed."

During Operation Enduring Freedom and Operation Freedom's Sentinel, the U.S. military, NATO (ISAF), and their Afghan allies drove the Taliban from power in 2001. The Afghans then formed a new interim-government under Hamid Karzai in Bonn, Germany; and quickly Hekmatyar took up arms again and led his groups of paramilitary fighters in attacks against the Karzai government and ISAF.

Even in my hometown in Kunar, Hekmatyar had supporters. One of my best friends and classmate's father murdered by his fighters in the '80s.

"What happened to Irashad's father?" I asked my dad. "I had never seen him in the village."

"Don't ever talk to Irshad about his father; I don't know if he remembers or knows what happened. His father was abducted from his house one day by *Hezbyano* [Hezbi-e-Islamic fighters]."

"Where did them take him?"

"I don't know but he still missing after decades," my mom said.

"I am sure he is dead by now," my father added.

I heard many stories about Hekmatyar's fighters; they were known for their guerrilla-style fighting against the Russian military and after the Russian withdrawal during the civil war in 1992. As a result of their attacks on civilians along with other fighting forces, Jamiat-e-Islami, Hezbi-Wahdat, Junbish-e-Islami, and so on, more than 50,000 civilians lost their lives only in Kabul, and a hundred thousand others left the country and immigrated.

When I started working for 1st platoon [1-32] at Combat Outpost Monti, we traveled back and forth to FOB Joyce where Chosin Battalion, 1/32 INF, 10th Mountain Division was stationed. In April 2009, we had to go to FOB Joyce and return to COP Monti at the end of the day. During the trip, 1st platoon [1-32] decided to fire at the surrounding mountains where we had been shot at before. Whether the HIG's fighters were there or not, we wanted to trick them into believing that we could see them before they attacked the convoy. That day, the tactic didn't work; when we arrived at Shin Kowrak the HIG militants launched a large-scale attack on the convey from both sides of the river. Every Humvee came under attack and HIG militants fired a couple of rocket-propelled grenades [RPGs] at our trucks and along with the small arms fire. I was sitting in the second Humvee truck when I saw the first RPG land in the dry field less than a hundred meters away from our truck. The field burst into flames, and the HIG militants believed that they shot one of our trucks because they saw the fire in the field burning.

> *"Allah Akbar, that was a great shot,"* Omari called over the radio.
> *"Allah Akbar, it's burning right now,"* Ahmadi replied.

Even though fire rained down on our convoy from all directions, we arrived safely at FOB Joyce with our trucks full of bullet holes.

"The first RPG was fucking close," SGT Hall was told the platoon at FOB Joyce.

"Were you fucking scared?"

"Fuck no, it was fun. Taliban sucks; they can't even fight more than five minutes." There was no doubt that SGT Hall was one of the bravest and fearless soldiers that I have ever worked with back in 2009, but we loved to make fun of each other.

"Yeah, John, Taliban can't fucking fight; they fight like losers," SPC March jumped in.

At the end of the day, we decided to stay at FOB Joyce until it got darker because Taliban and HIG militants never attack us at night, so we would be able to return to COP Monti without getting shot. Even after the American troops pulled out of Kunar Province, Shin Kowark remained insecure and an ambush spot for insurgents despite the agreement that HIG leader Hekmatyar made with the government in 2016.

Ch 19: Pursuit of HIG militants

1/32 INF, 10th Mountain Division
October 2009

"We are getting some fucking Taliban, John! Are you coming with us?" SPC Bravo asked.

"I don't know."

"Come on, you should come; it will be lots of fun," SPC Clark jumped in.

I didn't know anything about our next patrol until LT Kerr said, "John, call the Sub-Governor Mahmood and let him know that we are not gonna be fucking coming to Dangam for a couple of days." He continued, "We are going to fucking support the PRT in Shigal; make sure you have your radio, extra fucking batteries, and whatever you fucking need."

"Roger, sir."

"We will come get you when we leave," SFC Devine said when I turned to leave.

"You better old man."

Everyone in the barracks laughed and said, "That was a good one, John."

At the end of October 2009, we conducted another dangerous mission with the Provincial Reconstruction Team [PRT] from Camp Wright [A-BAD]. We went into Lawseen Valley where the PRT was going to check the progress and development of a girls' school and a small bridge that connected two surrounding villages deep in the valley. Both projects were under construction and funded by the PRT team in Asadabad. It was going to be the first mission by either Americans or Afghan troops into Lawseen Valley since 2001 when the area came under control of Hekmatyar and the Hezbi-e-Islami militants. This would also be one of the final patrols for 1st platoon [1-32] who was about to return home from a year-long deployment.

We left COP Monti at 4 A.M. to link up with PRT in Shigal District. First platoon [1-32] was joined by the Company Commander, Captain Bryant, and 2nd platoon [1-32]. Apart from the PRT's regular mission to provide humanitarian aid [HA] and school supplies for villagers, this mission would also deliver *Quran shareef* for the local residents. "Captain Bryan believes that bringing the Muslim Holy Book can change local residents' minds about Americans," Irfan told me.

People that lived in the valley were isolated, so it was easy for militant forces to manipulate their opinions of the Americans. Therefore, humanitarian aid [HA] and the Quran were going to be a great surprise and bring a better understanding of the Americans' intentions. We began our journey on the deadly dirt road into the valley around 5 A.M. The valley was beautiful, a breath-taking green covered with alpine, holly, and ciders on all sides. However, the dirt road became huge challenge and the most difficult part of the mission. We had to get out the truck for a ground guide the farther we drove into the valley to help navigate the dangerous loops and corners.

"It's fucking stupid," SPC Quick, our truck driver, said while driving on the rocky and zigzagging road. Big rocks hung over the road, dangling off of the high peaks and threatening to fall. We had to drive with great caution, not only because of the difficulty of the dirt road as we avoided overturning, but also because we suspected the enemy's ambushes, attacks, and IED strikes. Even with this caution, we received a call down that CPT Bryan's Humvee, one of the two vehicles behind our MRAP, had rolled over.

"Stop, stop the fucking truck!" SFC Devine yelled.

"His truck fucking went off the road!" SPC Cepeda shouted.

We found out soon that CPT Bryan and the rest of his men were okay. "Fucking lucky; the rocks and fucking trees stopped the Humvee from rolling over into the fucking valley," I heard someone say on the radio. The whole convoy stopped to help everyone in the truck out and make sure that they were not seriously injured. The worst part was that Qurans were in the same truck that rolled over.

"They've got to make sure that nobody from the village sees or finds out that the Qurans were in the truck that rolled over," I told SFC Devine.

"Yeah, I think they already took care of that, John, but thank you though."

"John, what's on the Icom scanner," SFC Devine asked.

"Let me check, but I don't think it works. The Duke is on in our truck."

"Oh, shit I forgot about that. I will ask everyone to turn it off for a little bit."

Unfortunately, this delay also provided extra time and opportunity for HIG militants to take positions or set up an ambush.

"Abu Sayeed, can you hear me?" Hamza called.
"Hamza, I can hear you," Abu Sayeed replied.
"Those people are coming for us."
"The trucks are very slow, but it looks a huge convoy."
"Hamza, Abu Sayeed, this is Muhajar. More than twenty trucks are on the way."
"Friends, ready and waiting," Hamza replied.
"Sangar, Sangar," Abu Sayeed was trying to call another militant.
"Abu Sayeed, I can hear you, this is Sangar."
"How's everybody doing?"
"We are good, waiting up here."
"Take great care and caution. Let us know if you need anything."

"What do you think, Johnny boy?" SFC Devine asked.

"I think we are gonna get shot at."

SFC Devine laughed and said, "Yeah, I am pretty fucking sure you're right."

Our biggest challenge still lay at the end of the mountain loops, corners, and curves when we finally arrived at the dead-end and couldn't drive any farther. "Let's get out of the truck," SFC Devine shouted. We had to walk for about two miles to arrive at the bridge and girls' school.

"John, anything new on the Icom?" LT Kerr asked after I linked up with him.

"Same old sir, HIG militants are talking about attacking us."

It was a spectacular view when we reached the top and could see the rest of the valley; the surrounding mountain peaks and hilltops looked so close to each other that you would think they were touching. We had air support flying over the valley, but we knew that the busy jungles, thick cedars, and holly trees made it far too easy for the HIG militants to hide, cover and position deep in the forest.

> *"Abu Sayeed, don't let them make it outta here alive,"* Sangay said on the radio.
> *"We are going to give them a lesson that they will always remember."*
> *"Be careful with helicopters."*
> *"Thanks to Allah, they can't see us."*
> *"Alhamdulillah! Thanks to Allah."*

There was one after another HIG militants cross-talking on the radio while we were still on our way to the school building after we checked out the bridge. We were slowed down when one of the female interpreters from the PRT team who was in her 60s couldn't catch up with the rest of the soldiers.   When we finally arrived at the school, I noticed villagers were evacuating their villages.

"John, what's going? Why is everyone leaving?" LT Kerr asked.

"We are gonna get shot at."

"I fucking know that, but why the fuck they are leaving the village?"

"Because they know what's going to happen."

"Stupid, fucking stupid."

We didn't spend much time at the school and headed back to the trucks after taking a bunch of pictures of the projects. The sun was gone, hiding behind the high mountain peaks that covered the narrow valley. We didn't walk too far from the projects when HIG militants rained down us from all over. "Get fucking cover!" I heard everyone shout.

First platoon [1-32] was pretty used to such fighting, but the PRT and the few civilians who accompanied them had never seen or experienced such fighting. It was a nightmare with all of the yelling.

"Please don't leave me here, son, please," I heard someone crying and begging for my help. I looked back and saw the female interpreter behind the rock, scared to death.

"Don't worry, nobody is going to leave you here," I replied.

"Thank you, thank you. I can't catch up with everybody; my legs hurt. Can you please walk with me? You are like my son," she said. When I heard her say, 'son', that really struck me, and there was no way I was going to walk without her to make sure she was okay.

"It's going to be alright; I have seen the worse. This fight is not going to last for too long," I replied.

"I am done; I am going to back to the states tomorrow."

While I was talking to her, Apaches returned from refueling and began engaging the HIG militants in the mountains and the whole fight came to an end after about twenty minutes. The Apaches gave us an opportunity to breathe and get the fuck out of there before we get shot at again. We all returned to the trucks that were parked at the very top while Apaches flew above us, but HIG militants were still talking about attacking.

"You think we are fine now?" Fatima, the interpreter, asked.

"Hopefully, but there are no guarantees; we still have to drive back. It's dark and I don't think they will attack but you never know. We've never been up here before," I replied.

We began our journey to leave the valley while Apaches were still escorting us out, but as soon as the Apaches left with the PRT personnel back to FOB Wright, 1st platoon [1-32] and the entire Charlie Company were hit with another large-scale attack by HIG militants. Stuck in the middle of a firefight, we kept pushing out of the valley, encountering more of the enemy's ambushes. The worst was when one of the trucks right before our MRAP came within inches of being hit by an RPG, and our truck got partially damaged by the shrapnel and small arms fire. Much of the attack came from the residential areas so we were unable to fire back.

"This is fucking stupid; fucking Taliban using civilians, John," SFC Devine complained after we finally made it out of the valley.

"Yeah, I fucking saw that."

"Hey, John what happened to the lady that was crying?" SPC Clark asked.

"Oh, she was okay; she works at FOB Wright."

"She was so fucking scared."

"Yes, she was, but she had a big smile on her face when she left for FOB Wright. I don't think she is going to work there anymore."

"Hahaha, the rest of the PRT needs to fucking go home; they were fucking scared," SPC Clark taunted.

"Nobody is like us, John," SFC Devine boasted.

Ch 20: The Battle of OP Bari Alai

May 2009

"John, tell the police chief that I am sorry, but we got to go back to Monti," LT Kerr said during a meeting in the Dangam District.

"Is everything okay? I didn't say anything wrong to offend him or make him mad?" The police chief asked after LT Kerr shorten the meeting.

"No, he is fine, we got a call for something else and we have to be back to Monti now. We will talk about when we get back."

Observation Post (OP) Bari Alai was a small outpost held by the Afghan National Army (ANA) while they were being trained by three U.S. and four Latvian soldiers. The OP was named after an ANA soldier who was killed in an IED strike just months before its construction. It was approximately 15-20 miles to the north of Combat Outpost Monti, between FOB Bostick (previously FOB Naray) and Monti (COP Asmar). The OP was built on a small hilltop by the Afghan National Army and the members of the Marine Embedded Training Team (ETT) following increased attacks, including ambushes and IEDs against Afghan and Coalition Forces in Nishagam also known as Ghazi Abad District of Kunar Province. Nishagam District was a Taliban safe haven where Taliban militants and other terrorists easily filtered in from Nuristan Province, which connected with Nishagam Valley in various parts. It was also vital for Afghan and Coalition Forces because all supplies traveled through Nishagam District a couple of times a month.

When I started working with the Coalition Forces at Combat Outpost Monti in 2009, I heard many horror stories from interpreters who supported many missions and daily patrols into the area. There was not a single patrol or mission that the Americans had conducted without a firefight, ambush, or IED strike because its rocky location, surrounded by high mountains and share borders with eastern Nuristan Province, Nari District, Asmar District, and the Durand-line, which made it much safer and easier for the Taliban insurgents and other militants to conduct terrorist activities. Nishagam District and OP Bari-Alai remained one of the most dangerous places for IEDs for Afghan and Coalition Forces even as the "War on Terror" moved to the southern Helmand province, which was run and secured by Afghan, Coalition Forces, and Latvian soldiers operating out of Forward Operating Base Bostick.

On May 1st, 2009, 1st platoon [1-32] was conducting its daily patrol in Dangam District of Kunar Province when a call came down from headquarters at Forward Operating Base Joyce; 1st platoon [1-32] was going to OP Bari-Alai to fight more than 100 Taliban fighters, who launched a coordinated uphill attack on the OP around 3:00 A.M. First platoon [1-32] not only provided security for Dangam Valley, it was also postured as a quick reaction force (QRF) in COP Monti and FOB Joyce. It was "Spring Operations" or the fighting season for the Taliban. Even though it was a little chilly and rainy, the Taliban began their spring operations by attacking Afghan and Coalition Forces throughout the country. There was a big increase in Taliban attacks, firefights, ambushes, IEDs and mortar attacks on Afghan and coalitions that spring, but 1st platoon [1-32] was always prepared to defend themselves and the people of Kunar Province.

"John, have you been to Nishagam District?" SFC Devine asked while we were heading back to Monti from Dangam District.

"No, but I've heard a lot about it. It's not a safe place; it's very dangerous." I didn't know what was going on, but I could tell that something was coming as we rushed back to the COP.

"I think we are going today."

"That's a very risky drive."

"I bet, but I got you, John," SFC Devine smiled.

"I got your back, sergeant."

I watched the soldiers of 1st platoon [1-32] fill with adrenaline as they prepared to go fight the Taliban. The fighting season had just kicked off, but the number of attacks towards COP Monti had already tripled. The Dangam District and the other districts were under frequent threats by the Taliban insurgents and other terrorist groups. First platoon [1-32] was comprised of less than 40 men, but they engaged 100 Taliban fighters who had overrun the fortified mountaintop observation post.

Even though everyone was tired after a long night in the Dangam District, they were ready for another fight. Nobody knew what time we were going to take off because there was fighting going on and rounds were fired from all directions. According to some primary intelligence, more than 18 ANA soldiers, including an interpreter, were taken hostages by the Taliban insurgents and some of the soldiers were killed during the clash. We could have left earlier, but the ongoing firefight made it harder for helicopters to land. Therefore, the whole platoon [1-32] was standing by. I thought after a little while that it wasn't going to happen because some past air assault operations got canceled at the last minute, but then SPC Clark shouted-

"John, Fuckin' John."

"What's up baby-face?" We called him "baby-face" because he was very young, but not younger than me though.

"You better be fucking ready; we are leaving in 15 minutes,"

He started running back to his barracks. I had to be at the HLZ early in case LT Kerr or SFC Devine had to make phone calls or something. I thought I was going to be the only interpreter, but Wahid was also at the HLZ. Wahid had worked with CPT Bryan for years, with far more experience than I had. He spoke English well and had lots of war and air assault experience.

"*Salaam*, you coming too?" Wahid asked.

"Yes, but I have never been to Nishagam."

"Yes, it's very bad up there. I was at the tactical operation command center [TOC] all day making phone calls," Wahid told me. "One of the interpreters that I know has been captured along with more than 15 ANA soldiers."

It was hair-raising and scary to think that an interpreter like myself had been captured. I never wanted to get captured by the Taliban; I would kill myself before they captured me.

"Seriously, do you know him?"

"I do, we worked together once. He is a very nice guy," Wahid replied.

I could tell that Wahid was scared to death; even though he had tons of war experience. On the other hand, I didn't have much experience and I was always thinking about having fun rather than safety. Even though we were going to the battle, I was excited about flying in the helicopter. I didn't think about what could happen like getting shot or injured.

"It's going to be fun; I have never flown in the helicopter," I told Wahid.

He looked at me and made a face so I could tell that he was angry, "it's not going to be fun; there is fighting going on! I had to talk to people all day long today."

"I know, but I like to fly in the helicopter."

While I was talking to him at the HLZ, I heard someone say, "10 minutes out, guys." Both LT Kerr and SFC Devine briefed everyone about what was happening in Nishagam-- "We don't know the exact number of the killed in action [KIA] and wounded in action [WIA], but both sides suffered casualties," SFC Devine reported.

"It's fucking pretty bad; the Apaches can't engage the fucking Taliban because they have taken Afghan soldiers and have taken civilian hostages," LT Kerr added.

Afghan National Army soldiers were forced to walk with them in the valley, and those who refused to do so were killed along the way. The briefing was mainly focused on the battle and recent updates about the enemy, and their movements, but it ended when we heard two UH-60 Black Hawk helicopters make their way into the HLZ. This was my first ever air assault mission, but I wasn't the only one, there were other soldiers from 1st platoon [1-32] who had never conducted an air assault since they had been at Combat Outpost Monti. When the first Black Hawk helicopters landed at COP Monti to pick us all up, we learned that there was no way they were going to land at the battlefield in Ghazi Abad District in Nishagam due to the heavy firefight and enemy snipers in the surrounding mountain peaks. We would have to jump out of the Black Hawks.

"John, you jump after me," SGT Hall shouted in my ear while we were in the helicopter. It was very hard to hear anything, but he shouted again, "YOU JUMP AFTER ME!"

I was confused as hell and didn't know what was going on until we arrived in Nishagam District, and I saw SGT Hall and the other soldiers jump out of the helicopters. SGT Hall gave me a thumbs-up gesture, and I did the same in return.

Even though it was going to be a short, couple meter jump, I wasn't ready for it. I was scared that I might end up breaking my legs. We were escorted by two Apache gunship helicopters all the way to the Ghazi Abad District where we were about to jump off the helicopters into a battlefield with the Taliban insurgents. I felt like I was in the movie *Black Hawk Down*. Everyone had to jump out of the helicopter as soon as possible and get covered. I was worried about it, but when we arrived it wasn't a big deal, and I followed the other soldiers.

We ended up jumping into farm land, which was recently watered so everyone got stuck because it was all muddy. I flipped over and hit the ground, my whole face and body ended up covered in mud while intense fighting and exchange of fire was happening. The second helicopter made its landing after circling a couple of times in the sky while Apache helicopters conducting cover fire targeted the Taliban's firing positions in the mountains.

It was cloudy and a little rainy which made the whole mission even harder for us, but we were all muddy and soaked anyway. After a little while, everyone managed to head to the district center and then onto the observation post to link up with other soldiers from FOB Bostick. The others had already been at the district center with their mortar team conducting fire missions since early morning. When we arrived, soaked and muddy, everyone looked at us like we were crazy, our faces painted with mud. They didn't know that we had to jump into a muddy farm field.

We still had a couple of miles to go to get to OP Bari-Alai, after we stopped by at the district center where soldiers from Bostick set up their mortar system. While 1st platoon was getting ready to leave the district center, a soldier from the 3-61 Cavalry Regiment was shot in the neck by the Taliban's sniper. It was still crazy all over the entire district; we had to hurry to go to support the OP because the Taliban could continue to attack at any time.

"We need to fucking hurry up," LT Kerr yelled while we were at the district center. "John, ask the ANA commander his name," LT Kerr instructed.

"Qumandan Rasool and these are my guys," Commander Rasool responded in broken English.

"Great, tell him that his guys are coming with us," SFC Devine told me.

"Okay, we are ready," Commander Rasool replied.

First platoon was joined by Commander Rasool and 12 ANA soldiers from Bostick as we headed to the observation post (OP). It wasn't a long walk itself, but the rainy weather and heavy loads of weapons, ammo, water and food slowed us all down and took us longer than we expected. We all made it to the Nishagam village, where we stopped for a short break before heading into the Taliban's territory. Even though we got escorted by the Apache helicopters and jets flying over the observation post (OP) and the entire valley, the Taliban's snipers were still targeting our patrol. We had to walk through the village, which looked like a ghost town. As we were leaving, my Icom scanner picked up a Taliban fighter who lived in the village and was watching us from his house.

> "Ayubi, you hear me? Ayubi, can you hear?" Omari, the Taliban spy in the village radioed.
>
> "Omari, I hear you. I am here with friends where the radio doesn't work very well," Ayubi responded.
>
> "May Allah keeps you safe out there; take great care of yourselves. There are helicopters flying everywhere," Omari said on the radio.
>
> "One of the friends said that two helicopters just landed next to the district center."
>
> "Yes, I saw them. They brought new soldiers," Omari confirmed.
>
> "Where are they? The snipers trying to find them," Ayubi asked.
>
> "There are 18 parrots, 12 crows and 2 puppies heading to the valley," Omari told his friend in code.
>
> "Where are they?" Ayubi asked.

"Out of my view now, but I could see them walking from the district."

"Must be in the village; let me call Qari Zubair," Ayubi said. "Zubair, Zubair, this is Ayubi, can you hear me?"

"Ayubi, I can hear you loud and clear," Qari Zubair responded.

"Omari said that they are in the village."

"We are here waiting," Qari Zubair assured them.

It sounded like the Taliban was going to ambush us on the way to the OP. Omari was reporting our movements, numbers of soldiers and even weapons (small arms and heavy weaponry) by using slang. 18 parrots, meant 18 American soldiers; 12 crows meant 12 ANA soldiers; and 2 puppies meant 2 interpreters. I was shocked when I heard him called us puppies because it was the worst and vilest thing to call someone, according to local culture and traditions.

"March, let the pilots know what John picked up on his radio," LT Kerr instructed.

"Roger sir, I'm talking to them right now."

"John, let the ANA know what's going on," SFC Devine added.

"I will but they have their own radio as well."

Commander Rasool was listening to everything they said.

"Allah is great! Punishment is waiting for them," Omari said.

"We are waiting desperately, but we can't do anything right now due to the wasp," Qari Zubair replied.

The mission continued to be a busy one for me because I was doing more than translation; I stayed up all night, listening to the radio to make sure that the Taliban's future plans and attacks got prevented.

Taliban insurgents were going to ambush us, but they were afraid of "the wasps," Apache helicopters. We stopped after intercepting the Icom chats to make sure Apache helicopters could scan the areas ahead of us. While we were waiting for the Apaches to give us the okay to move forward, we heard a bang. The Apache pilots were able to identify a small group of people hiding in the bushes about a mile away from us. It was the group of Taliban insurgents who planned to ambush us, but they got hit by the helicopter cover before even they fired a single round. I never heard Omari's call sign on the radio after that.

Even though it had been a dangerous trek, we made it to the observation post (OP) around 12:00 P.M. We found nothing but collapsed and destroyed remains of buildings, ammo cartridges and bullet marks on the rocks. The smell of ammo and shrapnel was everywhere. The Taliban had completely overrun OP Bari-Alai. Because the fight had ended and the casualties had been medevac'd, we thought the mission was over, and we would head back to Monti, but we had to stay longer than we expected for the hostages taken by the Taliban insurgents. Everyone was exhausted after a long, rainy day, but things started getting better at the end of the day when we barely heard a single shot.

"Anything on the radio?" LT Kerr looked at me, his face exhausted.

"Nothing much, the Taliban is just checking on each other, but Omari, the guy who reported our movement and spied on us is gone for good."

"That's fucking awesome, John. Let me know if you hear anything suspicious."

There were also reports that Afghan and American commando forces planned to carry out an operation deep in the valley to release the hostages from the Taliban insurgents, but it got pushed back when the Afghan government established a delegation team of local elders to go to demand that the Taliban release the soldiers or pay a huge price. The delegation went into the valley, but we didn't know how long the whole negotiation would take. The Afghan Defense Ministry also executed their plan by dropping commando troops along with Americans at various parts of the valley to block all the exits going into Nuristan Province. If that operation required support, our mission could last for weeks or even months. The situation was made worse because few of us had rain gear. I stayed up all night, curled up. Even those who had rain gear didn't get much of sleep because Apache helicopters and jet aircraft were flying over the valley all night. I finally fell asleep but woke up to an explosion and gunshots in the valley.

"John, *Salaam*," Commander Rasool approached.

"*Salaam Qumandan Saab*, what's up?"

"Have you heard the gunshots?"

"Yes, I just asked LT Kerr, and he said they are commandos."

The location of the hostages was identified within a village, but the Afghan and American commandos had few options because Taliban insurgents used civilians as shields. The commandos had been dropped at night and surrounded the Taliban while they slept. The Taliban insurgents had no way out, but rather than releasing the hostages, they attacked another small combat outpost up north to distract our focus on the hostages in the valley. However, that battle ended in less than 10 minutes without any friendly casualties, but some Taliban fighters were killed by the Apache helicopters.

> *"We can't do it. We already lost some of our friends," the Taliban call-sign Haidari pleaded.*
> *"Abu Baaker! What's going on up there?" Chinar asked.*
> *"It's pretty bad. We are trying to get the dead bodies but helicopters flew all night long," Abu Baaker replied.*
> *"May Allah grant them jinnah [paradise]; tell everyone to take a great care."*
> *"Abu Baaker! This is Sargar, let us know if we can help. We are trying to get up there, but can't do it now. The Americans are everywhere."*
> *"Be careful out there!"*

Finally, after none of the additional attacks worked, the Taliban decided to release the hostages. They started yelling at each other on their radios and asking their commanders to release the hostages as soon as possible; otherwise, they could get killed or captured.

"John, we are going back today," SGT Hall said after a couple of days.

"You better shower when we get back," I told him.

SGT Hall laughed and said, "You fucking need to shower; you smell like shit."

"Not worse than SFC Devine; I showered in the rain today."

"John, can you tell Commander Rasool thank you for everything? His men were incredible during this whole operation, but they can get ready to leave for the district center. I believe they are going back to Bostick," LT Kerr instructed.

"Thank you, this is our country and we are honored to fight and defend it," Commander Rasool replied.

Commander Rasool was indeed an incredible man from northern Afghanistan who had fought in Kunar for years. I had the honor and pleasure to work with him again in 2011 at Combat Outpost Monti while I was working for 101st Airborne and he had been promoted to captain. He was a great friend, soldier and leader who was tragically killed on an IED strike, during a combat patrol in Pech Valley a few years later. He is gone but never forgotten.

We left for COP Monti around 9:00 P.M., returning to the Dangam District which was also under constant threat from the Taliban insurgents. We found out that the hostages got released after a few days, but the attack on the OP Bar-Alai had already taken many innocent lives. Three Americans-- Ryan King, SGT James Pirtle and SSG William-- and two of the Latvians soldiers died while two others were critically wounded. Four of the ANA soldiers were killed and 12 were taken prisoner but were eventually released. Our unit from Combat Outpost Monti was the nearest coalition force [CF] unit to respond. The Taliban commander who led the attack, Commander Bakht Ali was killed during a firefight with

American soldiers almost a year later. He was known for his massive attacks including IEDs against Afghan and Coalition forces in the river valley, and for always having foreign fighters with him.

Ch 21: Food Poisoning

September 2009

"It was yummy; I ate tons of them," SSG Benson said as we finished eating.

"You probably have a food coma," SFC Devine told him.

"I can't stop eating either; it was very good," SGT Hall added.

"Did you notice that the soup was very good and sticky?" SSG Benson noted.

"I love *Dodai* bread. How do you guys make it?" SPC Case asked.

"It's very easy. My brother works at the bakery in Jalalabad," I responded.

"And you never brought me *Dodai* bread?" SFC Devine joked.

"John is full of shit," SPC March laughed.

"Yes, he is," SSG Anderson agreed.

"We are gonna give you to 'Nick Muhammad'," SFC Devine told me. Nick Muhammad was a local Taliban Commander in Dangam Valley.

"Good, he is my uncle," I joked.

The Taliban had recently failed once again to blow up our convey with improvised explosives devices [IED], and we knew that they would try to retaliate. However, we never expected that they would be able to poison our food at the district or police headquarters, where we always had meals with Dangam government officials and local tribal elders. You could never trust everyone, and the Taliban found an insider to do just that. First platoon's [1-32] friendships with local government and tribal elders were pretty known to the Taliban because 1st platoon [1-32] was always getting invited for meals and tea.

"*Turjuman Saab*, tell the Americans that we have an old proverb that goes 'a guest is a friend of Allah'," a local tribal elder once said while we were visiting his village deep in Dangam Valley.

"What does that mean?" LT Kerr asked.

"It means that Afghan likes guests," I replied.

According to the Afghan culture and tradition, if you are invited by an Afghan for a meal, you should accept and if not, tell the reasons; otherwise, the host could get offended.

Locals were very hospitable and lived up to the Pashtunwali code. When we went to their villages, houses or stores, we were always offered a meal with them or at least green tea.

"I remember when I was in Pech Valley, we had to eat with Afghan National Army all the time. They shared their own food with us, but we also brought soda, snacks, cookies, water, candies and other stuff," SGT Hall said.

"How did you like Afghan food?"

"Dude, the best food I ever had. I can never understand why Afghan food is so good," SGT Hall replied.

Even though 1st platoon, [1-32] did not need to purchase from the local market, stores and shops in Dangam, the soldiers did their best to support local business because one U.S. Dollar was equivalent to 70 Afghani, which meant a lot for the small business owners. It was one of the ways to create concrete and strong friendship and relationships with local businesses, whose owners were always excited to see 1st platoon [1-32] at the market.

"John, what's going on here today? I have never seen so many people at the bazaar before," LT Kerr asked.

"John's getting married to a goat," SGT Hall responded.

"Hahaha, you are an asshole, Sergeant, I mean, a real asshole," I replied.

"You don't even fucking know what a real asshole is?" SFC Devine chimed in.

"Yes, I do. A real asshole is like SGT Hall," I replied while everyone was laughing.

"John, you didn't fuckin answer my question," LT Kerr added.

"I think, the locals are preparing for *Loyee Akhtar*."

"What the fuck is that?"

"It's also known as *Eid-Adha* or *Eid Qurbaan* in Afghanistan."

"Translation, please?" SGT Hall jokingly asked.

"It's not Christmas, but it's a kind of three-day religious holiday celebrated and observed by many wealthy

Muslims by sacrificing animals to commemorate the Prophet Ibrahim's sacrifice of his son, Ishmael, to Allah," I replied.

"How often do you guys do that?" SFC Devine asked.

"Twice a year."

"Lots of booze and hookers?" SGT Hall joked.

"What? What is booze and hookers?" I asked him.

He looked at me very surprised and said, "John, you got to be kidding. You don't fucking know what booze and hookers are?" SGT Hall asked. I had no clue what was he talking about but kind of assume that it must be something related to *Loyee Akhtar*.

"We need to take him to the strip club once he gets to the States," SFC Devine responded.

When I heard mention of a 'strip club' I started laughing because I had heard many soldiers talking about these clubs even though I had never been to one.

"Hahaha, we don't have any of those here," I replied

"But you do have the fucking Taliban here," SPC March said.

"Fuck the Taliban!"

"Yes, fuck the Taliban! How do you say it in Pashtu? SPC March asked.

"*Taliban wagha-e-m.*"

"*Taliban wakha, wakhaa-e-m!*" SPC March copied. He couldn't say it right but was very close.

"What do you do during this festival?" LT Kerr asked.

"Family feasts and parties with lots of meat, but we don't have booze and hookers," I responded. Everyone laughed.

Eid Qurbaan was a little different in the Dangam District in 2009. Charlie Company [1-32] based at Combat

Outpost Monti decided to pay for the animals that each district [Asmar, Dangam and Shigal] was going to sacrifice for the Eid festival. This was the first time the Americans made this contribution in the region. First platoon [1-32] bought a cow for the Dangam District, which cost almost $500 USD, while the 2nd and 3rd platoons bought animals for the Asmar and Shigal districts.

"Holy moly, it's a fucking big cow," LT Kerr said at the sight of the platoon's gift.

"John, please thank him. This has never happened before; we always get meat from Asadabad that's not enough for everybody here," Shah Mahmood, the district governor requested.

"I hope, it feeds everybody," LT Kerr said.

"Oh, yeah, it's way too much. We are gonna have a great meal," Shah Mahmood responded with a big smile on his face.

Everyone in the district was grateful and excited for the meal, including the soldiers of 1st platoon [1-32]. They even took pictures and videos with the cow that was waiting to be sacrificed the next day.

"I heard we are having a party tomorrow," SPC Case said while we were leaving the district to go see the police chief whose office was about half a mile from the center.

"What party? Who said we are having a party tomorrow?" I looked at SFC Devine and replied.

"I don't know about a party," SFC Devine caught on. We both started fucking with SPC Case.

"John, I swear I will fucking choke you if you don't tell me the truth," SPC Case responded back. SPC Case was big and tall and could possibly choke me if he wanted to.

"Yes, we do," I relented.

SPC Case laughed and said, "Good, you just saved your ass."

"I think that the lunch is going to be at the district center tomorrow; that's where Walaswal Saab, the district governor, wants it," the police chief told us when we arrived at his office.

"John, ask him if I can kill the cow tomorrow," SFC Devine said.

"John, you know that he cannot," the district chief said.

"Nope, you can't unless you are Muslim," I replied to SFC Devine.

The police chief looked back at me and said, "John, if you want to, you can kill the cow."

"What's going on?" LT Kerr asked.

"The police chief said that I can kill it, but I won't."

"Why not, you fucking *p**%#*y*!?" SGT Hall added.

"No fucking way, I've never even killed a chicken."

"Come on John, stop being a little bitch," SPC March jumped in.

"They have people to take care of it."

***

We headed to the district center the next day around noon when the cow was killed, butchered and cooked. The district center was busy like there had never been a big festival before. The policemen were walking around with sleeves rolled up, with blood marks and spots on their clothes and oily hands, spreading the Eid greeting, "*Akhtar mo Mubarak shaa!*" We began walking to the meeting hall where food was served on the big table. There was meat soup, tons of meat, rice, Afghan bread and a little bit of vegetables.

"Holy smokes, it's a lot of food," SGT Anderson said.

"John, what is that?" SSG Benson asked.

"Looks like a meat soup."

"I love the BBQ, what do you call it in Pashtu?" SSG Anderson asked.

"It's kabab." I didn't know what BBQ looked like, but it seemed no different than an Afghan Kabab, and was everyone's favorite.

"Johnny, where is the fucking cold beer?" SGT Hall asked.

"You mean water?"

"Hahaha, it's alcohol not water," SPC Case chimed in.

"Who fucking cooked this?! This is yummy!" SPC Case asked while digging in.

"Your mom did," SGT Whited answered. SGT Whited was a very calm and smart person. He didn't joke very often, but when he did it was very funny and usually raunchy.

"Hahaha, your mom is a very good cook," SPC March joined in.

It was a great lunch with the table full of fun, jokes and memories shared of Thanksgivings, Christmases, 4th of July celebrations and so on. These were holidays that I had never heard of.

"Thank you so much for the food. it was very good, but we got to go," LT Kerr told Shah Mahmood at the end of the meal.

"I am glad you guys liked it." the district governor responded. He shook hands with shad everyone and said, "safe travels." While we were leaving the district center, I heard Shah Mahmood call me back, "I forgot to give you a hug." I laughed and ran back to him for a hug, which is a cultural tradition between Afghans when greeting each other or departing.

We arrived at Combat Outpost Monti safely without the Taliban ambush or IED strike. However, around 7 P.M. our symptoms of food poisoning began. I ended up going to the moral welfare and recreation center [MWR] right after we got back and found many soldiers of 1st platoon [1-32] talking to their families on the phone and computers while others were watching TV. I joined the ones watching TV, but suddenly I began feeling very sick with stomach pain, nausea, vomiting, a fever and a headache. I don't remember how I walked out of the MWR by myself, but I made it to the restroom which was just outside of the building. I began to feel worse and soon found myself on the ground. I thought, "this is it, I am going to die"-- not in combat with the Taliban, during an ambush or IED strike but by food poisoning. "John, you okay? John, are you okay?" Someone was yelling, but I couldn't respond or make out who was trying to help.

"I thought, you were messing around," Waheed, another interpreter, told me after I got better.

"I wasn't joking, man, I thought I was going to die, how did I make it to the clinic?" I asked him.

"I carried you. You couldn't even walk."

I started waking up after getting an IV and anti-diarrheal medicine. I was not the only person who got sick; I saw a bunch of other soldiers from 1st platoon [1-32] in the aid station.

I was eager to find out what happened and I couldn't wait to call the district governor Shah Mahmood.

"I am sorry, I don't know. I had people watch everything we cooked, but it's possible that the Taliban poisoned the food," he told me.

"John, ask him if the police got sick as well," LT Kerr wanted to know.

"Yes, we also weren't feeling good, but I am home now and I will find more about it once I get back to the office. Why don't you call Hajib Habib, the NDS Chief, to find out more," the district governor Shah Mahmood suggested.

The next day we were all feeling better, but were still trying to piece together what had happened.

"John, I talked to both the police chief and the district governor and they agreed with me that Mullah Sarwar is behind the poisoning," Haji Habib reported.

"That's what I thought; I never trusted that fucking guy," LT Kerr agreed. Mullah Sarwar was a local religious leader, tribal elder and very influential person in the valley. He was always invited to the meetings and weekly shura, but 1st platoon [1-32] had been suspicious of him since the first day we met him. Mullah Sarwar refused to shake hands with the Americans and me. He always tried to hide his face with his scarf whenever we were around. He used his influence, friendship and religious power to manipulate the village. We learned that Mullah Sarwar was a big sympathizer and supporter of the Taliban. He disappeared before any arrest or criminal charges could be made against him.

Ch 22: Battle of Kamdesh[4]

Combat Outpost Keating
October 2009

"Johnny boy, we are gonna need you!" SFC Devine called.

"I am about to go home on leave."

"I know, but I'm sorry we need you."

"No worries, I will see you in a little bit."

I had no clue what was going on when I headed over to his barracks still in my Afghan clothes.

"John, we're probably need you, we asked Hemat to work, but he is fucking very sick, otherwise I would take him," Lt Kerr explained.

"What about the rest of the other interpreters?" SGT Hall asked. "We can take one of them if John wants to go home."

---

[4] If you are not familiar with the Battle of Kamdesh, you should watch the movie *The Outpost*, but what I am writing here is based on my eye witness account of the battle in 2009.

"They are pussies. I already talked to LT Forcy, and none of them wants to go," SFC Devine told us. "John, I will get in touch with you when we know more, but what the heck you have it on right now?"

"It's Afghan traditional clothes."

"He looks like the Taliban," SSG Benson chimed in.

"John, the Taliban," SGT Anderson joked.

"I'm supposed to go home today. I wish I could travel with UCP uniform."

"Well, you can wear your uniform to Kamdesh," SSG Anderson shrugged.

Kamdesh literally means "Place of the Kom." It was an unofficial capital for the Kom tribe, but now it's a small town and a district in the middle of the Hindu Kush mountains in Nuristan Province. It's comprised of other small villages, which have their own language, culture, and traditions. It's a beautiful, remote mountainous region in eastern Nuristan Province that's approximately 350 kilometers from the capital city Kabul. People who live there are called "Nuristani", which means "beauty" or "light" because its people are beautiful. Kamdesh and Nuristan are popular for their natural beauty and are the consolidation point for two rivers flowing from Barge-Matal and the Nechangal mountains.

I had never been to Kamdesh before, but I heard my second oldest brother, Ajmal, talk about it while he was driving supply trucks. It had never been a safe place, and my brother had lost many fellow drivers to the Taliban insurgents. The image of tough terrain and a district center without buildings was something that I still remembered about Kamdesh from my brother's stories.

In addition, the local government was run by a local shura of 50 local elders who had long-held hostility with the Taliban insurgents as a result of decades-long conflicts over private property, water channels, and forest. These fights had killed many men from each side.

In 2009, this beautiful land experienced one of the bloodiest and most despicable battles of the war. COP Keating was a joint base for both Afghan and American soldiers from the 3rd Squadron, 61st Cavalry unit and was located deep in the valley, surrounded by high Hindu Kush mountains. The main goal of building COP Keating was to intercept and prevent the Taliban and other insurgent groups from transporting supplies to Kunar and eastern Nuristan Province and to be a base for counterinsurgency missions. The Afghan and American soldiers who watched over the valley from COP Keating and its observation post (OP), Fritsche, were under frequent and often simultaneous attacks from the Taliban insurgents, who attacked daily with snipers and mortars.

In October 2009, a daily attack turned into a large battle as hundreds of insurgents and foreign fighters tried to seize Keating.

More than 300 insurgents attacked the COP and OP from all sides with RPGs, mortars, snipers, grenades and machine-gun rifles. Meanwhile, in the Dangam Valley, 1st platoon [1-32] was busy as usual, conducting its daily patrols and missions, however, soon we were told to standby to possibly head to COP Keating to provide assistance. This would be another dangerous mission after the battle of OP Bari-Alai. It wasn't clear whether the mission would take place or get canceled, but we had to be ready.

"Make sure you get everything this time, Johnny," SFC Devine joked.

"I did, but I hope it never rains there," I told him, this timing packing the rain gear that I had forgotten at Bari-Alai.

SFC Devine laughed and added, "You never know buddy."

"Got enough batteries for the radio?" LT Kerr added.

"I got enough."

The whole time I packed, I hoped for word that the mission was canceled so I could go home. I had not seen my family in months. I missed my mom badly, and I had told her that I was going to see her soon before we were assigned to the mission.

At the end of the day, it turned out that we were going into the Battle of Kamdesh. I met up with everybody at the helicopter landing Zone (HLZ) where we got airlifted to COP Keating. When we touched down, it was a complete disaster zone— dead Taliban and Afghan security force and local police force bodies were everywhere. We believed that some of the police were insiders who supported the Taliban during the attack and had turned their weapons against the American troops.

The fight wasn't over yet. LT Kerr's platoon [1-32] was among the first support to arrive. We ended up landing at the nearest observation post (OP) in order to secure it from possible attacks and conduct search-and-clear operations before we descended to COP Keating. We had to walk through rocky terrain in the forest get to the COP. Even though the militants were on the run, Taliban remained in the area to evacuate their dead and wounded. We planned for an enemy ambush on the backside of the mountain. When we did engage, we didn't receive any casualties, but three Taliban insurgents were confirmed killed.

"Anything on the radio?" LT Kerr asked me.

"The Taliban speak more than one language here," I replied.

"I heard them speak Nuristani, Urdu, Arabic, Pashtu and one more language that I couldn't tell."

"Are they talking about us?" SFC Devine asked.

"I think so because I heard them talk about our helicopters landing."

We kept pushing and finally made it to the COP by 6 P.M. without more firefights. There was nothing left at Keating. Everything had been set on fire; while some of the barracks were still burning, the defensive barriers (HESCOs) and restrooms were already burnt to the ground. First platoon [1-32] conducted its search-and-clear operations in the remaining areas of the COP, but we didn't find anything other than the enemy's dead bodies and blood everywhere. I had not seen or experienced anything like the nightmare that took place in the Kamdesh District that day. More than a hundred Taliban insurgents and foreign fighters got killed during the attack. Our radio scanner intercepted people speaking Urdu, Arabic and local languages while they searched for missing fighters--

"Mobariz, Mobariz, can you hear me?!" Ezam called.

"Ezam, I can hear you," Mobariz responded.

"Mullah Saab says to let all friends know to take a great care with the aircraft."

"The Americans just dropped bombs closer to Bar Kaley [upper village]."

"Did you check on friends if they are okay?" Ezam asked

"I tried, but their radios not working," Mobariz said.

"Okay, may Allah keep you safe," Ezam spoke and right after that, there was a big boom in the background sounded like another bomb dropped.

In the aftermath of the Battle of Kamdesh, eight American soldiers were dead and twenty-seven wounded. The survivors of the Battle of Kamdesh and COP Keating were awarded high military prizes including SSG Clinton, who received the Medal of Honor by President Obama in 2013.

Some ANA soldiers and Afghan private security guards were killed and wounded during the attack. A local police chief who was taken hostage by the Taliban insurgents was brutally killed because he refused to help them against American and Afghan troops. There were other policemen who ran off the base and joined the Taliban against American and Afghan forces. Many of them were killed during the attack. The massive attack had been well-planned, and Taliban insurgents managed to attack the COP and OP from all sides. Many ANA soldiers fled their locations on the eastern side of the COP, despite the efforts and hard work of two Latvian advisors who tried to protect those firing positions. There were rumors that the Afghan forces couldn't keep their position due to shortages of ammo and close combat with the Taliban insurgents.

Shortly after the battle, we all evacuated the COP, and Keating was bombarded to make sure that it was completely destroyed so that Taliban or other terrorist groups couldn't use it. In retaliation, the Taliban insurgents began targeting locals, who had supported Afghan and American soldiers while they were at COP Keating. The Taliban brutally killed many local residents and their houses were set on fire. Those suspected of supporting Americans were isolated and unable to travel to any nearby towns for shopping because the Taliban believed that they would tell the Afghan and Americans about the insurgent positions.

This hard punishment lasted until the Taliban commander, Mulawi Sadiq, joined the Afghan government. He was popular for his extremism and major involvement in the attack against the Afghan and American soldiers at COP Keating. However, after the diabolic and outrageous activities by the Taliban against innocent residents in Kamdesh District after the troop's complete withdrawal on 6 October 2009, Sadiq turned against the Taliban. Once, he came under attack by the Taliban and his son attempted to carry out a suicide bombing to kill his father, but he did not succeed. Later, Sadiq would survive three other suicide bombing attempts, but nine innocent women who were farming got killed.

The former commander began to bring local tribal elders together to fight against the Taliban insurgents. Sadiq was able to establish a local shura comprised of almost a hundred tribal elders and residents from all villages of the Kamdesh District to ensure that the district was run in support of the Afghan government. Men, women and even kids who could find firearms were recruited to secure their own villages against the Taliban. Throughout the district, the main focus became survival. Parents began teaching their kids the basic skills for being a great fighter rather than have them going to school so that they could defend their families, farms, villages and houses from the Taliban and other terrorist groups.

Ch 23: Mission into Saabandi Village

Capture of the Notorious Taliban Commander
Nick Muhammad
2009

Everybody began giving each other exuberant high fives after we safely returned to COP Monti after a dangerous and risky mission at COP Keating.

"We did it, Johnny!" SFC Devine exclaimed.

"Yes, yes, it was pretty fun!"

"I don't know about that," SFC Devine joked.

"Did you fucking say 'fun'? Until we got into a fight with the Taliban!" SGT Hall quipped.

"We fucking scared them," I cheered.

"We are bad asses," SGT Hall confirmed.

"Well, I am, but I don't know about you," I joked.

SGT looked at me with a smile on his face, "What do you fucking mean? I am a badass."

"Mmmm, debatable."

SGT Hall was indeed a badass in the platoon [1-32], he was always at the front leading his squad.

We didn't waste time starting back on our normal and routine daily patrols/missions and weekly security meetings with the Dangam District officials and the local and tribal elders in Dangam Valley.

"*Salaam*, John, how have you been doing? I was worried about you for last couple of days. Your phone never works and I thought something happened," Shah Mahmood said when he called the next morning.

"I am sorry. I was gone in Nuristan, and my phone didn't work," I replied.

"Oh, how did it go? It was a tragedy; I heard about it. It was all over in the news."

"I am glad we came back. How's everything going with you guys?" I asked him.

"It's not too bad. I saw Haji Habib [NDS Chief], and he had a lot to talk about. When are you guys coming to visit?"

"I don't know, we just got back last night."

"Okay, you might need some rest. I will talk to you later."

We saw Shah Mahmood and Chief Habib the next day, and there was much to be discussed and planned before Taliban insurgents carried out their next attack on the Dangam District or OP Castle War Frog in the hilltops.

"John, tell LT Kerr that I have a huge piece of intelligence for you," Haji Habib started.

"Great, I am looking forward to it. John, tell him we were in Nuristan," LT Kerr responded.

"NURISTAN?!" Haji Habib exclaimed. You could tell from the horizontal wrinkles across his forehead and wide eyes that he was surprised by the news. "We heard about the attack," he added.

Haji Habib gathered a lot of information on Taliban, but whether it was all accurate or from reliable sources was always something that concerned LT Kerr. That day, everyone agreed that Taliban had planned to attack the district center and the observation posts.

"The Taliban will never attack as long you guys stay here," Hajib Habib claimed.

"Ha," LT Kerr laughed, "We like it here, but we have to do what our boss want us to do."

"Agreed, and same here for us, but what about this guy?" Haji Habib asked looking at SFC Devine.

"What about him?"

"You can leave him with us," Haji Habib kidded.

"Hahaha, he does look like an Afghan," LT Kerr agreed.

"Then where are my Afghan clothes?" SFC Devine asked.

"I have plenty of Afghan clothes that you can wear!" Haji Habib replied.

"Right size?" SFC Devine asked flexing his muscles.

While we were talking to Haji Habib, his aide came in with *Shuda* chai, dried fruit and cookies.

"Oh, *Shuda* chai," SFC Devine's eyes widened.

"Not for you," I teased him.

"Bullshit. I am gonna fire you," SFC Devine replied. SFC Kevin Devine loved *Shuda* chai, and that was the great part of having meetings with Haji Habib who was beyond hospitable and always treated us well.

"Oh, John, tell him that we met somebody a few weeks ago in Baidad village who couldn't speak because he had a hole in his throat, but I ordered a Servox electrolarynx speech device for him," LT Kerr continued the meeting.

"Really? That's so awesome. Where is the device? I want to see it," Shah Mahmood responded.

"It's not here yet, but it's on the way from the States."

"You think he is gonna be able to talk?"

"I don't know, but hopefully he does."

The man that we met in Baidad had a tracheotomy, a small hole in his neck, thirty years ago. The villager did not believe that he would ever talk again, but LT Kerr changed his life forever. I never heard of such a device, but when LT Kerr received it after a couple of weeks, it was a miracle for the local villager.

While 1st platoon's main area of operation was Dangam Valley, they also had extra duties like serving as a quick reaction force [QRF] at Combat Outpost Monti while other platoons conducted patrols and daily missions in the Asmar and Shigal districts. All three districts were under constant threat from the Taliban, but the Shigal District was likely to be the center and safe haven of Hezbi-E-Islami fighters that carried out attacks against both Afghan and American troops. As threats increased in Dangam and other districts, 1st platoon [1-32] patrolled and planned ambushes against the Taliban and other terrorists that had infiltrated into the Dangam Valley.

The Taliban's local commander, Nick Muhammad, who had been involved in many attacks against Afghan and

American troops, moved to Saabandi village in Dangam Valley.

"John, Nick Muhammad is in Saabandi," The police chief told me.

"How do you know he is in Saabandi?" LT Kerr questioned.

"I talked to Haji Habib, and we also heard about him from the locals." The police chief stated. "He is a dangerous man, but not as dangerous as you," the police chief looked at LT Kerr and added with a big smile on his face.

"I am fucking dangerous for the Taliban," LT Kerr agreed.

Saabandi village was about 10 miles away from the district center. It had always been a safe haven, consolidation point and supply route of the Taliban insurgents because it was closer to Bajaur Tribal Area [FATA] than the Dangam District was, and Nick Muhammad was always on the move.

"John, ask LT Kerr if he can do something about him. He needs to be captured or killed," the police chief asserted.

"I cannot agree with you more."

We didn't tell the police chief then, but 1st platoon had planned a mission to visit Saabandi village. We planned the mission to be carried out at night so that Nick Muhammad couldn't flee and escape into the Bajaur Tribal Area. Saabandi was located in the southeast of the Dangam District and was a very well-known village for the Taliban's activities, and it would take a lot of time, effort and reliable intelligence to capture Nick Muhammad. First platoon [1-32] was excited to visit Saabandi village before they wrapped up their year-long deployment, but I hated to go on night missions, especially where we had to walk or climb because I did not carry night vision goggles, and I was always worried that I would fall off and break my nose, arms or legs.

We left Combat Outpost Monti and arrived at the Dangam District around 8:00 P.M., but before we headed into Saabandi village, LT Kerr went with Hemat to let the police chief know about the possibility of friendly fire that may occur during our walk to and from the village in order to avoid a friendly force incident. While we waited to start the mission, some slept, but I couldn't because I was a bit worried about walking in the dark all the way to Saabandi village and back. I ended up talking with soldiers to find out more about WWE wrestling and Hollywood movies that I had been watching.

"What about WWE wrestling?" I asked, "Are they really fighting each other?"

"What do you mean by fighting?" SPC Tomeo the platoon's medic asked.

"The guys never get hurt," I explained.

SPC Tomeo laughed and started, "It's true, they do punch other." But then he laughed and said, "Nah, I'm just fucking with you. It's a fake sport."

"I like it. It does look like they are punching each other."

"John, do you wanna be a wrestler?" PFC Solis asked.

"I would love to, but I am very small."

"You can wrestle with Solis," PFC Cepeda suggested.

"Hahaha, you think so?"

While I was talking and joking, SPC March walked in—

"John, LT Kerr wants to know if you heard anything on the radio."

"Nothing in particular, the Taliban just talking about daily business."

"Alright, well, LT Kerr is in the truck. If you hear anything, let us know," SPC March replied.

At 1:30 A.M., everyone gathered for the mission briefing at the police headquarters in Dangam. While LT Kerr and SFC Devine talked about the mission, possible firefights and casualties, I saw a couple of flashlights, which looked like shooting stars across the sky right above us. I tapped Hemat on the shoulder more than once, waking him up to ask if he had seen them too.

"What flashlights?" Hemat asked.

"I just saw a few flashlights in the sky." I thought those flashlights might be the Taliban's signal used at night to inform each other.

"I didn't see them," Hemat told me.

"What's up, John?" SFC Devine asked.

"John saw some flashlights," Hemat responded before me.

"Where did you see them?" LT Kerr asked.

"Right above us and farther in the valley, close to Saabandi."

"On the ground or above in the sky?"

"Above in the sky, sir."

"Oh, that's the bird," LT Kerr clarified.

"Aircraft, John," Hemat explained.

"Let me know if you guys see any flashlights in the valley," LT Kerr said and then continued the briefing.

"Apaches are just a few miles away at FOB Wright in Asadabad," LT Kerr told the group.

The Taliban may not have been afraid of us, but they were scared of Apache and Kiowa gun-shift helicopters. The Taliban called the helicopters "wasps" because the Apaches and Kiowas always chased the Taliban like a dog runs after a stranger. The Taliban couldn't easily hide due to thermal surveillance cameras and other sensors mounted on those helicopters.

"Hopefully we don't need air support, but you never know. Saabandi village has never been visited by the Americans before," SFC Devine briefed.

"We need to be very fucking careful," LT Kerr warned.

First platoon [1-32] divided into three groups; a group of soldiers ended up staying with the trucks at the district center. SFC Devine led the second group and headed to the observation post (OP) on the east side of the district to watch over our movement deep into the valley as we would be surrounded by hills, huge rocks, trees, caves, and a little water in the river. The third group, led by LT Kerr, was assigned to go after the Taliban Commander Nick Muhammad and his fighters in the heart of Saabandi village.

It was tough walk, through rocky terrain and complicated by bushes, trees and the river, but we arrived at the village around 4:00 A.M. The walk left me with scratches on my arms, legs and face because I could hardly see in the dark. First platoon [1-32] showed up at the front porches of the Taliban militants while they were sleeping. We found a guy walking to the mosque, who happened to be the mullah. He shook when I said, "*Salaam Alaikum*".

"John, can you see if I can talk to him really quick?" LT Kerr asked. The mullah refused to speak to us at first, but then looked confused when he realized that Americans are much nicer than he expected, and he agreed to talk for a little bit.

"*Walikum salaam*," the mullah replied, struggling with his words because he was so scared.

"You are going to be fine. They aren't going to hurt you," I told him.

"Are you sure?"

"What's up, John?" LT Kerr interjected.

"He thinks we are going to hurt him."

"No, we won't, we just wanna fucking talk to him."

"*Turjuman Saab*, I can't talk for too long because I have to go and perform the morning pray call."

"John, ask him his name," LT Kerr continued.

"Malawi Anas," I told him.

"How do you spell it?"

"M.U.L.A.W.I A.N.A.S,"

"Okay, he can go."

LT Kerr let the mullah go because we were focused on looking for Nick Muhammad who supposed to be there for morning pray along with other villagers. After another half an hour, villagers began leaving their houses for morning prayers at the mosque, but none of them wanted to speak with us.

"We gotta fucking talk to somebody," LT Kerr was becoming frustrated. Everyone could tell how badly the entire village had been brainwashed and manipulated against the Americans. While I was looking for someone to speak with us, the whole village quickly turned into a ghost town. Luckily, I was able to stop a sheepherder, who was herding his sheep and goats.

"Salaam Alaikum."

"Walikum salaam."

He was also scared but willing to speak with us. He carried a battle-ax that was pretty sharp.

"Sharp ax," I commented.

"Yes, I sharpened it last night."

"What are you using it for?" I asked, talking to him at a distance to make sure he wasn't dangerous.

"I cut holly trees and bushes while herding my goats and sheep," the sheepherder responded.

I didn't think he had ever seen Americans, but I bet he had heard so many bad things. He was surprised when I pointed at the soldiers providing security and said, "Don't worry, they are not here to harm you and your family."

"Engineer Saab, I have to go; my sheep and goats are gone," the sheepherder said as we realized that the animals had wandered. People in the villages would use the word, "engineer" for interpreters because they didn't understand.

"Yeah, he can go," LT Kerr told him after a few questions.

After that, we ended up also talking with a local elder who wore a turban, long beard and mustache.

"Salaam Turjuman Saab, how are you?" the old man asked.

"Oh, we are good. Ask him how is he doing," LT Kerr replied.

"I am good now, I was feeling not very good this morning, but I heard you guys were here. *Turjuman Saab,* I was at the district a few times," The local elder continued.

"John, do you remember him?"

"No."

It was very surprising that the local elder showed up and wanted to speak with us because this never happened in places that were dominated and controlled by the Taliban. He was putting his life at risk just to speak with us. No one would be able to protect him and his family from the Taliban's threats once we were gone.

"John, tell him, we are here to help, and ask his name," LT Kerr instructed.

"Malak Zar Muhammad," the local elder replied.

"My name is Kerr," LT Kerr said after they both shook hands.

Malak Zar Muhammad had a lot to say; his facial expressions, body language and resiliency spoke more than a million words. The local elder looked around and said, "*Turjuman Saab*, I went to Chaghasray (another name for Asadabad) last month, where I saw the new schools, roads, and a clinic. If someone gets sick here, we have no road, and we have to carry the patient all the way to the district," the local elder continued, "Interpreter *Saab*, tell him I didn't go to school. I would like to send my grandkid to school here, but don't have any building for the school."

"They need to support the local government so they will help and build a school building for them," LT Kerr responded.

"Interpreter *Saab*, did you tell him that 'one flower doesn't bring the spring'?" Malak Zar Muhammad questioned. It was a traditional saying.

"He is trying to tell you that he can't do anything by himself while the majority of his village supporting the Taliban because they have no other option," I explained.

"I see."

Malak Zar Muhammad looked around to make sure there is no other villagers and said, "the mullah of our mosque speaks nothing but hatred and propaganda against the government and Americans."

LT Kerr looked at me and asked, "is he talking about the same person we talked to earlier this morning?"

"Yes, yes, he is not a good guy. He radicalized and brainwashed our kids," Malak Zar Muhammad pled.

"John, tell him, that the mullah didn't want to speak with us this morning."

"I know, Interpreter *Saab*. I have to go now."

"John, thank him and tell him we will see him in the district."

"Okay, be careful," Malak Zar Muhammad said while leaving. But while he walked back to his house, he stopped for a second and looked at us more than once. That struck me as creepy. While he had kind words, we could never know if he had been sent by the Taliban commander to find out about us. On the other hand, he could get killed, tortured, or lose family members, his house or property if he really meant what he had said because Saabandi village had been governed and controlled by the Taliban for years.

"What do you think, John?" SGT Hall asked.

"I don't know. He was very good with his words, but you never know, sergeant."

"True."

"John, anything on the radio?" LT Kerr questioned.

"I am listening right now. The Taliban are not talking about us in particular, but it seems like something is going to happen," I replied. "It could be an ambush on the way back or a firefight here. The Taliban is trying to find out our location and if we have already left."

> *"Qari Saeed, Qari Saeed, can you hear me," Fida asked on the radio.*
>
> *"Fida, Fida, I can hear you."*
>
> *"Malawi Zobair wants to know if the Americans are still in the village," Fida responded.*
>
> *"I am not there, but let me call Abo Mubashir," Qari Saeed radioed back.*
>
> *"Abo Mubashir, Abo Mubashir, Abo Mubashir, can you hear me?"*
>
> *"Qari Saeed, I heard you talking to Fida. The Americans are still in the village. I don't know the plan," Abo Mubashir joined the conversation.*

I was listening to the Taliban's radio when around 6:30 A.M., the sun rose above the mountain peaks. The village came alive; families began leaving their houses with their kids.

"What is going on, John?" SGT Hall asked while LT Kerr was talking on the radio.

"Not a good sign, I think we are going to get shot at here. Whenever families leave, it's a sign that fighting will follow."

"You got to let LT Kerr know."

As I updated LT Kerr on the situation, I heard Apaches approach the valley.

> *"Qari Saeed, Qari Saeed, can you hear me? Can you hear me?" Fida was back on the radio.*
>
> *"I can hear you, Fida," Qari Saeed confirmed.*
>
> *"Wasps just came. Tell our friends to stay where they are."*

"We are still here, but some friends already took off."
"Call them on the radio and tell them to hide somewhere and
do not move. Wait for the wasps to fly away."
"Okay, I will call them and let them know."

The Taliban talked about some of their fighters that had left to ambush us on the way back, but the Apache helicopters scared the hell out of them. Along our path, we couldn't stop females or ask them questions due to Afghan culture and tradition. We also weren't accompanied by Afghan security forces to help us talk to families fleeing their homes. We didn't know that some of the people we assumed to be women wearing chadari and burqas were male Taliban fighters, including Commander Muhammad. In the end he escaped using this tactic.

The Taliban's radio never shut off, and they kept talking about the attack, but it never happened.

"Let's get the fuck outta here," LT Kerr said as we started the trek back. We headed back to the district, but on a different route and trails to avoid possible IEDs or an ambush attack. It was much easier to walk back to the district center because it was daylight, and I could see everything and every step I took. It was rare and surprising that we didn't get shot at in Saabandi village. I was tired like the rest of the soldiers and couldn't wait to get some sleep and relaxation before we head back out to the district the next day or two.

Ch 24: Dangam District under Attack

After we returned from Saabandi village, Taliban commander Nick Muhammad and his fighters from the Bajaur Tribal Area [FATA] gathered again in Saabandi to plan an attack on the Dangam District.

The district governor, Shah Mahmood, smiled and updated us when we saw him, "Nothing new, but we do hear things about a Taliban attack. I heard that Nick Muhammad is back in Saabandi with more people from Shultan, Shigal, Ghazi Abad, Marawar, Ganjgal and FATA to attack the district."

"You think they will attack during daylight or at night?" LT Kerr asked him.

"I don't know much, but you should talk to Haji Habib."

"John, tell LT Kerr that Nick Muhammad and his fighters plan to attack the district," Haji Habib confirmed when we made our way to his office.

"Okay, have you talked to anybody in Asadabad?" LT Kerr asked.

"I did, and I got a cipher earlier today that some foreign militants joined Nick Muhammad's fighters to carry out a massive attack."

"We are gonna fucking kill them again if they attack."

"But they won't attack while you guys are here," the police chief added. "John, tell him that they are scared of you."

"Let us know how things go, and I will see what I can do," LT Kerr responded while we were heading back to Combat Outpost Monti.

We left for COP Monti and arrived safe after a day of meetings, but around 10:00 P.M., I received frantic phone calls from the district governor, the police chief and the national directorate security chief one after another. The first call was the horrified voice of the police chief, "John, can you hear me, we are getting shot at from all over the place right now!" I could hear the gunshots, screaming and yelling in the background. While I was talking to him, the district governor was trying to get hold of me.

"Let me talk to the district governor and I will call you back," I told the police chief.

"Okay, but please hurry; it's getting crazier here. We need help!"

"*Salaam*, John, the Taliban are attacking from all sides. They are shooting at the district from Cheshan mountains," the district governor, Shah Mahmood, told me before I could say a word.

"I was talking to the police chief before you called, and I am going to let LT Kerr know," I replied. "I will call you back. Let me talk to Haji Habib now," I told the district governor while Haji Habib was now also calling.

"What's up, John?" both LT Kerr and SFC Devine asked as I entered the barracks. They were both awake, working on the computers, but the lights in the barracks were off.

"The district is under attack," I informed them.

"What? Who said that?" LT Kerr wanted to know.

"I just talked to everybody at the district."

"Okay, let's go outside," LT Kerr directed.

When we went outside, we saw a big flash and explosion in the valley because it wasn't too far from COP Monti.

"Holy crap, let's go to the TOC [tactical operation command]."

We arrived at the TOC to find a few NCOs and fire support officers running back and forth because they already knew what was going on.

"Good, we need you to call the police chief and ask him where the Taliban are shooting from," LT Forcy, the fire support officer said.

"I am on the phone with him right now."

"It's getting bigger and bigger. The Taliban fired more than five RPGs at the district, but missed, and a few rockets landed short." The police chief updated me.

"What part of Cheshan mountain? John, I am gonna need you to show me here on the map," LT Forcy broke in.

"The part of the mountain that's right next to the village," the police chief directed.

The Taliban had chosen a portion of the mountain that was pretty close to the residential area so that Charlie company at COP Monti couldn't drop a bomb or conduct fire mission due to civilian casualties. While I was talking to LT Kerr and LT Forcy, the district governor called again.

"John, I have been trying to get hold up you, but your phone has been busy." He sounded upset, like he thought that I was not answering his call on purpose.

"Sorry, but I was talking to the police chief."

"Is LT Kerr going to help us? The Taliban are using PKM machine guns, rockets and AK-47s!"

"John, ask if everyone in the district is okay," LT Kerr instructed.

"Yes, we are fine at the district, but I don't know about the police up on the observation posts. Ask LT Kerr if he can send those smaller helicopters," the district governor said.

"John, tell him we are working on it, but the nearest air support that is available is in Jalalabad," LT Kerr replied before adding to me, "John, don't tell them, but we are probably going to go; if you wanna go get ready."

I left the TOC to get my body armor, and on my way, I could see the tracers and hear the explosions even from Monti. While I was walking to my barrack, I saw SFC Devine running to the TOC. "John, we are going to Dangam!" he shouted as he passed.

Around 10:30 P.M., we headed to Dangam and to our surprise, made it without facing an IED or firefight. It was the middle of the night and no one-- the police chief, district governor and the NDS chief—knew that we had arrived. That included the Taliban.

"Zarqawi, can you hear me?" Qari Saeed called on the radio.
"Qari Saeed, I can you hear. What's up?"
"Where are those rounds coming from?"

"I don't know, they are not coming from the district or the observation posts."

"Find out if the Americans are here," Qari Saeed directed.

"Okay, let me call Fedai, he probably knows or saw the trucks driving to the district."

"Fedai, this is Zarqai can you hear me?"

"I can hear you, Zarqawi."

"Did you see the American trucks?" Zarqawi asked.

"Yes, they were driving to the district but I couldn't call you; my radio didn't work," Fedai responded.

"Zarqawi, this is Qari Saeed, I heard Fedai. Let everybody know that Americans are here."

"What's the plan now?" Zarqawi asked.

"Let me talk to Mulawi Saab," Qare Saeed responded.

"I just talked to Mulawi Saab and he wants everybody back," Fedai directed.

"Okay, but be careful."

"There is no checkpoint but I see something firing at us," Ghazi another militant reported as he joined the conversation.

"They are the Americans, Mulawi Saab wants everybody to stay back and take great care and makes sure they don't see you guys up there."

Taliban nightmares came true when they heard that the Americans [1st platoon, 1-32] were there at the Dangam Valley. The Taliban militants found themselves with no choice because if they didn't want to leave, they could get killed. The firefight ended without a friendly casualty, but a dozen of the Taliban militants were killed during the attack and dozens were critically wounded on a fire mission from COP Monti. We returned to Monti around 1:00 A.M. without telling the

Dangam government officials that we were ever there when we went back out to see them the next morning.

"John, you guys didn't tell me that you were coming last night," the police chief said surprised.

"We didn't know if we were," LT Kerr assured him.

"Thank you. It was a surprising visit, but worse for the Taliban."

"It would never fucking happen if we are here."

"*Salaam Alaikum*, how are you?" SFC Devine asked when we next saw Haji Habib.

"*Walikum Salaam*," Haji Habib responded with a smile.

"John, did you teach him?" Haji Habib asked me.

"What did he say?" SFC Devine butted in.

"He said that you are his bitch."

"Bullshit, what did he say?"

"He asked if I taught you those words."

"Tell him I was in Iraq," SFC Devine told me.

"So, he must speak lots of Arabic," Haji Habib assumed.

"A little bit, not a lot."

"What about you, John, do you speak Arabic?"

"I do, I went to school for Arabic."

"Where did you go to school? I didn't fucking know that," SFC Devine asked.

"In Jalalabad, there is an orphan school where I went for Arabic."

"Ask Habib if he can speak Arabic," SFC Devine said.

"Hahaha, I can't, but we pray in Arabic and do all sort of religious stuff in Arabic anyway!"

"Anyway, how are you doing? We came out last night, but didn't stop by the district," LT Kerr got down to business.

"I am good, just a little tired; I didn't sleep very well last night. It was bad until you guys showed up," Haji Habib updated.

"I bet. I wanted to stop by last night but we had to back to Monti and we didn't have time. I just talked to the police chief and he thought that you might be gone."

"Yes, I was going to go home this morning, but I had to go to Asadabad to the main intelligence office."

"It's going to be a quick one, and I will make sure you go to Asadabad," LT Kerr assured Habib.

Haji Habib laughed and added, "No worries, I got a lot to talk about." He continued, "Nick Muhammad brought many Pakistani Taliban with him to capture, confiscate, and burn down the district buildings, but fortunately that didn't happen."

"Do you know anything about Taliban casualties?" LT Kerr asked.

"I am still trying to find out more about them, but Khitab and Zarqawi are two Pakistani TTP (Tahrek-e-Talibani Pakistan) members that have been confirmed killed."

"Hell yeah, he is fucking gone!" SGT Hall yelled standing at the door.

"What about their injured fighters?" LT Kerr continued.

"Of course, they take them to Pakistan."

"John, tell him, thank you and to let us know if he hears anything," LT Kerr said closing the meeting.

Haji Habib looked at me and said, "John, you better answer the phone when I call you." Then he smiled, "I am just joking with you. You know everybody likes you."

We left his office to meet Shah Mahmood whose office was a couple of blocks away. As soon as we walked into his office, Shah Mahmood stood up and asked LT Kerr to use his chair. It was a sign of appreciation for what 1st platoon [1-32] had done the night before.

"Thank you so much. I don't know how to thank you; it was a great help last night."

"John, tell him we wanted to fucking help, and we did. I am glad my fucking soldiers did great last night."

"You guys did an amazing job. When you guys left here last night, we heard the Taliban talking very angrily because they failed to capture the district."

The district governor called us "invisible soldiers" because of the way we had come and gone without notice. "We didn't know that you guys were here last night until the first checkpoint in the bazaar called us and let us know. From now on, we are going to call LT Kerr 'Commander Zarawar'" Shah Mahmood finished.

"What does that mean? LT Kerr asked.

"Brave," I told him.

LT Kerr laughed and said, "Thank you. I'm glad we helped last night."

It wasn't the first time that a district governor had called LT Kerr a brave soldier. LT Kerr and the entire platoon was known for their bravery, valor, courage and incredible fight against the Taliban.

We wrapped up the meeting, but before we head back to Monti, we stopped by OP Castle War Frog to check on the policemen. They were great friends with 1st platoon. The policemen were good, except Muhammad who received a minor injury from an RPG, but refused to go home.

Ch 25: "Living Hell"

The Battle of Barge-Matal, Nuristan
August 2009

Barge-Matal was one of the most remote districts of Nuristan Province to the northeast of Combat Outpost Monti. I had never heard of it before August 2009, but it was there that I witnessed more than I could have ever imagined.

The Taliban believed that everyone who lived in Barge-Matal supported the government and were infidels who must be executed. More than one hundred Taliban fighters, along with foreign militants, attacked Barge-Matal District right before the country's presidential election. While it was easy for the Taliban to infiltrate Barge-Matal from the Chitral area of Pakistan, it was complicated for the Afghan government to send ground troops, supplies and reinforcements because the many of the roads had been destroyed over years of fighting or were now under the Taliban's control. After facing small resistance forces of local police, the Taliban captured the nearby villages and burnt the area to the ground.

"It was bad; my soldiers left everything behind and walked for miles. As soon as the Afghan police left, the Taliban raised their flag, burned down the whole town, houses and the girls' school building," COL Shams, an Afghan Border Police commander later said. COL Shams had a lot of experience in the district. He was born and raised there, and he used his influence and relationships to obtain direct access within the Taliban to learn about their plans and battle tactics in order to help the American and Afghan troops throughout our operations.

The collapse of Barge-Matal became big news; it was a lead headline in every local newspaper and it was even covered by some international media. One of the reasons that it received so much attention was that it took place right before the presidential election while the focus of the government was on politics rather than securing its own people. The Taliban boycotted and rejected the election and threatened those who were going to cast their votes.

At the same time, President Karzai wanted to secure votes in Barge-Matal, so he asked his U.S. counterparts to conduct an air assault mission with Afghan forces to recapture Barge-Matal. Even though some U.S. military officials did not want to be up there, Chosin Battalion [1-32] operating out of Forward Operating Base Joyce was assigned to retake Barge-Matal. In July 2009, 3rd platoon [1-32] led by 1LT Jake Meraldi; Battalion Headquarters Company led by LTC Mark O'Donnell; battalion scouts with more than 80 Afghan National Army soldiers and border police, commanded by Col Shams were dispatched into Barge-Matal by CH-47 Chinook Helicopters for a 72-hour operation. In the end, the mission lasted for more than a month with casualties both for Afghan and American soldiers. At the end, the big question remained- who was going to govern and support the people of the Barge-Matal when coalition force left?

While I was at Monti before my leave, I had heard horrible stories out of Barge-Matal about the brutal fighting that never seemed to end. I never thought that 1st platoon [1-32] would be called to replace 2nd platoon [1-32].

"What's up, John?" LT Kerr asked.
"Sir, I want to go home for a couple of days. My brother just called me, and mom is sick in the hospital."
"Sorry, buddy. I don't think we are going to Dangam anytime soon, so have many days do you want?"
"Probably a month," I joked.
"No way, Johnny boy, we need you," SFC Devine chimed in.
"Probably 4 days," I responded.
"Yeah, that's fine with us, but we probably need you if we go to Barge-Matal," LT Kerr warned.

It felt great to be home with my mom who told me again and again, "I am not sick, but you make me sick because I always worry about you." She did worry and fear for me. I was her favorite son because I was the youngest among my brothers.

It was the second day of the trips and I planned to visit my uncle with my mom when I received a text message from SFC Devine "Johnny, we need you back here as soon as possible." I thought that Devine was fucking with me. as he always did, but I had to call him to make sure he wasn't messing around. I hadn't even spent half of a day with my family, and I planned to visit my uncle for dinner.

"Yes, sorry buddy, we need you here by tomorrow afternoon," SFC Devine confirmed. I didn't even ask him about the mission, but I had a pretty good understanding that we were going to Barge-Matal. I had no idea what to tell my mom because I had promised her that I was going to be at home for a couple of days. She had been so excited to have me there, so I didn't tell her that I was leaving until the next day. I also didn't want to tell my family that I was going to Barge-Matal because they all knew how bad it was there. I got off the phone with SFC Devine while my mom was sitting with the rest of the family who was visiting.

"What's going on?" my mom asked.

"I got transferred to Kabul," I lied without thinking.

Everyone began celebrating. "That's great! There is no fighting in Kabul," my mom cheered. She knew that I had been trying to go to Kabul for a while because it was much safer. My mom always asked if I could work in Kabul or somewhere safer than Combat Outpost Monti. "I am so happy today and feel much, much better now that you are no longer working in Asmar at Monti. That place is dangerous," my mom said.

I left early the next morning for Combat Outpost Monti while my mom was still sick but was beginning to feel better.

"I will be back very soon," I promised her.

"Okay, may Allah keep you safe and healthy. Call me us when you get there and let us know," my mom instructed.

I made it to downtown Jalalabad and had planned to get some Afghan kabab with fresh *doodai* bread that everyone in 1st platoon loved, but it was too early for restaurants to be open.

I ended up waiting for a little while but still was set to make it Monti on time.

"Are you ready? I talked to a taxi driver, and he is going to take you all the way to Asmar," my brother told me.

"Yes, I am ready, but do you know this taxi driver?" I asked.

"I don't know him personally, but another driver that I know recommended him."

I had to make sure that I rode with someone trustworthy because I had a long journey, and the trip ahead of me was full of illegal Taliban checkpoints. Even though I always covered my face with a scarf, I would still be in danger.

"Johnny, what's up buddy? How was the trip?" SFC Devine asked when I arrived back at the COP.

"It was good, and I brought some food," I told him.

"What you got?" SGT Hall shouted from the other side of the barracks when he overheard.

"Some kabab and fresh bread."

"Hell yeah, I want some!" SGT Hall and the others had already eaten lunch, but they still wanted the fresh food.

"Where is my *doodai*?!" SFC Devine asked, sifting through the packages.

"I didn't get any *doodai* for you."

"Bullshit, John. I am gonna kill you," he joked back.

While we were talking about the food, LT Kerr got back from the TOC, and he and SFC Devine began talking about the mission that was going to happen late that evening.

We were going to Barge-Matal after 2nd platoon lost two of their brave soldiers, SPC Alexander Miller and SPC Justin Coleman. They both were killed by the Taliban's small arms while watching the Taliban's movements in the cornfields and deep in the village. First platoon [1-32] would drive to FOB Joyce where we planned to be airlifted by CH-47 Chinook helicopters to FOB Bostick in Nari before we headed to Barge-Matal.

Before we left for FOB Joyce, SFC Devine asked, "John, you got everything you need? We are not coming back soon."

"Yes, I do," I responded, but I hoped it was going to be a week, or at the longest two weeks, for our mission. In the end, it lasted for more than a month. I carried tons of batteries for Icom scanner and an AK-47. It was not mine; I had borrowed it from Sahil, an interpreter who worked for the Medal of Honor recipient, Dakota Meyer and his Embedded Training Team (ETT). Sahil had been given the weapon to carry on missions while working with the Marines and supporting Afghan National Army soldiers on daily patrols and operations.

I had learned to load and fire an AK-47 while training Afghan police and national army soldiers. The interpreters did not usually carry weapons, but this one was way different mission than the ones we had done for the past year. Hekmat had said, "John, it's less translation and more fighting because the villages are already empty."

Late in the evening we left for FOB Joyce and arrived without getting shot at in between COP Monti and Joyce.

"Let's rock and roll, bitches," SGT Hall shouted. We had made it to the helicopter landing zone [HLZ] at FOB Joyce to get airlifted to Bostick when the word came down from the

TOC that the mission was postponed due to stormy weather in Nari.

"Get some fucking sleep, we are leaving tomorrow afternoon," LT Kerr said after we waited at the HLZ for a few hours.

"Fuck this; it's so fucking stupid" I heard everyone grumble in response. It was a pain in the ass to bring tons of gear and supplies back to the barracks.

The next day, it felt weird walking around FOB Joyce with an AK-47 while everyone else had an M4 or M16 rifle. Every soldier that I passed stared at me, and some even asked to let them take pictures with the AK-47. My weapon soon became an issue with the 1SG from Headquarter Company, who insisted that I shouldn't bring a weapon because one of the interpreters who worked for the Marine ETT at FOB Joyce accidentally shot his foot as well as an Afghan National Army soldier. I wouldn't have cared if I couldn't bring it, but SFC Devine and LT Kerr assured the 1SG that I was going to be okay.

We finally flew out of FOB Joyce around 4:00 P.M. and arrived at FOB Bostick in Nari. We were set to fly into Barge-Matal at 1:00 A.M. the next morning.

I saw Hekmat, a fellow interpreter, at FOB Bostick while we were about to leave for Barge-Matal. Hekmat had spent almost a month in Barge-Matal, and I could see the hardship, suffering, grief and sorrow on his face.

"How did you like it, Hekmat?" I asked.

"I hated it; it was worse than Korengal Valley," Hekmat responded. Hekmat was an interpreter for American troops in Korengal Valley in 2007 where he had witnessed and suffered acts of war worse than I could imagine.

"You will find out once you get there," Hekmat said. "Take great care and do not leave for outside unless you have to; there are Taliban snipers everywhere in the mountains that targeted people out in the open.

That night while we waited at the HLZ for our flight to Barge-Matal, a medic ran over and told us that SPC Miller's body had arrived. Everyone from 1st platoon [1-32] went to see it before we left. I could not believe that SPC Miller was no longer with us. I had never seen 1st platoon so sad and heartbroken before. He was a great friend, a brave fighter and probably the youngest soldier that the Chosin (1st of the 32nd Infantry Regiment) sadly lost. It was a sad night; every soldier was heartbroken and grieving. SPC Miller was gone but will never be forgotten. He fought selflessly for his country and for the people of Afghanistan. Rest easy warrior.

The platoon broke into tears while waiting for our flight into the shit show that was about to happen. It was a cold, windy and raining lightly. "Let's fucking get outta here," everyone said. Finally, it was confirmed that we would soon head into Barge-Matal.

"Listen up, guys, the helicopters left J-BAD and are arriving soon," SFC Devine announced.

"John, let the Afghan National Army soldiers know," LT Kerr added.

A little while later, we heard Apache helicopters flying over the mountain tops. "10 minutes out," SFC Devine confirmed.

***

"John, you okay? Be careful; it's a fucking shithole," someone shouted as we prepared to load up for Barge-Matal.

"John, you're riding with me," LT Kerr said before we got on the CH-47s.

"Roger, sir," I replied.

I ended up sitting next to the gunner of the CH-47 helicopter. It was fun to watch through the gunner window; I tried to find a house or compound in the valley that still had lights on, but I couldn't see anything except trees, icy mountain peaks, the river and the flashing strobe lights of the helicopters. The farther we flew, the colder it got, and you could tell that we were no longer in Bostick. The weather dramatically changed from a warm 70 degrees to 30 degrees. The CH-47 that I was flying in felt like it was going to crash or hit the tress in the valley or icy peaks of the Hindu Kush mountains.

"Five minutes out, "the gunner shouted in my ear while using hand signals for the rest of the soldiers on board. The CH-47s finally approached the HLZ on the southeast side of the district. I couldn't wait to find out what people talked about when they described Barge-Matal.

Our helicopter landed in a cornfield surrounded by the river and high mountain with only a small path out. It was dark and the forests made it even darker.

"You okay, John?" someone asked when I plunged into a water ditch.

"I'm okay, but I can't see shit."

"Fucking hell!" I heard another soldier yell when he fell into one of the ditches.

"Stay fucking quiet! We are in fucking Barge-Matal!" someone yelled at him.

"We fucking need to get out of here before sunrise," LT Kerr directed. We had to walk for a few miles to get to the village that was at an elevation of close to 10,000 feet. The village was separated by a fast-flowing river from the district center.

"Watch out, John, that's a fucking river!" SGT Hall called. "If you fucking fall off, you'll drown!" I was walking at the edge of the river like the rest of the soldiers, but even a small misstep could lead us to death. The water was freezing, and even if we didn't drown, we could easily die from hypothermia. Despite the night vision goggles that the soldiers wore, there was not a single soldier that didn't fall at least once on the way to the village. The forest and rocky terrain made the trip more complicated than we expected, and by the time we made it to the village, everyone was soaked and exhausted.

We met up with soldiers from Chosin [1-32]. "Follow me. You guys are staying here," one of the soldiers who had been there for over 20 days directed us. We entered a small, musty room that would be our barracks. The ceiling was so low that we had to duck to enter and exit.

Everyone wanted to get some rest before we went out on patrol a few hours later. I wanted to wash my face and uniform because I was soaked and muddy.

"Do you know where the shower is? I need to wash my face; I think I got some dirt in my eyes," I asked Farid, an interpreter from Joyce.

He laughed, "We don't have a bathroom or a shower. You can go to the river, but it's not safe; you could get killed," Farid responded.

"Do you have any water?" I asked.

"I do, but it's only for drinking. We don't get enough water and only eat one MRE a day because we don't get re-supplied often. You can wash your face in the river water if you guys go out on patrol," Farid added.

I ended up just going to sleep, still dirty, but woke up to SPC Carlson warning me that we would be going out on patrol in 10 minutes.

"John, you ready to get some fucking Taliban?!" SGT Hall asked while everyone else was preparing for our first patrol.

"Always."

SGT Hall laughed and asked, "How many magazines you got?"

"Two here and one in the backpack," I replied.

"John, remember, one shot, one kill," LT Kerr joined in.

"But wait for us to run out of ammo first," SFC Devine joked.

"I got your old butt, sergeant."

"Bahaha, that's fucking funny," SGT Hall and SSG Benson replied.

"Hahaha, I am younger than you," SFC Devine defended.

"Yeah right, you couldn't even walk last night," I shot back.

We continued to joke as we prepped, and at 10:00 A.M. we began our first patrol into the village that was known for the Taliban attacks and snipers. It was a recon patrol with a couple of soldiers from Chosin [1-32] as our guides. Even though we were very aware of the Taliban's combat tactics, fighting, and attacks, 1st platoon [1-32] needed to better understand the area of operation [AO].

"The fucking Taliban snipers are everywhere. You go out to the open, they will try target you," one of the soldiers kept telling us. "When we got here, we couldn't even walk around."

His buddy pointed to the mortar pit and said, "I was there when a Taliban sniper shot at me, but he missed."

"You are a lucky bastard," SGT Hall assured him.

"Ha-ha, I think so too," the soldier replied.

"How often are the snipers set up? LT Kerr asked.

"Sunrise till sunset, but they suck at shooting," the soldier responded.

"The village that we are going to is very dangerous. The Taliban always sneaks in and attacks the high school where the battalion [Chosin, 1-32] tactical operation command is," our guide continued as we made our way closer. Both the village and local bazaar were less than a few miles away, but we had to walk across a wooden bridge that was a main target for the Taliban snipers. Only if you were lucky enough, and a fast-enough runner, would you survive the Taliban's snipers.

I wasn't worried about getting shot at the village, but I did worry about getting shot while crossing the bridge, where my body would fall into the water and get taken by the current. The bridge was so shaky that every time we stepped it felt like an earthquake.

"Stop, we have to run through one by one," LT Kerr told us.

The platoon divided into two smaller groups to run across the bridge so that one could provide security for the other. The first squad of soldiers managed to run and make it without getting shot at.

I was about to start running when I heard soldiers from the other side of the bridge who had already made it waving and saying, "You got it, John!". I ran like I never had before, and even though a Taliban sniper fired, I made it. "Ha-ha, you ran faster than Forrest Gump," SSG Benson joked when I reached the other side.

Across the bridge, there was a small town and the village, but most of it had been burned down to the ground.

"Do you see the rocket-propelled grenade?" I asked.

"What fucking rocket?" LT Kerr responded.

"The one half-stuck in the wall."

"Oh, that's crazy!"

When we arrived at the village, it looked like a ghost town with collapsed buildings, burned wooden beams, shrapnel and bullet holes everywhere. I had played *Call of Duty* once, and I remembered how the game looked-- "Is this a *Call of Duty* game?" I asked SPC Bowdish. "Hahaha, it looks like it," he replied. Both the town and village were dead quiet, but what remained told stories of brutality and suffering.

"Where is fucking everybody?" LT Kerr asked.

"They are still waiting to return to their homes," I responded.

"John, what about those who lost their houses? Look at that one—it's completely burned," PFC Solis wondered.

"I don't know. They'll figure it out."

It was heartbreaking to see the houses and town destroyed. Patrolling the neighborhood was not easy and became even more complicated because one team of soldiers had to secure each of the buildings while the other kept lookout. We never knew if a Taliban fighter could be hidden in one of those neighborhoods or in the cornfield.

We arrived at the building surrounded by a cornfield, hill and jungles, where SPC Miller was shot and tragically killed. "This is the window where SPC Miller got shot and killed," PFC Simpson said, breaking into tears. Everyone had had crying episodes every day since they saw SPC Miller's body at FOB Bostick.

"Put the M249 machine gun in the fucking window," SGT Hall told SPC Cepeda. We would set up in the same window that SPC Miller had used to surveil the cornfield and rest of the village.

"We are gonna turn this place into a bloodstream of the infidels," Qumundan Wali, the Taliban commander broadcast on the radio.
"Inshallah," another Taliban militant responded.

"They know where we fucking are," LT Kerr said frustrated.

"John, TOC wants to know what fucking language they are speaking and what channel are you listening to," SFC Devine told me.

"A mix of Pashtu and Nuristani. I'm on channel 456.864.00," I replied.

"We are fucking here to fight the fucking Taliban," I heard one of the soldiers say while we were searching and clearing the houses in the village. 1st platoon [1-32] took the highest security measures to defend against any possible attack as the Taliban kept talking about us. We were supposed to be back at our firebase after a few hours, but 1st platoon continued to search every last house in the village, and all the while the Taliban snipers kept shooting at us.

"Where is this fucking guy shooting at us from?" SPC Roach said while we were on the second floor of the house, watching the tall and thick cornfield.

"We need to fucking find him," SGT Hall confirmed.

"I want to fucking beat the shit out of him before I fucking kill him," SPC Cepeda chimed in.

SGT Anderson looked at me and asked, "John, what do you think? Where this fucking guy?"

"He can't be too far."

While we were talking, the Taliban sniper targeted a couple of soldiers a few meters away from us.

"Get to fucking cover!" LT Kerr yelled.

We took cover, but it sounded like the sniper was only a few hundred meters away from us; you could tell by the sound and impact.

The nightmare finally came to an end that afternoon when we spotted the shooter in a cave about half a mile away from the village. The cave was in the hill, covered by all sorts of trees and bushes, which had provided him with a good hiding place. First platoon [1-32] wanted to go after the sniper, but the TOC had already dispatched jets to drop a bomb on the target.

"60 seconds," LT Kerr advised. "20 fucking seconds."

"20, 19, 18, 17,16, 15…" everyone shouted, and some soldiers even pulled out their cameras to record the bombing.

The target was dangerously close-- less than 800 meters away from friendly forces, but the pilots still managed to destroy most of the cave and kill the Taliban sniper. "Fuck yeah!" Cheers rang out after the bomb hit. We-- SGT Hall, PFC Cepeda, SPC Roach, SPC Carlson and PFC Simpson and I were on the second floor, watching the cornfield when the bomb hit the cave. I thought the entire room would collapse, as wood pieces and debris from the roof and outside poured over us. The blast felt stronger than I expected. The ringing in my ears lasted all day.

"Anything on the Icom radio, John," SFC Devine asked.

"Nothing. He is fucking gone."

"Alright, let's go fucking check out the cave," LT Kerr directed.

"John, let me know if you hear anything about us moving to the cave," SFC Devine followed up.

We had only targeted one of the Taliban snipers, and others continued to shoot as us as we made our way to the cave.

"Fucking hell, he's got more than a hundred fucking rounds on the stack and ready to be fired," one of the Marines observed as we entered the partially destroyed cave. We ended up staying there to search and clear the area until sunset when the other snipers stopped shooting at us. It was only 7:00 P.M., but the surrounding mountains, rocky pine trees and tall and thick cornfields made the village seem dark, like it was midnight.

"Let's fucking get outta here before it gets too dark," LT Kerr said. We returned to the firebase, but we would go out again the next day.

"Good job, Jonny boy. You did great," SFC Devine said when we returned to the firebase.

Ch 26: Sniper Hunting

Another day and another patrol in the Hindu Kush Mountains of Nuristan Province. Our second patrol was a joint one with Afghan National Army soldiers from the 2nd Battalion [201st corps] the following day.

"John, tell the ANA that the patrol got pushed back due to fucking air support," LT Kerr instructed.

"*Turjuman Saab*, my guys are ready," MAJ Samad the ANA commander assured me.

While we were waiting to roll out, the high school building came under the Taliban's attack from the cornfield on the west side of the village where the tall plants in the field and surrounding forest provided the Taliban the perfect cover to attack.

"Mortar mission!" a soldier from the mortar team shouted.

Battalion mortar teams fired both 81- and 60-mm tubes to provide fire support for troops on the ground and target the Taliban's target reference point on the west side of the district; each fire mission included more than 50 rounds and after days of retaliation, they had turned the west side of the valley into a firepit with a constant cloud of smoke that remained.

"Get to fucking cover!" everyone yelled after we got shot at from the north of our firebase.

"Where is this fucking coming from?" LT Kerr yelled.

"I think it's from the fucking north," someone responded.

"Let's go fucking get this mother fuckers," the mortar sergeant yelled, directing his soldiers.

The Taliban fired an RPG from what we had believe was a "safe zone" in the north, but it never reached our location.

"Get out of the fucking way," LT Kerr shouted at soldiers while walking out of the building with an AT4.

"You are good to go, sir," SGT Hall called.

LT Kerr just couldn't wait to fire an AT4 light anti-armor weapon at the Taliban. The AT4, an 84-mm unguided, anti-armor weapon is the American version of a rocket-propelled grenade.

"Yay, sir!" everyone cheered after LT Kerr shot the AT4.

"Fuck you Taliban!" SPC Carlson shouted.

"Mortar team is going to conduct a fire mission," a mortar sergeant shouted.

"Fire mission, Fire mission!" 1st platoon's soldiers chanted. Battalion mortars [1-32] played an incredible and suppressive role in destroying and targeting Taliban's locations and target reference points deep in the Hindu Kush.

After the engagement with the Taliban at our base, we waited to go out on patrol only to find out after hours of waiting that it had been cancelled.

Even though we didn't go out, Apache helicopters still engaged and targeted Taliban fighters while they were supplying ammo and food to their fighting positions in the mountains for the next day. The whole night was noisy with aircraft flying over the valley, and before everyone went to bed, the aircraft dropped a couple of bombs that shook the entire valley like an earthquake.

"Good morning, sergeant," I greeted SFC Devine early the next morning when I arrived to prepare for our patrol with the ANA. We were joking with some others about who finished the last of the morning coffee when LT Kerr walked in. Even though he was just waking up, he was ready to rock and roll.

"Did you talk to ANA?" LT Kerr asked me, "Let them know that we are going to meet around 10:00 A.M."

"Where do you wanna meet them, sir?" I asked.

"By the fucking bazaar right before the village."

It was the first joint patrol with the ANA soldiers since we had been in Barge-Matal. We left the firebase on our way to the bazaar, but we had to cross the bridge that was the snipers' main target before reaching where the ANA were waiting for us. We all ended up making it without falling or being hit.

"*Salaam Turjuman Saab,* ask LT Kerr the plan," LT Zamarai asked when we met.

"John, tell him that we must search and clear those houses," LT Kerr responded.

LT Zamarai made a face and explained, "There are no villagers in those houses right now; they had gone before we got here to retake the district."

"True, but we never know if the Taliban snuck in last night," SFC Devine replied. The village was at the edge of the mountain where the Taliban could easily penetrate and hide in one of the buildings because they were all connected like a ladder.

"*Turjuman Saab*, I can hear people talking on the other side of the building," an ANA soldier told me after we got done searching a few houses.

"The ANA soldier thinks that he heard people talking," I relayed to SGT Hall and LT Kerr. "Behind that building," I directed them to the two-story building that we were about to search.

While we were talking, the Taliban attacked the school building where the rest of the battalion's personnel were still stationed. We were only a couple of hundred meters away from the Taliban, but the tall and thick cornfield, trees and bushes blocked our view, but we could hear them. "*Allah Akbar!*" we heard one of the Taliban yell while we took cover under a collapsed building.

"John, tell the ANA that we need to fucking get outta here," LT Kerr yelled.

"*Turjuman Saab*, I see the sniper, he is hiding behind the tree with an RPG," an ANA soldier said while he was trying to find a good spot to shoot at him.

"John, what the fucking is he doing?" LT Kerr asked.

"I am going to shoot the Taliban," the ANA soldier replied.

"John, tell him to not fucking fire at him. Our soldiers at the school are taking care of him," LT Kerr commanded. "Everyone needs to calm the fuck down; we need to get the fuck out of here. I don't want my fucking soldiers to die here under this fucking broken-building."

LT Kerr made the right decision. We had no other choice than to let him alone. The Taliban fighter had an RPG that could have killed us all, especially if the ANA soldier missed.

"John, tell the ANA that we need to get the fuck out of here one-by-one and quietly, to the east side of the village. Once we get there, we are gonna fucking shoot this mother fucker," LT Kerr commanded.

We managed to get out of there, but right after we left, the Taliban attacked and started shooting at the building where we had just taken cover. We attacked from the east side as planned and soon the shooting stopped.

"John, tell the ANA that they did a great job; I think we fucking shot him," LT Kerr told me.

"Yes, I shot him in the head," The ANA soldier who had a PKM responded.

We later found the body of the Taliban fighter, he had been shot, and his body was left behind on the battlefield. We handed it over to the Afghan border police at the end of the day.

"Did you shoot your AK, John?" PFC Simpson asked.

"Yes, I shot a few rounds," I replied.

"Make sure, it's clear now," SFC Devine instructed.

"Yes, it is; SGT Hall just checked it. That was fun"

***

"This is fucking stupid," LT Kerr radioed.

After the second patrol and near-death experience, 1st platoon [1-32] was tasked to chase Taliban snipers into the mountains on the southeast of our post. The Taliban's snipers were a daily headache for both Afghan and American soldiers. They shot dozens of soldiers at the school and around the firebase because the Taliban had control of the high mountain tops, giving them the upper hand. We set out on our patrol to ambush, kill or capture the Taliban snipers in the Hund Kush. It was going to be a tough operation after we experienced close combat with the Taliban the previous day.

We had to be up in the mountains no later than 4:00 A.M. in order for 1st platoon to catch the Taliban unprepared. Everyone was excited, so we left the firebase around 1:00 A.M. to get to the portion of the mountain that we believed the Taliban's snipers had been using. It was much more complicated than we expected due to tough, rocky terrain, forest and slippery slopes, but we finally made it to a small animal shelter. It was an old-fashioned room, built probably decades ago for animals, where local villagers kept their goats and sheep during summer. We ended up searching the room but didn't find anything except dried animal feces and hay.

There were a few caves and huge rocks about fifty feet away from us, where anybody could easily hide. We searched the caves and then went even farther, pushing the patrol out to secure the parameter and find a great spot for the ambush before sunrise. Sunrise was the Taliban snipers' favorite time to start shooting at us down below in the valley.

"John, anything on the Taliban's radio," SFC Devine asked before he went out with the first squad to check out an ambush location.

"Nothing yet," I replied.

"Okay, let me know if you hear anything."

SFC Devine had left the animal shelter, and LT Kerr was talking to the TOC on the radio when we heard a Russian PKM and then small arms fire targeting our location up in the mountain.

"Fucking hell, where is this fucking coming from?" LT Kerr shouted.

"Get fucking covered," SFC Devine yelled while we all tried to figure out who was shooting at us. Both the AK and PKM sounded pretty close, but not close enough to ruin our plans of an ambush.

"What are you doing, John?" SGT Casey asked when he saw me with my AK47 at the window.

"Nothing. I just gotta make sure the Taliban doesn't come here," I replied.

SGT Casey laughed and said, "It's not going to happen."

"Don't fucking shoot that thing, John," LT Kerr yelled.

"I won't, sir."

"I am trying fucking find out what's going on?" LT Kerr told us.

"Anything on the radio?" SSG Casey questioned.

"No, it's just the Taliban's music."

While I was talking with SGT Casey, we heard LT Kerr complain, "Fucking ABP [Afghan Border Police]." LT Kerr was angry that tactical operation command [TOC] hadn't let the ABP know about our patrol. It was them shooting at us, thinking that we were the Taliban.

"Stupid bastards. Why the fuck didn't TOC let the ABP know?! I almost lost my fucking guys up here!" LT Kerr radioed. "Don't they fucking have a liaison officer at the TOC?"

Tactical operation command [TOC] believed that they had informed the ABP prior to the mission, but some sort of miscommunication occurred. No one was hurt, but it had put us on alert. It was hard to differentiate between weapons that ABP used and the Taliban. They both used Russian AK47 and PKM machine guns that sounded the same, but the direction of the shooting had helped us identify that it had been friendly shooting. Still, the shooting revealed our location and we would be unable to execute the ambush that we had planned.

We headed back to the firebase, navigating our way down the steep slopes. A couple of soldiers ended up losing their balance and slipped while the mortar team conducted a cover mission to keep the Taliban from attacking as we made our way down the mountain.

"John, I am glad you didn't shoot your AK47," SGT Casey said when we got back.

"Why is that, sergeant?"

"Your gun sounds like a fucking Taliban gun. The guys down here wouldn't know whether it was the Taliban or you shooting," SGT Casey joked.

Ch 27: Lucky Morning

There is no doubt that the battle of Barge-Matal was one of the toughest and longest battles that I was part of. It was a complex challenge for both Afghan and American soldiers, who agreed that Barge-Matal is a place that they never wanted to go back to. The daily firefights, sniper shootings, rocket attacks and missions left many soldiers, both American and Afghan, suffering from psychological illness. An ANA commander who served in the district for over a month shot himself in the leg in order to get evacuated. For me, the hardest part of being in Barge-Matal was that I had no ability to communicate with my family for almost a month. When I was at COP Monti, I talked to them at least twice a week, and now I feared that they would think I was dead.

The village was old-fashioned, its buildings made of wood and clay instead of concrete. The rooms were so small that we could hardly fit more than three people in any one. We had no shower for almost a month, and those of us who didn't have baby wipes stunk. We didn't have enough water, and everyone was instructed to use the bottled water only for drinking. After weeks, though, I needed to wash my face after seeing myself in the mirror, caked with dirt, it wasn't even me. I found an old pipe system that went by our building, but I wasn't sure if it had water. I fixated on the possibility that there might be water, and I plotted every day how I might try it while avoiding sniper fire.

One morning, I woke up at 7:00 A.M., it wasn't a sunny day in the valley, but it was sunny up in the mountains. It was a little bit colder as usual, but I was still ready to wash both my face and hair that was so matted it looked like it had never been washed before. I decided that it was the day that I would try the pipe system to see if it had a water supply. I was so excited that I even forgot to put on my body armor and helmet for protection against the snipers before heading outside. I made it to the hose, but the faucet lever was too old, and I couldn't open it with just a turn. I noticed water drops while I was trying to turn the faucet lever and was hopeful that this meant there would be water. I managed to turn the lever after a few attempts, and water began to flow. I washed my face and then ran back to the building to grab my toothpaste and shampoo.

I went back out, and after brushing my teeth, I put a handful of shampoo in my hair; I heard a bang within seconds. I thought it was still the buzzing in my ears from the shooting the day before, but quickly realized that the Taliban snipers saw me. I don't remember how I made it back into the building, but noticed big bruises on my legs and arms from slipping on the way. The Taliban's sniper fire rained down where I was standing. It was a miracle that I survived.

I still had shampoo in my hair and eyes when the others arrived.

"What fucking happened?" LT Kerr asked still waking up.

"I was out there, and they started shooting at me!" I responded.

"Fucking lucky, man."

"What the fuck is in your hair?" SGT Hall asked.

"It's a shampoo," I responded, "I was just around the corner washing my hair."

Everyone laughed, but I didn't care about shampoo or how I looked because I was just lucky to have survived.

"John, you got to find this motherfucker," SPC Bowdish to me.

"Hell yeah, let's go find him!"

"You were lucky, I saw those marks," PFC Landsdet said.

"I know. The rounds landed within meters away from me," I replied.

"We are glad you are okay brother," SPC Cepeda added.

We returned to COP Monti after more than a month of daily fights, rocket attacks, and snipers, but when we left Barge-Matal, the entire district and surrounding villages were successfully cleared from the Taliban. More than five thousand mortar rounds were dropped on the Taliban deep in the valley and caves where they were hiding. The U.S. Airforce was a big part of the operations, and Coalition aircraft flew and conducted more than 40 raids, using the heaviest bombs [110,000 pounds] against the Taliban. When the rest of the coalition forces finally withdrew from Barge-Matal, they left the local police forces to take care of the district and the observation posts that were built while we were there. Icom chats and intelligence poured in that more than a hundred

Taliban got killed and hundreds of others were wounded during the entire operation to retake Barge-Matal.

While we were in Barge-Matal, the Taliban claimed that they killed more than a hundred Americans and Afghan soldiers. They were masters at propaganda to raise moral among their fighters.

In truth, 39 soldiers from 1-32 received injuries and three incredible soldiers-- SPC Miller, SPC Coleman, and another great soldier, were tragically killed along with seven Afghan soldiers who received injuries. The soldiers from 1-32 who received injuries during the operation of Barge-Matal were given purple hearts for their heroic sacrifices.

If you ask any soldier, including me, if they want to go back, the answer is simple— "no."

2009 was a year of both good and bad memories. The scar on my right arm serves as a permanent reminder of these memories and the role we played in the operation that successfully cleared Barge-Matal from the insurgents.

Ch 28: Final Patrol with the 1st Platoon Boys

December 2009

"John, I am putting you in my backpack and getting you outta here; I don't want you to die," SFC Devine told me as 1st platoon prepared to end their tour. SFC Devine promised to help me get the paperwork to leave Afghanistan, but I didn't know that the process would take years.

In December 2009, 1st platoon [1-32] began to return home from a difficult and risky, year-long deployment in the Hindu Kush mountains of eastern Afghanistan. As 1st platoon [1-32] was preparing to reunite with their families and friends back in the United States, they left hundreds of memories with the people of Dangam, government officials, and local tribal elders.

For many soldiers of 1st platoon, it was the last deployment of their army career and the closing of a chapter before they transitioned to civilian life. It would take months, if not years, to adjust to that new life.

SSG Dole had already submitted his paperwork for retirement, and was technically retired, but he ended up supporting 1st platoon [1-32] during the battle of Barge-Matal.

"John, I don't have to go to Barge-Matal; I am done with the army, but I wanted to go," he told me. I was a little confused why someone who was already retired still wanted to go to war and engage in a battle that could kill him.

"Well, it's a long story-- I submitted my papers and got them approved, but I wanted to stay here until the end," he explained. SSG Dole had always been quieter than the others, but he was a great sergeant.

"What do you wanna do when you get out?" I asked.

"I don't know, but I definitely want to spend time with my family. I will probably go to school to get my degree."

"Good luck with that, it's pretty impressive," I replied.

First platoon [1-32] had established incredible friendships with local government officials, tribal elders, and villagers of Dangam Valley. The band of brotherhood between 1st platoon [1-32] and local tribes such as Mushwani and Salarzai was unbreakable.

"John, tell SFC Devine that we will miss them," Gul Wali, a local tribal elder from the Mushwani tribe, who had been fighting the Taliban since their rise to power in the '90s told me. The awesome thing about 1st platoon [1-32] was that they knew so much about local culture and tradition that mistrust and misunderstandings were always avoided.

"John, you are not going with them, are you?" District Governor Shah Mahmood asked.

"I wish."

SFC Devine laughed and looked at Mahmood and said, "John, is gonna get outta here, I am doing his paperwork."

"No, no, we need John," Shah Mahmood replied.

"*Khamaar*, the dragon, looks like an Afghan," The police chief said and laughed "He can stay too."

SFC Devine smiled at him and replied, "I wish, but it has been a very great year and the new guys are very good people. I know them; I used to be in the same unit. John, tell them that the new guys are arriving at Monti and I am going to bring them out here tomorrow."

"Okay, but we are not done yet, we have some gifts for you guys," The police chief added. "John, you know it is our tradition."

Dangam District officials and local tribal elders always honored Americans with feasts and gifts. It was a great way to establish and strengthen friendships that were very vital during the fight against the Taliban.

"He said that it's our culture and tradition to honor guests," I translated for SFC Devine.

"That's what I thought he said." Devine chuckled.

"Good job, just make sure you don't forget what you learned here," I joked.

"Hell no, I will speak much better Pashtu than you when you get to the States."

The farewell party was even funnier when SFC Devine put on Afghan clothes that the district governor got for him. "I am from the Mushwani tribe," SFC Kevin Devine joked while everyone was laughing so hard. SFC Devine, a Native-American, indeed looked like an Afghan.

"Tell him he can stay with us and get married here," the police chief joked.

SFC Devine laughed saying, "My wife would kill me."

"Our women are not like Americans; they won't kill you. We marry more than one woman," The police chief said.

"Ha, in some states you can have more than one wife," SFC Devine half-joked.

First platoon did a lot for the people of Dangam Valley, including building a micro-hydro energy power system and a concrete building for the policemen at the observation post, a project that turned a small room that looked a cave into a beautiful building better than anything the police could dream of. It was now a place where the police could feel secure while they worked.

We returned to Combat Outpost Monti at the end of the day and found that most of the new soldiers of the battle company [173rd] were already there at Monti.

It was hard to say goodbye to people that I had fought shoulder to shoulder with against the same enemy that tried to kill us every day for almost a year in the Hindu Kush Mountains of Kunar and Nuristan Provinces. I couldn't believe it was the final patrol with 1st platoon [1-32] boys. During my time with Charlie Company [1-32] Infantry, I endured countless dangerous and risky situations that could have left me killed or seriously wounded. Some of my brothers were not lucky; many of our missions were heavy in casualties. Through it all, we became a family. I worried that I would never see them again after they left, but social media helped me connect with most of them. I didn't know anything about social media until one of the soldiers created a Facebook account for me and taught me how to use it.

***

"The next unit is the 173rd. I used to work with them, and the guy who is going to replace me is my best friend," SFC Devine told me. "His name is Pat [SFC Flanagan]; we went through basic training together."

"Did you say 'Fat'?" I asked.

"Ha-ha," he laughed and replied," Not 'f-a-t', 'P-a-t. You'll probably like him more than you like me."

"Who said I like you?" I joked.

"Whatever, I know you're gonna cry because I'm leaving."

He was right, I was very sad to see 1st Platoon [1-32] leaving COP Monti, and I didn't know anything about the incoming unit, 2nd Platoon, Battle Company, 2nd Battalion (Airborne), 503rd Infantry (of the famed 173rd Airborne Brigade Combat team.) I couldn't believe my best friend, brother and instructor was leaving, and I thought I would never see him again. Before he took off, we talked for hours at the HLZ. For SFC Devine, who had been in the army for more than 15 years, his multiple tours to both Afghanistan and Iraq were not enough.

"If I ever get out, Johnny boy, I'd like to help my mom with her business," SFC Kevin Devine told me. His mom sold flowers and had a greenhouse in Martha's Vineyard. "Take great care, Johnny boy, and keep in touch."

"I will, sergeant."

It was really hard and upsetting to see him leaving, but it was great that he was returning home safe and secure after such a challenging deployment. I didn't know then that it would be SFC Devine, and his mom, who would later work for years in order to help me navigate the complicated visa process and paperwork to come to the United States. It would be a long process, nearly seven years, I would finally make it and we would be reunited at Fort Bliss in El Paso, Texas.

Our U.S. soldiers returned home, but their memories and bravery against the Taliban insurgents stayed with the people of Dangam and its government officials. I was also honored to participate in some major battles while supporting 1st Battalion, 32nd Infantry, and the 10th Mountain Division (LI) operating out of Combat Outpost Monti in 2009. I want to mention some incredible men that I had the privilege to fight alongside including warriors who have been honored for their heroism by the President of the United States when they received the Medal of Honor:

> Sergeant Dakota Meyer, USMC – He was located at COP Monti alongside us in 2009. LT Kerr, who was promoted to Captain, was standing next to Sergeant Meyer when he received his Medal of Honor from President Obama.

> Staff Sergeant Clint Romesha, U.S. Army – He was operating out of COP Keating during the Battle of Kamdesh where I fought and worked to save soldiers' lives.

> Staff Sergeant Ty Carter, U.S. Army – He was also at COP Keating during the Battle of Kamdesh.

2nd Platoon, Battle Company, 2nd Battalion (Airborne), 503rd Infantry posing for a picture before conducting their daily patrol out of Combat Outpost Monti on March 24th, 2010.

Ch 29: Sky Soldiers

Battle Company, 2nd Battalion (Airborne), 503rd Infantry, (173rd Airborne Brigade Combat Team)

I joined 2nd Platoon, Battle Company, 173rd Airborne when they came to relieve 1st platoon [1-32] at COP Monti. I provided them with the same skills and knowledge of local culture and traditions as well as understanding of the area of operation (AO). For many soldiers of 2nd platoon [Battle Company, 173rd], this deployment was going to be a piece of cake, but for those who had never been to Afghanistan, it was going to be a challenge. I wasn't worried about the heavy workload and operations, which I was used to, but I was worried about making friends and forming bonds like the ones I had with 1st platoon [1-32].

Battle Company, 2nd Battalion, 503rd Infantry, of the 173rd Airborne Brigade Combat Team, are known as "Sky Soldiers", and deployed out of Vicenza, Italy. The 173rd Airborne Brigade Combat Team was one of the United States European Command's conventional airborne strategic response forces for Europe. Battle Company had already completed some of the toughest tours in Afghanistan and operated against the Taliban in the Korengal Valley, the

"Valley of Death," in 2007-2008. Korengal was one of the most dangerous places during the War Against Terror, and the Company lost exceptional soldiers and experienced too many combat injuries, while they fought hard with honor and great bravery. Now however, they were going to encounter fewer domestic fighters and more foreign insurgents as they operated out of Bajawar. I was beyond excited to meet these incredible fighters.

Second platoon's experience is documented in the film *Restrepo*, shot between 2007 and 2008. I watched *Restrepo* a couple of times, and there is no doubt that it is one of the most powerful documentaries about the war in Afghanistan. Even though I had been to Korengal Valley with my brother, Ajmal, years before and was familiar with the tough terrain, high mountains and beautiful forest and waterfalls, *Restrepo* brought old memories back to life. *Restrepo* was not just a short documentary, it showed the bravery, courage, and fearless fighting of 2nd platoon [Battle Company, 173rd Airborne]. When I began to watch it, I had goosebumps; I even told Ajmal about it. I had never thought that I was going to be working for the same soldiers one day.

"How did you like it there, sergeant?" I asked SSG Hoyt when we were talking about *Restrepo* once.

He changed his chew and replied, "It was alright, John."

"I've been to Korengal once," I told him.

"Did you fucking say, you've been to Korengal?" SGT Stichter jumped in, surprised to hear that I knew the valley.

"Yes, I went there with my brother. He was a truck driver," I responded. SGT Stichter could hardly believe it.

"I remember, John was fighting us," SSG Hoyt said laughing.

"How old are you, John?" SPC Cantu asked.

"Can't tell you."

"Come on, you are not a girl," SPC Cantu retorted.

"I don't know," I explained.

"Are you fucking serious, John?" SPC Cantu taunted.

"Let's say 20 years-old," I guessed.

"No, you are not 20, John," SGT Sosebee responded.

"What's your birthday?" SPC Cantu asked.

"I don't know. I never had one."

"What day were you born?" SGT Cortez jumped in.

"I don't know, I never found out."

"What is your paperwork say?" SPC Cantu asked.

"March 3rd."

"That's your fucking birthday, John," SSG Hoyt ended the debate.

Fighting in Dangam Valley was not as bad as Korengal Valley, but the enemies were the same. There were going to be a lot of firefights, possible IED attacks, and close combat with enemy fighters for a couple of months during the spring operations deep in the Hindu Kush mountains and along the Durand Line.

"How's spring season here?" SGT Lizama asked.

"It's fighting season, lots of fighting," I replied. "Well, it's not nearly as bad as Korengal."

"Nothing here looks like fucking Korengal," SSG Hoyt said. "This is going to be a piece of cake." SSG Hoyt was a great NCO [non-commissioned officer], squad leader, fighter and friend.

I missed 1st Platoon, [1-32], but I was also excited to work for 2nd platoon. 2LT Gasperini was a platoon leader and SFC Flanagan was a platoon sergeant; they were both great people. I heard a lot about SFC Flanagan before he even arrived at Combat Outpost Monti from SFC Devine who went to basic training with him and served in C Company, 2-504th PIR of the 82nd Airborne with him later. "He is my homie, he will take care of you, Johnny boy," SFC Devine assured me.

Finally, I met both SFC Flanagan and 2LT Gasperini; they were both very quiet and not as boisterous as SFC Devine.
"John, I heard a lot about you," SFC Flanagan said.
"I hope it's all good, sergeant."
"John, I heard a lot about you and I am excited that we are gonna be working together," 2LT Gasperini added.
I could tell from 2LT Gasperini's first impression that he was a gentleman. I never heard him cuss. When working with him, I would need to try to break the habit of using the foul language that I had picked up while working with 1st platoon [1-32]. The "f-word" was LT Kerr's favorite, and it was readily used by 1st platoon. It seemed to mean just about anything to a soldier.

Later, I met 2LT Gasperini and the rest of the soldiers at the barracks where everyone was waiting to learn about Afghanistan's multi-ethnic society, its culture and traditions. Afghans are very sensitive to their cultural and traditional values. Many soldiers from 2nd platoon were pretty aware of Afghan culture, but for some new soldiers I would provide background (and dispel the assumption that everyone used camels, donkeys and mules for transportation!). It was a short class but a great opportunity to meet the new fearless fighters like SFC Flanagan, SGT Hoyt, SSG Trapp, SGT Crisafulli, SSG Frazier, SGT Stichter-Forward Observer, SPC Copeland-DOC, SGT Sosebee, SGT Diebler, SGT Jones, SGT Cortez, SGT Lizama, SGT Brown, SPC Cantu, 2LT Gasperini and many others.

"Nice to meet you, John," Everyone shouted at the end of the class. I couldn't wait to be part of such a great group on daily patrols, and operations.

***

"John, we are going out to Dangam," 2LT Gasperini said as he passed me walking to the Tactical Operations Command [TOC].

"Roger sir, I will meet you at the motor pool," I replied.

At the end of December 2009, 2nd platoon began patrolling in Dangam Valley in support of Operation Enduring Freedom X. The objective of our first patrol was to have a key leader engagement with Dangam government officials and local tribal elders as well as to conduct reconnaissance of the Dangam Valley for possible Taliban fighting positions [TFP] deep in the Hindu Kush Mountains.

I was excited to go out on the first ever patrol with 2nd platoon and get to know each other better before the fighting season kicked in. Snow was still up on the surrounding mountains, and it was still a little chilly, but you could get shot in Dangam regardless of the season or weather. It was not fighting season yet, but the Taliban were already stocking up supplies, ammo and recruiting new fighters for upcoming "spring operations." Second platoon [Battle company] was well-prepared and ready to fight.

2LT Gasperini was a smart officer with great and fearless fighters around him; they all adhered to *Pashtunwali*, an ethical code and traditional lifestyle among the people in Dangam Valley and the indigenous Pashtuns. *Pashtunwali* could be used both for force protection and as an offensive force. A great example is Muhammad Gulab, a Pashtun in Shuryak Valley, bordering Korengal, who harbored and saved the life of a wounded U.S. Navy SEAL during Operation Red Wings in 2005. Muhammad Gulab put his own life, and the lives of his family members, at greater risk than we could imagine to save the life of the wounded SEAL because of Pashtunwali tradition.

"John, tell the district governor that we are here to help and continue the friendship that you guys established with SFC Devine and his soldiers," 2LT Gasperini told me.

"We are looking forward to working with you. Dangam was pretty bad district before *Khamaar* and *Zarawar Zalmy* got here," the district governor replied.

"Who are *Khamaar* and *Zarawar Zalmy*?" 2LT Gasperini asked. He was surprised to learn that these were the nicknames that were given to LT Kerr and SFC Devine for their bravery and fearless fighting against the Taliban.

"*Turjuman Saab*, tell 2LT Gasperini that we are gonna help and support you as much as we helped and supported *Zarawar Zalmy*," a local Mushwani tribal elder, Noor Muhammad, said during another meeting later that day.

"*Turjuman Saab*, we lost many great leaders fighting the Taliban; we have been fighting them forever now."

"We are here to help. Let us know if you see the Taliban," 2LT Gasperini told him.

2LT Gasperini and the entire second platoon [Battle company] was able to establish and create an incredible friendship with Dangam government officials and local elder tribal elders within weeks.

***

"John, you riding with the lieutenant," SFC Flanagan said before we left for Dangam Valley one day. We got on the trucks and headed out, but while we were driving, the platoon noticed people with AK-47s, RPGs and PKMs along the road.

"John, who are those people?" LT Gasperini asked.

"They are road security, sir." The highway was funded and constructed by one of the U.S. PRT teams who operated out of FOB Wright. Because it was a dirt road, making it easy to plant IEDs and plan other ambushes. All the laborers, including the security personnel, were from Dangam Valley and were required to report any suspicious activities.

"What do you think, should we talk to them now or on the way back?" 2LT Gasperini asked over the radio, and then added to me, "Do you know their commander?"

"Yes, I do sir, I have spoken with him many times."

Commander Muzamil was a security commander in charge of the Asmar-Dangam highway; he was also an influential tribal leader of the Mushwani tribe in Dangam Valley. This would be a great opportunity for 2nd platoon to get in contact with those who secured the Asmar-Dangam highway [Route Santiago] where the Taliban always tried to use IEDs and hire local recruits.

"*Salaam alikum*, ask them if we can talk to them, John," 2LT Gasperini greeted the security forces.

"Yes, *Turjuman Saab*," one of the security guards replied; he had an RPG setting right next to him.

"My name is Gasperini and I am the commander for of these guys."

"*Turjuman, Saab*, tell him that our commander went to Asmar this morning. He won't be back for a few hours" the security guy replied.

While I was talking to him, SFC Flanagan pointed to another security guard with PKM and a bunch of rounds strapped to his body with radio trying to talk to some soldiers, "John, what's he trying to say?" SFC Flanagan asked.

"*Turjuman Saab*, I was listening to the Taliban and they are talking about you right now. They know that you are in Dangam."

"What's up, John?" SSG Hoyt asked.

"He picked up Taliban's conversation. I got the frequency that the Taliban is using, but they are confused about our location."

It was loud and clear that the Taliban were attempting to plan an attack, but they didn't know that 2nd platoon had fought much worse in Korengal, and although they were new to Dangam, they would be ready to fight. The Taliban had sympathizers in the valley, but 2LT Gasperini and his team were well-positioned to fight back by establishing friendships like this with the local company who provided security for Asmar-Dangam highway. The majority of the security was provided by the Mushwani tribe of Dangam who had their own long history of fighting with Taliban. The biggest challenge for us in forming a working partnership with them was that they didn't have official uniforms and carried AK-47s, RPGs and PKM machine guns. You couldn't tell whether they were the Taliban or local security from distance.

2LT Gasperini sought to address the issue at his next meeting with the sub-governor. "They don't have uniforms, and it's very hard for the helicopters to tell the difference between good and bad guys," 2LT Gasperini explained.

"Yes, I agree with you, but I don't know what to do," Sub-Governor Shah Mahmood responded.

"We can talk to their commander, but I would like to buy uniforms for them," 2LT Gasperini added. It was great problem-solving by 2LT Gasperini and his team because the Dangam government officials and the security personnel both were scared of the helicopters that patrolled the valley for this same reason.

We tried to assure Shah Mahmood that the helicopters wouldn't fire unless they were under attack, but we knew that purchasing uniforms was the best solution.

The security personnel couldn't wait to get their uniforms, but obviously the mail could take months to arrive at COP Monti. Both the security guards and Dangam government officials began asking about the pending arrival frequently.

"It's coming, sir, my father already bought them," 2LT Gasperini explained. 2LT Gasperini was using his own money for the uniforms with the help of his father who was a retired army colonel.

When the uniforms finally arrived, we decided to surprise the security guards by bringing them to their tents. The security guys had a couple of small tents that they put up for shelter from the rain along the Asmar-Dangam highway.

"*Turjuman Saab*, tell him, thank you so much. He saved our lives," the security guards asked me to tell 2LT Gasperini. You could tell how happy and thrilled those guys were after they received the very small gift from 2nd platoon. "No problem. Let me know if I can help more," 2LT Gasperini replied.

Ch 30: The Deaths of Taliban & AQ Leaders

The Deaths of Taliban CDR Nick Muhammad and AQ Operative Abu Khudifah

In late March 2010, 2nd Platoon, Battle Company, 503rd Infantry, 173rd Airborne conducted a route reconnaissance mission deep in the Hindu Kush mountains along the Durand Line, Dangam Valley, Kunar Province. We wanted to observe the Taliban's activities because in that zone there were no Afghan border police or Pakistani militia forces to control Taliban movement. There were thousands of trails that the Taliban could use to enter Dangam. March was usually the beginning of the Taliban's spring operations, but 2nd platoon still managed to patrol deep into the Hindu Kush mountains, close to the Durand Line along Bajwar, a large safe haven for the Taliban and other terrorists.

During our briefing before leaving Monti, we discussed how to best travel deep into the valley.

SFC Flanagan turned around and asked, "John, you think we can drive these big-ass trucks far into the valley?"

"I think so, sergeant, but the farther we drive in Dangam valley, the narrower it gets," I replied.

"Did first platoon [1-32] ever drive the MRAP trucks there?

"Yes, but not very deep into the valley because the road is very narrow and only big enough for the Humvee trucks."

"Let's fucking try," SGT Jones concluded.

We left COP Monti on Friday morning around 9:00 A.M. It was a beautiful, peaceful day. Unlike in the United States, Afghans do not work on Friday because it considered the day of rest, like Sunday is for Christians. But daily life for farmers was consistent, they didn't take days off. We found many people working on their tiny farms and small pieces of land while we were driving into the valley. Dangam Valley was a mountainous region, where a little over 1% was flat land and the rest of the valley was occupied by the tall Hindu Kush mountains.

"John, what are those people doing?" 2LT Gasperini asked.

"They are farmers, sir."

"Oh, that's cool. Are women helping them too?"

"Yes, they mostly prepare food, water, or tea for the farmers. They are families. Some families own the land and some works for other families."

"Okay, so if you don't have a farm, you can work for other people?" SPC Cantu asked.

"Kinda of, but it's not a daily wage."

"So, it works differently than in the United States," SPC Cantu concluded.

"I don't know how things work there but probably. We do things in the Afghan way," I smiled.

"Have you ever worked on the farm?" I asked SPC Cantu.

"Yes," he replied, "what about you, John?

"My entire childhood. I had to help my parents."

It was great to see families working on their farms, growing crops and raising livestock with their kids playing around, but as we approached the district center it got quieter. We stopped to check a few washouts and culverts for IEDs along the road.

"John, where did you guys find the IED?" 2LT Gasperini asked

"Oh, that was in Baidad village, the first village we just passed," I responded. "It was on the road right before the water spring. I will show you on the way back."

We didn't find anything after a few stops so we continued our patrol. We were good so far, but the fact that were people out farming didn't mean that the Taliban wouldn't try to attack, using the civilians as human shields. We finally arrived at the local market of Dangam District without getting shot at or hit by an IED, but we still had a long risky road and tough terrain ahead up us into the heart of the valley where the Taliban operated freely against both Afghan and American soldiers. When we drove through the local market, it wasn't busy as it used to be; fewer shops were open, but that also could have been because it was Friday.

We kept pushing our patrol forward, but we had to stop when some of our mine-resistant ambush protected [MRAP] vehicles couldn't turn a corner. The MRAP trucks were oversized vehicles, and they wouldn't be able to drive deeper into Dangam Valley due to narrow and small roads. We would all need to get out of the trucks and continue on foot.

"John, you think we can walk out here?" 2LT Gasperini asked.

"Yes, but it's a long-ass walk, sir." I kidded. "But sir, I love to walk."

The Icom scanner had been quiet, and I wondered if the vehicle-mounted counter radio-controlled electronic jammer system, the "Duke," was on. The Duke system not only acted as a counter-measure against radio-controlled IEDs, it also blocked the Icom. I confirmed that the Duke was turned off, and then waited for a few minutes while everyone got out of the trucks and talked about our next move, but there was still nothing on the radio. I wondered if there was something else wrong with it.

Suddenly, while we were preparing to walk, SPC Cantu heard a pop-shot. It was a very small, haphazard shot that could hardly be heard. "Did you guys hear that?" SPC Cantu asked.

"Yeah, I heard a pop-shot," I confirmed.

"Are you guys fucking sure?" SSG Hoyt asked.

"Anything on the radio, John?" SFC Flanagan added.

"Nothing yet, sergeant. Just some static sounds."

The patrol stopped and everyone looked at the surrounding mountains through their weapon scopes, but it was hard to see in the dense forest and through the rocks and tall trees especially because it was foggy. It was tense, and we knew that it was likely that we could get shot at, at any moment. The trucks turned around, but 2LT Gasperini called for a fire mission. "Here comes the boom, John," SPC Cantu pointed. The first artillery round landed on the hilltop where we believed that the Taliban were hiding. The fire mission was short, ending after a multitude of rounds. After the fire mission, we began to head back to Combat Outpost Monti, but as soon as we arrived at the local market, the remaining stores and shops were closed and the rest of the people were leaving. It was not a good sign to watch locals leaving the business because whenever it happened while 1st platoon [1-32] was around, we got attacked.

"John, why everybody is leaving?" 2LT Gasperini asked.

"Weird sir, but we are going to get attacked," I asserted.

"Did it happen when you were with 1st platoon [1-32]?" 2LT Gasperini questioned.

"Yes, and then we got shot at," I replied.

2LT Gasperini informed everybody to be on alert, but it wasn't clear where we would be targeted. Attacks always happened when crowds rushed to leave the local markets. Our convey drove back to Monti slowly. I was sitting in the second Humvee with 2LT Gasperini, SPC Cantu [RTO], SPC Zajac [gunner], and a driver; as soon as we left the market and reached a narrow corner where two mountains from east and southeast came together, there was a boom. AK47, PKM, and RPG fire started raining down on us from all directions. It was horrible. "Fucking Taliban!" I heard on the radio while 2LT Gasperini and SPC Cantu communicated with the other vehicles and with Monti. The vehicle in front of us, a MRAP with SFC Flanagan inside, was attacked but survived the three rocket-propelled grenades [RPGs] that landed underneath it blowing the back tires.

I had been in firefights, ambushes and direct and indirect rocket attacks while I was with 1st platoon [1-32], but this was indeed one of the worse close-combat situations with the Taliban that I experienced. We got stuck in the middle of the firefight while the rest of the convoy stopped at the corner, about 50 feet away, and also under intense enemy fire. The adrenaline rush was so high that I didn't think about getting wounded or dying. I noticed a cloud of smoke pop up from a small bush to my 9 o'clock; it was the man with RPG who kept firing at our convoy.

"Cantu, Cantu!" I shouted after I saw the smoke through a small window of our Humvee truck.

"What's up John?" SPC Cantu replied while 2LT Gasperini was talking on the radio.

"Do you see the smoke?"

"What fucking smoke? Are you talking about the MRAP?"

"No, it's the fucking guy firing RPG at us! To our 9 o'clock!" I directed him.

"I see it, I got to let fucking PFC Zajac [the gunner] know," SPC Cantu yelled.

As I looked back to double-check while I was talking to the gunner, my window got hit by small fire. I thought I got hit in my forehead.

"Holy fuck!"

"Are you okay?" 2 LT Gasperini shouted to me.

"I am okay, sir, but my window got shot!" I replied.

"It's a ballistic glass," SPC Cantu assured me.

"I guess I am lucky, sir."

He laughed.

There was not a single truck that didn't get shot at least once, but the MRAP at the very front and our Humvee became the main targets due to the short distance and advantageous angle both for small arms and RPGs of the Taliban. Reinforcements were already on the way from COP Monti, and after things calmed down a little bit, we made it to the nearest village, just a couple hundred meters away from where we got ambushed. Even with the firefight over, the artillery fire mission from COP Monti, and later the air support, continued to target and destroy the Taliban's fighting positions.

We got out of the truck after we arrived at the village where the reinforcements from Monti, including the company commander, Captain Nagy, had just arrived.

I began to pick up Taliban radio transmissions --

"Muhajar, can you hear me? This is Fedai."

"Fedai, I can hear you; did you check on everybody?" *Muhajar asked.*

"I am trying to, but their radios not working."

"Mulawai Saab is very anxious about everybody."

"Muhajar, this is Qari, if you hear me please let Ghat Mulawai [the superior mullah] know that we got some problems here. I can't talk to everybody right now. There are wasps flying," *Qari continued.*

"Okay, take care and let us know as much as you can," *Muhajar instructed.*

"They are still here," Fedai confirmed.
"Be careful," Qari told the others.
"Yes, but some friends need to get out of here badly," Fedai replied.
"Mulawi Saab says that we can't do anything right now. Wasps are everywhere," Qari told him.

With the ambush over, the Taliban's higher leaders and fighters were trying to find out the status of their friends whose radios weren't working. After the artillery fire mission, aircraft were on-station to drop bombs on the remaining targets, but some of the Taliban fighters had taken cover, using civilian property, houses, and buildings as their shield against us. Still, many Taliban fighters got killed and dozens were wounded, while 2nd platoon [Battle Company] only received some minor injuries. The Taliban couldn't collect the dead bodies until the next day, and some of the dead bodies that were left behind on the battlefield to be collected by local residents. We learned that the wounded militants were evacuated after we left, including the notorious Commander Nick Muhammad, who was taken into Pakistan for treatment.

We arrived back at Monti and the soldiers went to debrief. I didn't have to be at the meeting so began walking back to my room when my phone rang-- *"Salaam,* John, he is seriously injured," Police Chief Shahzada said, not even waiting for me to answer.

"Calm down, *Qumandan Saab,* what is going on? Who is seriously injured?"

"Commander Nick Muhammad got seriously injured," Police Chief Shahzada confirmed.

I stopped the police chief from talking further and went to find 2LT Gasperini and SFC Flanagan.

"John, we need him to give us as much information on the Taliban as he can," SFC Flanagan instructed.

"Yes, we are gonna need it for the battle damage assessment [BDA]," 2LT Gasperini added.

Back on the phone, the police chief told me, "I have been trying to find out more through the families who live deep in the valley. They saw Nick Muhammad carried on a bed by the Taliban right before the Saabandi where he lived. Another police officer's family in Gooriga called and also said that they saw a bunch of wounded Taliban there."

We hoped to find out more but the police chief told us that he needed to take another call. After about two minutes, he called me back, "Sorry," he said, "I had to speak with the same family that told me about Nick Muhammad. They just told me that Nick Muhammad passed away."

The Dangam policemen worked in the same districts where they had families, friends, and relatives that cooperated, identified, and informed them prior to attacks or about the situation in the aftermath. We later learned that Nick Muhammad was not the only one who died on the way to the hospital in Pakistan. Khudifa who was believed to be an Al-Qaida operative from the Middle East also got killed during the firefight. His dead body was left behind at the battlefield until the next day, until local sheepherder found and buried it.

Ch 31: Daab Valley Firefight

March 2010

"You need to be very careful in Daab Valley," my parents always said. My parents knew that I was working at COP Monti, only a few miles away from Daab Valley.

"They used to kill soldiers just to get their rifles," my mom told me when she found out that I was traveling to Daab Valley.

The valley had been dangerous since the 1980s when the communist regime governed the country. Both of my parents and my older siblings remembered how unsafe it was for Afghan and Russian soldiers to drive through Daab valley.

"Those people would fight you with axes, knives, swords and old English rifles to attack supply and fuel trucks," my oldest brother, Ahmad recounted. Ahmad was not a truck driver, but he had heard horrible stories about Daab Valley because we lived not too far from it. Daab Valley remained dangerous and deadly for many Afghan truck drivers who struggled and put their lives at risk to feed, support, and help their families. Decades later, the people of Daab Valley still ambushed Afghan and American supply convoys. It sounds bizarre civilians would put their lives on the line to collect fuel and weapons from the conveys, but many local villagers mistook the Americans as Russians and wanted to continue to fight back.

Daab Valley was one of the most rugged, mountainous valleys in Kunar Province. The Kunar River ran through the Daab Valley, flowing south, but areas with high elevation were forested, sustained with grassy mountain meadows. The rocky, steep landscape with the fast-moving river made it a great hideout for the Taliban and other terrorists from which to attack Afghan and American forces. Daab Valley had been popular supply route for the Taliban as they came from Bajawar, Pakistan because it was very close to the border. However, it was also a supply route for dozens of Afghan and American small firebases and FOB Bostick [Nari] who received deliveries twice per month. There wasn't a single time that supply trucks didn't get attacked or shot at. American military forces made a huge effort and spent millions of dollars to escort and secure the supply trucks traveling on the unpaved road that had been destroyed by Taliban's IEDs and rocket attacks. Daab Valley was about 10 miles from COP Monti, and every American unit stationed there had conducted overwatch missions, patrols, and operations to secure, escort, and bodyguard supply trucks traveled through the area. I had been to Daab Valley with 1st platoon [1-32] many times, and I was never able to get the picture of more than fifty trucks and fuel tankers that had been burned-down to the ground out of my head. A beautiful valley turned into a junkyard.

In March 2010, Battle Company [2-503D] planned to carry out a company-sized operation to clear, secure and protect the Daab Valley from the Taliban right before one of the supply convoys arrived. It wasn't a much different operation from the ones in the past, but this time I got to use a new scanner system called "Wolfhound." Wolfhound was a cooperative radio direction finding system; it was much better and smarter than the small radio that I had carried for years, but it also weighed about 20kg [44lbs]. The system had 8 antennas facing both up and down along with a remote control that tracked and intercepted the direction, distance and conversations of the Taliban deep in the Hindu Kush mountains.

"John, it's pretty easy, anybody can help you how to use it," SFC Flanagan said.

On March 7, 2010, all three platoons and the headquarters element left COP Monti at 5:30 A.M. to conduct a search-and-clear operation in Daab Valley and its surrounding villages. More than hunting down the Taliban, the operation was also an internal test of leadership from the fire team to the brigade level. It was a sizable military convoy comprised of more than thirty vehicles and both Afghan and Battle Company [2-503rd] soldiers. It was quiet when we arrived at 6:00 A.M., and everyone began their day without a firefight, rocket attack, or IED strike, but this would not last.

"What's up, John? How do you like the new thing?" SSG Hoyt asked about the scanner.

"It's pretty damn good. I already got a couple of frequencies for the Taliban."

"That's awesome. What the fuck are they talking about?"

"It's on and off right now, but they are actually talking about us."

OEF*IN
EASTREN PART
OF THE COUNTRY
11:20:44

"Kamran, Kamran, this is Abu Obaida; can you hear me? Americans are here. Be careful, they are everywhere."

"Yes, I heard they are here, but we need some hay [ammunition]."

"What kind of hay?"

"We need some for cows [Dish-ka]."

"Kamran, Kamran, can you hear me? this is Badar. Do you see their trucks in Daab valley?"

"Yes, they are everywhere. There are few trucks by the village where some soldiers began climbing into the valley."

"Let everybody know to be very careful."

Right after the sunrise, the entire convoy came under attack while some soldiers, including 2nd platoon [2-503D], were up on the mountain. The attack was well-coordinated, and so effective that we could hardly help the other platoons when it started. But after a few minutes, 2nd platoon [2-503D] got to the other platoons, who found themselves under intensive fire, and were able to offer support. While we were trying to help the others, we came in very close contact with the Taliban who occupied the mountain peak just above our position. Soon, we had two Apaches and two Kiowa circling right above us to engage the Taliban fighters.

"John, are they still fucking talking?" SFC Flanagan asked after the impact of rounds.

"Not the ones up here, but some of them are talking about the guys in the other platoons." There were two other platoons less than half a mile away from our position who also had contact with the Taliban.

"Hold on, John," SFC Flanagan cut me off while I was talking to him.

"PFC Nicholas cook got shot," PFC Cantu [RTO] had just reported. PFC Nicholas Cook was mortally wounded and needed an air medevac immediately, but since there was no suitable helicopter landing zone [HLZ], his platoon tried to medevac him on the ground while the fighting was growing worse. Medevac helicopters continued to circle, but they couldn't land; meanwhile, Battle Company tried to bring the MATV trucks into the valley but it didn't work.

"Qari Ozair, don't let it land! Shoot it with an ax [RPG]," Abu Obaida said on the radio. Qari Ozair was a local Taliban commander who leading the group of Taliban during the fight.

"The Taliban is going to shoot the helicopters while they are trying to land," I yelled to 2LT Gasperini.

Even though the Taliban had threatened to shoot down the helicopters, and under intensive, non-stop fighting, one of the pilots was able to bring the helicopter into the valley and retrieve the wounded soldiers.

As the Apaches and Kiowa helicopters targeted dozens of the Taliban militants, the firefight slowed down.

> *"Talha, Talha, this is Mulawi Saab, let me know how everybody is doing?"*
> *"Mulawi Saab! Wasps just fired at our friends. I can't get a hold of them right now."*
> *"We are praying for them. Let everyone know to stay where they are; wasps are taking the whole sky,"* Mulawi Saab replied.

Even with the helicopter presence, some Taliban remained and continued to engage with other platoons who were stuck, but 2nd platoon [2-503D] was able to provide suppressive fire into the enemy's fighting positions to let the rest of the platoons got out of there. We had four gunship helicopters, two Apaches and two Kiowa, flying over the valley and mountains while we tried to depart, but they couldn't engage the Taliban due to their proximity to the friendly force.

Battle Company [2-503D] assisted and ultimately got everything under control after attacking the remaining Taliban with mortars, hellfire missiles and JDAMS [Joint direct attack munitions]. Their artillery fire missions blanketed the entire valley as we fought through the afternoon.

Get the Terp Up Here!

After the fighting, many Taliban, including Qari Ozari and Mulawi Talha had been killed. Even though each and every one of us had put all of our energy and effort into the fight to save the life of PFC Nicholas Cook, he sadly died on the way to the hospital due to wounds that he received in one of his eyes.

During the operation, my new Wolfhound system proved to be life-saving because it helped us identify enemy forces, their movements, directions, and plans to prevent future attacks. It was a chaotic, sad, and heartbreaking day for everyone, but everybody did their part of the job by fearless fighting with the Taliban. Finally, we returned to COP Monti after an exhausting day.

Ch 32: Escaping the RPG

"Where the fuck those rounds are coming from," SSG
 Trapp shouted.
"It's fucking coming from the other side of the river,"
 SGT Crisafulli replied.

***

"John, this could be our fucking last mission here,"
SGT Cortez told me.
 "Yeah, I heard that."
 "You better come with us," SSG Hoyt added.
 "I would love to, sergeant."

This could be the last mission for 2nd platoon [2-503D]
in Daab Valley before they reunited with their brigade in
Wardak Province sometime in May 2010. It was an early
mission; we had to leave COP Monti at 4:00 A.M. It was quiet
and beautiful when we arrive at Daab Valley. Because it was so
early you could hear the sounds of nature and the river as it
rushed along its bed, bubbling over rocks. It was quite peaceful
to live in the serene quietness of the early morning and chilly
weather for a bit before we would get attacked.

We stayed in the vehicles until sunrise. Around 7:00 A.M. it was sunny up on the mountain peaks, but not yet in the valley. 2LT Gasperini, SSG Hoyt, SGT Stichter, Copeland-Doc, SSG Trapp, SPC Cantu and I began walking along the dirt road by the river to set up the firing and mortar positions because we never knew when the Taliban would attack.

While we were walking, SGT Stichter asked, "John, what was that guy talking about on the loudspeaker earlier?"

"Oh, are you talking about the Mullah?" I heard him preaching and addressing the villagers earlier," I responded.

He laughed and said, "I thought he was fucking talking about us."

"Not exactly about us, but he did say things about Jihad," I replied.

"I knew it!"

After a little walk, we found a great spot for the mortars, and after SFC Flanagan arrived, we planted them and returned to the trucks.

"What's up?" I asked Copeland when I saw him knocking on the window of our Humvee truck around 9:00 A.M. "Lieutenant needs you," he replied.

I got out of the truck and walked towards 2LT Gasperini who was less than 100 meters away, talking to SFC Flanagan.

"I am listening to a couple of Taliban's frequencies back and forth here. They are planning to attack. They heard that the convoy is on its way up here," I told them.

While I was still talking, we heard small arms fire. "Where the fuck are those rounds coming from?" SSG Trapp shouted.

"It's fucking coming from the other side of the river," SGT Crisafulli replied.

"2 o'clock! They are fucking shooting RPGs from the other side of the river!" SGT Cortez yelled.

"They are fucking hiding in the bushes!" SSG Hoyt shouted.

"Get to fucking cover!" I heard when a second RPG landed 600-700 meters away.

"Let's fucking get out of here!" SSG Hoyt yelled.

It was "run Forrest run" after we heard the second RPG land, and we managed to escape just before the third round [RPG] landed where we had just been taking cover. It was hard to run with the Wolfhound system, and I had never thrown myself on the ground to get cover as hard as I did that day.

The Taliban shot another RPG at one of the trucks, but it landed short in the water. He never got the chance to fire another because one of the gunners shot him dead.

When the convoy arrived, we headed back to COP Monti. Unlike other days, the convoy was heavily escorted by the road clearance patrol [RCP] and Apache helicopters. Even though the convoy came under attack in Daab Valley, it made it out safely without even stopping. When we got back to the COP, I got stitches in my arm from when I had dived for cover in the gravel.

Ch 33: Goodbye to 2nd Platoon
Battle Company, 2-503rd

May 2010

"Are you kidding?! They [2nd platoon] just got here!" District Governor Shah Mahmood told me.

In May 2010, 2nd platoon [2-503D] wrapped up its short deployment at Combat Outpost Monti and continued the remainder or their deployment in Wardak Province in central Afghanistan. Many Afghans, tribal elders, government officials, policemen, and locals in the Dangam District didn't believe that 2nd platoon [2-503D] was about to leave them.

Even though 2LT Gasperini was a young, newly-graduated officer with only a little knowledge of Afghanistan, he was surrounded by fearless, smart NCOs and fighters like SFC Flanagan who supported and assisted him in establishing solid and long-lasting friendships with local people and tribal elders from various backgrounds, cultures, and traditions. Despite the fact that he was a young lieutenant, he was one of the smartest officers that I had the honor to work with.

"John, tell 2LT Gasperini that I probably will forget the rest of the English I learned," Shah Mahmood joked.

2LT Gasperini looked at him and with a big smile on his face said, "You've gotten a lot better, and you speak very good English, sir."

"Why are you leaving?" Shah Mahmood asked.

"My guys like it here, but it's not up to us, sir. Our chain of command wants us to leave."

Shah Mahmood laughed and said, "I wish our government officials and military leaders respected their superiors."

"It will eventually happen, sir; our military is very old military," 2LT Gasperini replied.

"John, tell him we had an old military too, but a lot happened," Shah Mahmood replied.

"You still have great soldiers and fighters," 2LT Gasperini assured him. Shah Mahmood looked a bit emotional and said, "Thank you, sir, I hope you all come back to visit without those trucks and weapons."

"We couldn't have done our work without your help and support, sir," 2LT Gasperini looked sincerely at the district governor. It was supposed to be a brief meeting, but it turned out to be the longest we had together.

2LT Gasperini and the rest of the platoon headed back to Monti for relief in place/transfer of authority [RIP-TOA] with the incoming unit, Alpha Company, Task Force No Slack, 1st Brigade Combat team from the 101st Airborne Division, Air Assault. When we returned in the afternoon, Monti was suddenly overcrowded by soldiers that I didn't recognize. COP Monti was a small outpost where everybody knew each other.

The dining facility was a small building that would overflow with more than ten people; therefore, many soldiers ended up eating outside the chow hall. I ended up going to the MWR because every seat, table, and chair near the chow hall was full.

Before 2nd platoon departed, 2LT Gasperini shared news, "Oh, you are going to Bagram and will be working for a general," he told me. "I will send you the email I got from him."

"Awesome, thank you, sir."

"There is some great news on the way for you, John," SFC Flanagan encouraged. "You will love it there."

I was super excited about moving to Bagram to work for a U.S. Army general. It was a really big deal for someone who had spent years in combat in the Hindu Kush mountains.

"----- Forwarded Message ----
Sent: Wed, May 12, 2010 11:50:41 AM
Subject: (UNCLASSIFIED)

John - Here is the email the General sent back to me. He is a very good man, and he is trying to help. He hopes that you can work directly under him. I will let you know as soon as he gets back to me.

Come see me as soon as you read this.

--- On **Tue, 5/11/10, Martins, Mark S BG Deputy Commander, JTF 435** wrote:
From: Martins, Mark S BG Deputy Commander, JTF 435 <
Subject: RE: Rich Gasperini (UNCLASSIFIED)
Date: Tuesday, May 11, 2010, 10:37 PM
Classification: UNCLASSIFIED

Cris--roger all, and great. Was in Asadabad last week and know your AO pretty well. Met your Bn Cdr, in fact, and learned of move to Wardak.

This can work out well, though let me do some checking. I can talk to the MEP ACOR here in Parwan and try to set this up. Because that is the same firm that employs our interpreters, I'll bring him on--if workable--very quickly and start putting him to good use (and in a setup where I can be the General on his packages).

Hope all is well. Kunar is hauntingly beautiful.
Keep up the good work, and thank you for your service.

v/r
Mark Martins
Brigadier General, U.S. Army
Deputy Commander, JTF 435
Parwan, Afghanistan

-----Original Message-----
From: Cris Gasperini
Sent: Wednesday, May 12, 2010 1:02 AM
To: Richard Gasperini; Martins, Mark
Subject: RE: Rich Gasperini (UNCLASSIFIED)
Dear Sir,

I am fully aware of the high OPTEMPO in which you operate, so I am truly thankful for your willingness to take the time to assist us with this matter. Nasirullah (John) is an impressive young man who has proven to be my most valuable asset during this deployment. His command of Pashto, Dari, Arabic, and English makes him a very reliable interpreter, and his interpersonal skills and dedication to the COIN mission make him stand out amongst his peers. John has faithfully performed these duties for three successive Coalition Force units in Kunar Province. All this despite the physical risks he takes by accompanying us on daily patrols along the AFPAK border and the mental strain he endures from regularly receiving death threats on his cell phone.

My unit – 2D BN, 503D IN (ABN), 173D ABCT – is moving this month in order to reunite with our Brigade in the Wardak Province. In an effort to coincide with our departure, John has decided that the time is right for him to leave the front lines and find employment in other areas of ISAF. He originally planned to seek employment with Coalition Forces in Jalalabad, but he was absolutely thrilled when I informed him of the possibility of working with JTF-435. Upward advancement is tremendously difficult for local nationals such as John, so I truly believe this opportunity could open a myriad of doors to him. Moreover, I think it is a place where he could continue to excel and positively contribute to Operation Enduring Freedom.

A Jalalabad-based company called Mission Essential Personnel (MEP) contracts John to CF, and his site manager is named Scott Kreller (....). My unit is currently conducting RIP-TOA with an incoming unit from the 101st Airborne Division, so I will be leaving Kunar within two weeks. John is currently training his replacement, and he plans to leave Kunar within the month. He is prepared to begin new employment by June. Thank you again for your help, Sir. I know your time is precious, so I do not like absorbing too much of it. Please advise if there is a POC with which I could place John into contact. He is standing-by, eagerly awaiting the opportunity to assist JTF-435.

Very Respectfully,
1LT Cris Gasperini
Classification: UNCLASSIFIED"

***

It was beyond unbelievable that I was going to work in Bagram, a place that my mom always hoped for me because it was much, much safer than Combat Outpost Monti. I didn't know if my mom and the rest of the family would believe it after I had lied to them about both Kabul and Bagram while I was working for 1st platoon [1-32]. Still, I couldn't wait to share the news with them about the new job.

"*Salaam Abai*, I am going to be working in Bagram."

"What? Where is Bagram?" she asked.

"It's very close to Kabul," I told her.

"Are you sure you are not going to Nuristan again?" she asked suspiciously.

I laughed, "No, I am not going to Nuristan; I am going to Bagram. It's much safer and nicer."

She laughed and replied, "I don't know, I can't trust you anymore."

"I am not lying this time. I wish you could read English; I would send you the email I got. Where is *Dadda*? I wanna talk to him."

"He is here but he won't believe you either," my mom taunted.

"Yes, he will. Put him on the phone."

"*Salaam Dadda*, I am going to Bagram," I told him when he picked up.

"Yeah, I heard you talking to your mom. You are not messing with us this time?" my dad was skeptical.

"No, I am not. I just got the email says that I will be working in Bagram."

"That's awesome, but when will you be there?"

"Probably in a couple of weeks."

"That's great. I hope you are not lying again."

"I am not lying this time," I promised my dad.

My parents were excited for me, because they had been worried about me being in the war zone, combat, and front line for years. "I have lived my life, and I never thought that I would live very long, but I don't want to see anything bad happen to you while I am still alive," my mom always said.

Bagram Airfield [BAF] was the largest U.S. military base in Afghanistan. I was not just thrilled to work in Bagram, but I also couldn't wait to get my Special Immigrant Visa [SIV] started. You had to have a recommendation letter from a U.S. military general, and that would have never been possible at Combat Outpost Monti where generals rarely spent time. Both 2LT Gasperini and his father, who was a retired U.S. Army colonel, were trying to make my dream come true. It seemed, though, that the dream was swept away when

Second platoon [2-503D] left Combat Outpost Monti to reunite with their brigade in Wardak Province.

I ended up working for CPT Michael and Alpha company, Gator, [Task Force No Slack, 1st Brigade Combat Team, 101st Airborne Division (AALT)] still out of Combat Outpost Monti. CPT Michael didn't know that I was packed and waiting for my call to leave Monti for Bagram.

It was nice working for the Company Commander CPT Michael, but I missed working with platoon leaders and soldiers because I still received tons of phone calls from government officials, and tribal elders of Dangam District.

"Where have you been hiding stranger?" The district governor said on the phone.

"Hahaha, I am still here in Asmar at Monti," I replied.

"I am glad you still here, but you are not coming out here; I met some new people from Alpha Company, but you were not with them," the district governor probed.

"I work for their commander, but I miss coming to Dangam," I told him.

It wasn't long after that that I learned that I wasn't going to Bagram, even though my company, Mission Essential Personnel [MEP], had asked Captain Yoder from the Civil Affairs team, who managed the interpreters at Combat Outpost Monti.

"John, we need you here. There is no way that Alpha Company would let you go work somewhere else," Captain Yoder told me after about a month. It was very disappointing, but I knew that my deep knowledge and experience would benefit Alpha Company as they learned the area of operation

[AO]. I never told my parents and family that I was not going to work at Bagram Airfield. They were very excited, but I understood that things happened for a reason.

I continued working for Captain Michael who had served in Iraq and was eager to confront the Taliban militants in the Hindu Kush mountains and along the Durand Line.

I finally shared the disappointing news that I wouldn't be transferred to Bagram with my mom and the rest of the family. They had been waiting to hear that I was no longer in a war zone, on the front-lines and in combat. I wanted to tell them the truth because sooner and later, they were going to find out. It was sad and frustrating, I didn't want to lie to my family again, but I also didn't want my mom to worry. In the end, I lied again--

"Mom, I did go to Kabul for a month, but I didn't like it there," I told her.

"Why didn't you like it there? It's very beautiful, safe, and secure," she questioned.

"I don't know, it wasn't like Asmar [Combat Outpost Monti]."

She asked me to quit, but I insisted that I was going to work for a little while longer to get a house for them.

"What about Jalalabad?" she asked.

"I am trying to get to Jalalabad."

"Okay, I am rooting for you," she cheered up.

Tea drinking with locals.

Ch 34: Ahmad and the Suicide Attack

18 May 2011

"How is Lala doing?" I asked.

"He is doing okay," Ajmal, my second oldest brother, responded like nothing was wrong.

"Why his phone is not working?"

"Mmmmm," Ajmal lost his words and couldn't answer.

My family refused to tell me that my brother was hurt in a suicide bombing and was struggling for his life.

May, June and July of 2011 turned out to be the deadliest months with IED strikes, vehicle-borne-improvised explosive devices [VBIED], suicide bombers, and direct and indirect attacks on Combat Outpost Monti almost tripling. The Taliban announced their spring operations against the Afghan and American soldiers, and instantly many districts were under an increased threat. It was a busy deployment for Alpha Company as it increased and extended its presence by conducting more and more patrols and operations in response to the Taliban's attempts to capture surrounding villages and

335

district centers. Some days, I had to participate in more than one patrol or mission per day.

My family lived in Jalalabad where there had been a series of suicide bombings and VBIED attacks. In May, a VBIED exploded in the heart of the most populated area of Jalalabad City. A suicide bomber drove his truck, full of explosives, into a van that was carrying new Afghan cadets, killing them all and seriously wounding many civilians.

A month later, I found out that my oldest brother had been seriously injured and was fighting for his life. Shrapnel was embedded throughout his body. I was furious at my family for not letting me know.

"Why didn't you let me know?" I yelled at Ajmal on the phone.

"We thought, you might end up getting killed or kidnapped on the way home or to the hospital." In this respect, Ajmal was right; the Taliban were always coming after interpreters and their families.

Lala was still in the hospital when I finally got a chance to speak with him. He sounded weak and struggled to talk. I also learned that he lost his temporary memory. He was struggling with his transient global amnesia, sudden and temporary memory loss, due to the attack. It was short a conversation with him and I was emotional because he wasn't the same person as before the attack. He was in severe pain even though his doctor gave him tons of pain killers. I decided that I needed to go visit him in the hospital.

With CPT Yoder's permission, I left for home after one of our daily missions, but I was not sure that I would make it because it was a very dangerous trip back to Jalalabad in those days. The Taliban had checkpoints along the road, looking for people who worked for the Americans and Afghan government, most of all for interpreters. Interpreters were believed to be traitors, the eyes of the American soldiers, *dogs*, and infidels. Luckily, I made it to Jalalabad, despite the taxi breaking down in a Taliban hotbed.

When I left Combat Outpost Monti, I didn't tell anybody at home that I was coming to visit my brother because they would never let me visit due to the risk I was going to take. There was no doubt that the Taliban would cut my body into small pieces after torturing me if they ever caught me. When I arrived at the hospital, everyone was shocked. I couldn't recognize my brother when I first saw him. Even after a month of recovery, he was still wrapped up in bandages from head to toe.

After a short visit, Ajmal told me, "Go home, it's not safe here; I heard that some injured Taliban militants were brought here last night," he spoke softly to make sure that nobody heard him talking. It was normal that wounded Taliban who couldn't make to Pakistan would be treated in the hospitals under the government's control. In these cases, the fighters would lie and claim to be innocent bystanders.

I went home to see my mom and the rest of the family. My mom was worried about me and my brother, "I didn't want to lose both of you, and that's why I told everyone not to inform you about your brother got wounded," my mom told me. "I know that you act like you are a grown man, but I still think of you as the baby who broke all of my glasses, dishes, and whatever you could find at the house."

I laughed and replied, "I didn't do any of those things, old lady."

I understood her concern, but I would always risk the danger for my brother. He was my best friend, mentor, supporter, believer, and most importantly a backbone, role model, and hard worker for the rest of the family. Everything I had, accomplished, and was able to pursue was a result of my brother's guidance and support.

I wanted to find out more about the suicide attack before I headed back to Combat Outpost Monti, but I still had to wait for my brother to get discharged from the hospital. When he did come home, he struggled to remember everything that happened to him, "I was going to see Ajmal at the bus station, riding my bike, but when I arrived at the most congested and overcrowded part of the city, there was a big explosion and then I didn't know what happened," Ahmad recounted.

"I was trying to get hold up him to let him know that I was okay," Ajmal added. He had been at work about a mile away from where the suicide bomber attacked. There was no way that he could have known that Ahmad was in the middle of the blast zone fighting for his life and praying for a miracle to help him survive.

Ahmad hadn't realized that the American soldiers provided the first response after the suicide bomb went off because it was less than a mile away from the U.S. military base FOB Fenty [Jalalabad Airfield]. "I learned later if the American soldiers hadn't stopped my bleeding, I could have died there."

My family didn't find out until the next day that Ahmad was in the hospital; they thought he was either killed or kidnapped because I was working for the Americans. "I looked around the entire city for him and made phone calls, but I couldn't find any news about him," Ajmal told me. Like the other injured who arrived at the hospital alone, the hospital staff posted Ahmad's picture on a board in the hospital for family members, relatives and friends to search. That was how my family finally discovered what had happened.

I later realized that back at Monti, I had been working the radio station during the time of the attack. I had broadcast news of the attack that injured Ahmad without knowing how my own life would be impacted by the report.

I am happy to say that my brother survived the heinous attack, but not without the lasting marks of shrapnel pieces in his back, legs and even chest. He returned to live with his family of six beautiful kids who I don't want to imagine having to live without him.

Ch 35: My Own "Band of Brothers"

Alpha Company, Task Force No Slack, 1st Brigade Combat Team, 101st Airborne Division (AASLT)
2/327th No Slack
June 2010

"God damn it," Captain Michael yelled while beating the dashboard of the MTV truck. "I can't fucking believe it," he was talking to himself.

I didn't know what was going on.

***

Captain Yoder invited us to watch a couple of movies about the 101st Airborne when they first arrived at Monti. Born and raised during the Taliban regime, we were not allowed to watch movies or even listen to music on the radio, so now, I always enjoyed watching movies. The movie that CPT Yoder talked about was *Band of Brothers*. I had seen it before, but I didn't realize it was about the 101st Airborne [AASLT]. I appreciated the fearless fighting in the movie, but I also knew that the sort of battle that the 101st Airborne would face here in the Hindu Kush would be dramatically different.

"The 101st Airborne is known in the U.S. military for their assault operations," CPT Yoder said. Captain Yoder was in his late fifties, and I called him the 'history book'. He had millions of experiences and deep military knowledge. I felt like I was taking a history class at school whenever I asked him about something because he loved to get questions and answer them.

"What about eagle patch on the soldiers' arms?" I asked him after the movie.
    "I forgot to tell you that 101st Airborne Division is also known as the 'Screaming Eagles;'" CPT Yoder explained.

We learned a lot about the 101st Airborne, and we couldn't wait to start working and supporting them in their daily patrols. The 101st Airborne would become a big part of the air assault missions and operations against the Taliban, AQ and other terrorists deep in the Hindu Kush mountains. It was time to become part of the real stories and fighting, this wouldn't be a movie.

June 2010 was the deadliest and most dangerous time for Combat Outpost Monti and by the end of the month some of the incredible, brave soldiers from Alpha Company, 327th Infantry, 101st Airborne would tragically lose their lives in an improvised explosive device [IED] strike.
    On June 7, 2010, 2nd platoon was to head out to secure Daab Valley and Browalo Khowar for a key leader engagement with local residents and tribal elders. LTC J.B. Vowell was the battalion commander leading the meeting, which aimed to discuss security and potential projects with local residents and

tribal elders. It was a beautiful, sunny day at Combat Outpost Monti and we hadn't received enemy contact, which was not normal.

I got done with breakfast and was leaving the chow hall when I saw First Sergeant Robert Barton walk in with his full gear on. He was a great man who took great care of his soldiers. He was brave and funny and always had a smile on his face whenever I met him.

"John, how do you like working for us?" he asked me a few days before the mission.

"I love it, sergeant."

"That's awesome. I am glad you like working for us," he replied while I was talking with Captain Michael and Company Executive Officer Cody Grimm.

"John, don't listen to him," Grimm joked.

"John is my favorite interpreter," 1SG Barton replied.

I worked a lot with CPT Michael, CPT Grimm, and 1SG Barton, and I was looking forward to learning from their experience.

Around 8:00 A.M., I grabbed my body armor and radio and headed to the gazebo table where I supposed to meet up with CPT Michael and the rest of the platoon while 1SG Barton and 2nd platoon had already gone. The gazebo table was a smoking area, meeting table, and a briefing spot where CPT Michael often met his Afghan counterparts, government officials, and tribal elders because it was right outside of the tactical operation command [TOC].

When I arrived, we made our way to the vehicles and hopped in. We were still waiting on CPT Michael who was behind talking with CPT Grimm. Suddenly, I saw CPT

Michael run back to the TOC, but he returned to the truck in less than a minute. I thought he forgot something. He opened the door and got in the truck while I was talking with SGT Horton-RTO.

"God damn it," CPT Michael yelled while beating the dashboard of the MTV truck. "I can't fucking believe it," he was talking to himself. I didn't know what was going on until SGT Horton said, "first sergeant's truck got hit by an IED."

I couldn't believe what just happened. This must be a joke because I just saw Barton in the chow hall and talked to him for a bit before he went out. All at once, too many thoughts flooded my mind about 1SG Robert Barton. I saw him the night before playing with CPT Grimm and other soldiers in the building hall where the soldiers had wrapped him in a body bag while others pulled it back and forth on the concrete floor, just joking around. Loud music was blaring and they were having so much fun. This was what helped cope with the constant fighting, stress and loneliness at COP Monti. Now, I simply couldn't believe that 1SG Barton was no longer with us.

We finally left Monti with the devastating news of our loss hanging over the trucks. Everyone was heartbroken and mourning everything that had happened. Captain Michael was angry and emotional; he kept punching the dashboard of the MTV truck and talking to himself while the rest of us were speechless. It was a short drive but felt like it took forever. When we arrived at the scene of the attack, we were all still in shock. The beautiful, sunny day no longer seemed beautiful; the smiles on soldiers' faces had turned into tears and heartache. A whole part of the dirt road was destroyed by the Taliban's IED. It looked like a big rectangle hole that would be excavated by roadwork machines. The entire Humvee truck was gone, you wouldn't have known that it ever existed. Everyone searched for the soldiers that had tragically lost their lives.

Some pieces of the truck landed in the craggy mountain face and fast-flowing river. While everyone was looking for the rest of the truck, I saw LTC Joel B. Vowell, the Battalion commander, standing in the cold water of the river. He was looking for his soldiers and pulling out pieces of the truck. In that moment watching LTC Vowell, I learned the true meaning of leadership. LTC Vowell was a great commander, leader and friend that I have heard both officers and noncommissioned officers at Combat Outpost Monti speak well of. LTC Vowell was not only a great commander, he was a fearless soldier who always fought with great honor, dignity, respect and courage against the Taliban deep in the Hindu Kush Mountains in Kunar province. I had the privilege to work with LTC Vowell, and supported him and his soldiers in many operations and daily missions.

I had heard the word, "Leadership," for many years, but never understood what it really meant until that day. I was honor and privilege to work beside 1SG Robert N. Barton, who I accompanied on many operations and daily patrols before he died with those 4 soldiers in a tragic IED attack.

While we were mourning and looking for pieces of the truck, the Taliban celebrated their victory over the radio--
"Qari Zubair, can you hear me? This is Omari," Omari called on the radio. *"Alhamdulillah, we killed many* infidels!"* *Omari exclaimed on the radio.*

"Mashallah, it's a great victory for Mujahidin," Qari Zubair joined in.
"Mulawi Saab is very happy about what our friends did today."

"We are gonna fucking find them," I heard CPT Michael say while we were on the way back. There was no way that the Taliban could get away with this; they were going to pay the price. When I returned to Combat Outpost Monti, there were still some soldiers who had stayed behind to look for the mastermind of the bomb. Monti was dead and silent. The outpost that was always busy had turned into a place of sorrow. The MWR was closed for everyone, and I ended up staying in my room until I got the call from SGT Carlton. When I left to meet him in the Shura Room, I didn't know about the seven detainees that had been brought in for investigation.

"John, we fucking got them. They are fucking in there," PFC Dustin said. He and a few other soldiers were standing with their M4s and M240 machine guns ready go right outside of the room. I walked into the room to find the detainees in the handcuffed in the corner.

"John, we are gonna split them up; some of them will stay outside in the garden while we investigate the others," PFC Anthony [THC] said.

While I was talking with PFC Anthony, I heard the detainees claim, "we are innocent; we didn't do anything."

"Do you have to cover your face?" PFC Anthony asked. I always covered my face in these cases, but this time I had forgotten.

"Well, it's too late; they saw and talked to me."

"Are you sure you don't need a facemask?" PFC Anthony insisted.

"Yeah, I have been their main fucking target anyway."

He laughed and said, "Okay, let's fucking do it."

We took the detainees in for interviews individually while the others remained with the team in Orange-Garden. The whole process took a few hours. Before I left, we ensured that the detainees received food and water and could use the bathroom. I then headed back to my room to wait to hear what the leadership decided to do with the fighters.

About half an hour later, PFC Anthony called to tell me that one of the guys was being sent to Bagram for further questioning. He asked that I call the sub-governor to arrange a police truck to pick up the others for transport off of the base.

I went to bed around 2:00 A.M. with the mindset that I would get some extra sleep the next day, but I didn't know that the tribal elders would show up at the entrance gate early the next morning trying to speak with Captain Michael. "*Salaam,* John, I am sorry if I woke you up, but there are ten elders here with me who want to speak with Captain Michael," Captain Rasool, the ANA Commander, said when I picked up his early call.

It was almost 7:00 A.M., but I still debated if I should wake CPT Michael up or have someone at the tactical operations command [TOC] do it. I was still rubbing my own eyes because I didn't get enough sleep when I decided to head to Captain Michaels' barracks.

"What about the detainees?" Captain Michael asked still waking up.

"They will probably say that he is innocent," I counseled.

"He is gone; I can't do anything about him. If he is innocent, he will come home," Captain Michael replied. Still, he agreed to meet with the group. As he sent me for some water and cookies for the guests, I heard Captain Rasool say, "John, Captain Michael is a great man, if I lost my soldiers, I would never ever meet those guys."

"*Turjuman Saab*, we have been waiting out here since 6:00 this morning," one of the tribal elders said to start the meeting. The other elders looked a bit frightened and yet absolutely stunned when they saw Captain Michael hand out water, juice and cookies.

"*Turjuman Saab*, did you teach them about Afghan hospitality?" one of the elders asked.

"No, but they know."

"I bet you guys know what happened yesterday; I lost my soldiers," Captain Michael said after greeting everyone.

"Yes, we heard the blast but we didn't really know what happened," one of the tribal elders confirmed.

"Well, it was a bad day yesterday," Captain Rasool added but was cut off by another elder who pointed at the Afghan and American flags, both at half-mast and said, "I am a former military officer, and I know that lowered flags are a symbol of mourning." He continued, "I am sorry to hear of your loss, but you arrested one of our villagers who is innocent. When we left the village this morning, his children were crying."

Captain Michael again tried to explain that six of the seven detainees had been released and that if the seventh was found to be innocent he would also return home.

Captain Rasool looked at elders and said, "Americans are very nice; he just lost his men, but now he is here talking with us and serving snacks, waters, and soda."

"We are here to help you; we were coming to your village to talk about projects yesterday. My boss drove all the way from FOB Joyce in Sarkani to help you," Captain Michael added.

The elders had nothing else to say, they looked uncomfortable, and embarrassment spread on their faces. One of the elders took a long breath and said, "*Turjmaan Saab*, tell him that we wish we could do something about it. We don't feed them or let them use our houses but the Taliban has weapons and forces people to support them."

We wrapped up our meeting after almost two hours and escorted the elders back to the entrance checkpoint. While we were walking back to the gazebo, Captain Rasool looked at Captain Michael and said, "John, he is very great man. If I were him, I would shoot every one of them in the head." Captain Michael smiled and replied, "We will get the masterminds." As Captain Michael promised, a couple of months after the attack, the terrorist who was behind the catastrophic IED that killed five brave soldiers of Alpha Company was finally killed by a sniper during an overwatch mission.

Ch 36: Shin Kowrak

Summer 2010

Just eight days after the death of five brave soldiers of Alpha Company, another fearless soldier lost his life during an enemy ambush in Shin Kowrak [Hill 1311]. CPL Benjamin Osborn tragically died while everyone was still reeling from the tragedy of the IED attack. On June 15, his patrol came under enemy attack while driving through Shin Kowrak [Hill 1311] in the Shigal District to the south of Combat Outpost Monti. Shin Kowrak was popular for militant attacks and was a well-known ambush zone. The majority of the insurgents there were HIG fighters from the surrounding villages and smaller valleys who could retreat back to their villages after the attacks to avoid further engagement. Hill 1311 was a very small portion of the Shigal District, but it was far more infamous than the district itself for its instability, insecurity, and daily terrorist activities.

That day, more than twenty militants fired on Alpha Company's location from both sides of the river. Even though it was a short firefight, CPL Osborn, who was only 26 years-old got shot, and tragically died while fighting back the enemy fighters. I didn't know him very well, but I had the honor and opportunity to support him on many patrols. He was a great gunner, friend, and a kind, and brave soldier. It was a tragedy that only one bullet took his precious life.

After CPL Osborn died, Alpha Company 2/327th, No Slack continued hunting Taliban and other terrorists deep in the Hindu Kush mountains. Captain Michael was beyond angry at the Taliban and couldn't wait to get revenge and retaliate. Daily patrols, missions, and air assaults tripled against the Taliban, and more bombs than ever were dropped on the Taliban's strongholds.

"John, I probably killed more Taliban than anybody who ever worked at Monti," CPT Michael told me. He had personally been out on every mission. After weeks of consecutive fighting, he had become a deadly force, and HIG militants feared his soldiers. In August 2010, Captain Michael launched his final air assault mission in Shin Kowrak [Hill 1311] to punish those who killed CPL Osborn before he would transfer his authority at Monti to Captain Billig.

***

It was an unusual Friday because had not started with a rocket attack on COP Monti. There was no mission planned, and it was quiet because the Afghan workers had a half-day of work on base so that they could go to Friday prayers. The loudspeakers from the mosques were about to go off when I received a call from the district governor of Shigal District.

"*Salaam*, good morning, John!" Zahir Safi greeted me, but sounded panicked. It quickly became obvious that this was not a normal call to request a meeting. "Do me a huge favor, and please let Captain Michael know that we need some help."

The Taliban had set up an ambush in Shin Kowrak at Hill 1311 on both sides of the river. They searched vehicles and raised their flag. They were now waiting to launch a large-scale attack on the Afghan and American forces.

"I asked the police chief but he doesn't have enough fighting forces and heavy weapons to go out after the Taliban," Zahir Safi continued. "I just talked to Wahidi, the provincial governor, too because I received non-stop phone calls from locals in the area."

I hung up with Zahir Safi and left to inform Captain Michael. I found him and a few non-commissioned officers [NCOs] watching live intelligence surveillance and reconnaissance [ISR] in the TOC. I didn't know at the time that they were watching live footage of Shin Kowrak [Hill 1311]. While I was debriefing CPT Michael, Zahir Safi called back to report on the Taliban's weapons. They were using their usual weapons— Dish-Ka, recoilless [88mm] RPGs, PKMs and AK-47s.

"Okay, I gotta talk to my boss," Captain Michael told me to relay to Zahir. "Governor Wahidi spoke with LTC Vowell."

We were not sure if we were going to help or if a bushmaster company [quick reaction force] from FOB Wright would be tasked for the mission.

While we waited for our answer, Zahir continued to call non-stop for updates. "John, tell the commander that I wouldn't ask if I could do it, but I don't have enough manpower here," he said. "If he is not sending his men, please have him send a helicopter to scare them away." Zahir Safi was trying to maintain the trust that the people had placed in his local government for security and safety, and he believed that his job was on the line if he didn't help.

"I don't have the exact number but I am pretty sure it is not more than twenty men," Zahir Safi continued to update us. "They don't have any uniforms, just traditional clothes."

CPT Michael finally received our orders, "John, don't tell him but we are going at noon."

"It's a short fucking air assault, but we have to very careful," Captain Michael said during the pre-op briefing. "The Taliban are on both sides of the river and are armed with 80mms, RPGs, PKM and Ak-47s." It was always scary and surprising to learn about the enemy's power. It was even more dangerous this time because the RPGs, Dish-Ka and recoilless that the Taliban had could shoot down the helicopters. While everyone was receiving a briefing about air assault, SGT Horton interrupted, "the helos just took off from J-Bad."

I loved air assault missions because I was able to fly, but this air assault was going to be risky. We finally headed to the helicopter landing zone [HLZ] and I got ready to counter the enemy forces.

"Hey, that's a nice shirt you got," I told SGT Horton while we waited for the helicopters. It had a gator logo on the back.

"Yeah, my mom sent it to me. Florida has tons of gators; people eat 'em."

"Huh, eat them?" I asked. I had no idea what a "gator" really was.

"Yeah, it tastes like chicken," he joked.

The helicopters were still ten minutes out when everyone shouted as a big boom came from a nearby farm to the east of Combat Outpost Monti. "Incoming, incoming, incoming!" We were under a rocket attack. Everyone ran to the bunkers closest to the HLZ as the helicopters approached but then quickly managed to circle around and redirect back to FOB Wright. The rocket attack on Combat Outpost Monti stopped after the mortar crew dropped 105mm artillery shells and mortars on enemy targets. None of the enemy rockets landed inside Combat Outpost Monti, but our artillery shells killed three insurgents and wounded dozens.

After the rocket attack, I wasn't sure if the mission would continue, but after the district governor let us know that the Taliban was still in the area, we got ready to leave. I headed back to the HLZ, but instead of Black Hawk helicopters, I heard Apaches and then saw them flying over the ridgelines. I was a bit confused; I asked SGT Horton, "What's going on? Are we flying in Apaches?"

He laughed and said," No, they are our security, John."

Twenty minutes later, two UH-60 Black Hawk helicopters finally arrived at Monti and by 1:00 P.M. we took off for our air assault mission. I was in the first UH-60 Black Hawk helicopter with Captain Michael, SGT Horton and a few other soldiers from third platoon. During the short flight; I noticed that there were about twenty cars stopped to be searched by the Taliban as we flew over the district. Even from a distance, you could tell that it was not a normal day at Hill 1311.

The HLZ was close to the hilltop where HIG militants had set an ambush. Before we landed, they were locked up by two Apaches circling right above them, otherwise, they would have been able to shoot our helicopters with an RPG or recoilless rifle [82mm].

"We got to be outta here in half an hour," Captain Michael shouted. Everyone spread out and positioned to fire. HIG militants rained PKM and small arms fire on us from the east side where they had been searching vehicles. We were stuck in the middle of a firefight with nowhere to take cover. I could hear the rounds land in the sand and rocks around us; they sounded like hailstones.

We had to get up to the top of the hill, but it would be risky. "Can you let Captain Michael know that they are going to fire at the Apaches?" I yelled to Sergeant Horton. "The fighters are talking about us, but they are scared of Apaches right now."

Bush Master [QRF] from FOB Wright fought the HIG militants on the east side of the hill while we were climbing to the top.

The Apaches also tried to provide us cover and spotted some militants crawling up the hill, but they couldn't engage them due to the close proximity to the civilian houses on the backside of the hill. Even if the fighters used these homes for cover, we wouldn't fire on them.

We finally made it to the very top where HIG militants left both heavy and small weapons when they fled to the houses. In our 30-minute mission window, and without our Afghan soldiers, we wouldn't be able to pursue them.

> *"Mulawi Saab, this is Zarqawi talking."*
> *"Zarqawi! You are coming loud and clear; how's everybody doing?"*
> *"Almost dead, but we made it out."*
> *"I am very thankful to Allah that you are all okay; I was praying for you all."*
> *"Mulawi Saab, this is Bilal talking. We are good, but Fatih is no longer with us."*
> *"May Allah grant him, Jannah [Heaven],"* Mulawi Saab replied.
> *"Amen, Haqqani got wounded but he is doing better,"* Bilal added.

HIG fighters continued to check-in with one another on the radio while we flew back to Monti with the enemy's confiscated weapons-- recoilless rifle [82mm], RPGs with seven rounds, PKM, and five AK-47s with zero casualties. When we got back and I turned my phone back on, there was message from the district governor praising Captain Michael's effort, bravery, and incredible work.

"John, tell the Commander [Captain Michael] I owe you a party here in the district. Thank you so much for everything you guys did today. I just got off the phone with provincial governor and he is very, very appreciative."

Ch 37: Impersonating President Karzai

In August 2010, Alpha Company 2/327th No Slack and its battalion, operating out of FOB Joyce left for Daab Valley to provide security and protection for a logistics convoy. The convey was driving from Jalalabad Airfield [J-Bad], which would not be an easy journey for more than fifty jungle trucks and fuel tankers. Taliban attacks and IED strikes along the road were expected challenges. Road clearance patrol [RCP] always tried to find IEDs along the route, but sometimes they were unable to uncover the bombs because the Taliban used plastic, animal's skin, and other hardcovers to hide and keep their IEDs undetectable. However, the greatest threat that the convoy faced was from the local residents that attacked the fuel tankers to get the cargo.

I was part of the overwatch mission to listen to the Taliban's radios and talk with local residents if we had to while waiting for the convoy to arrive. Some days the convoy took hours, maybe even the whole day, to get to Daab Valley. Afghan National Army soldiers were also part of the overwatch mission, but they came under attack way before the supply trucks arrived. The Taliban launched RPGs and PKMs from across the river, injuring two ANA soldiers. The ANA soldiers were hit by RPG shrapnel while smoking outside of their Humvee, but they were lucky that the majority of the shrapnel was blocked by their truck.

"I saw the RPG when it landed, and I thought they were goners; it was bad," Zabihullah, an ANA soldier told me.

"*Turjuman Saab*, do you see the hole right there? That's where it landed," Zabihullah pointed. The RPG had landed about 30 feet away from them.

"John, tell the ANA soldiers that they are fine, but they need to be out of here as soon as possible," our medic said. "I gave them bandages; they won't bleed anymore, but they should go to the clinic."

We drove them back to Monti with a few trucks while the rest stayed in Daab Valley. While we were gone, the rest of the guys in Daab Valley and Barworo Khowar got shot at it, but nobody got hurt.

"John, we gotta go back. If you need anything, you need to fuckin hurry up," SGT Horton said as soon as we returned to Monti.

I ran to the TOC to get batteries. Our trucks were still running in the motor pool ready to depart to offer support for the guys under attack. When I was leaving the TOC, I saw our fire support officer LT Blume shouting, "John, John! I fucking need you! I know you guys are about to go back out, but I need you to make a call for me."

"What is up, sir?"

"Can you fucking call the district governor and ask him if he heard anything about civilian casualties in Shall Valley? I don't even fucking know where this place is."

"Shall Valley is the one across from the Daab Valley," I told him.

We didn't know that the ANA had been attacked there about 20 minutes before. I called District Governor Zalmay and he told me, "John, I haven't heard anything about civilian deaths, but I heard some Taliban militants got killed during cross-firing from Daab Valley."

"Tell him that I got an email from the president's office through our chain of command saying that we killed civilians at the cemetery in Shall Valley," LT Blume relayed.

District Governor Zalmay laughed and replied, "The Taliban always uses civilians and holy sites such as cemeteries because they know Americans won't attack those places."

LT Blume was relieved to hear that we weren't responsible for civilian casualties. However, it was weird for Combat Outpost Monti to receive an email from the president's office; it had never happened before.

We headed back out to Daab Valley, and finally the convoy was able to make it out. We had just returned to Monti for the second time when I received a phone call from Gul Wali, the Intelligence Chief at the National Directorate of Security, in Asmar. He told me, "There is a local who works for the president's protective service who made the call and lied about the civilian casualties. It was Taliban fighters that were killed."

Once again, the Taliban called their own casualties "civilian" in order to manipulate the local and national media to work against the American and Afghan forces and government.

Captain Billig out on patrol in the market outside of Combat Outpost Monti. 2011.

Ch 38: Captain Billig

"Sir, why didn't you join the Air Force? It's an easier job." I asked him during one of our missions.

Captain Billig smiled and replied, "The Air Force has no history-- you fly, drop bombs and that's it; but we make history."

I didn't know then what history Thomas Billig was talking about, but it wasn't long after we began working together that I found out.

In September 2011, Captain Michael was promoted to Major and got transferred to FOB Joyce. He left Combat Outpost Monti, but he was not forgotten--

"John, where is the other commander?" one of the ANA soldiers asked.

"What other commander?"

"The big, strong man who loved to fight the Taliban," he replied.

"Oh, he is in Sarkani [FOB Joyce]. He works there now," I replied.

"I remember when he went after the Taliban one day," the ANA soldier said, "It was scary but he didn't care."

"I know. He didn't care. He just wanted to fight."

When CPT Michael left, Captain Thomas Billig took over and became the company commander; I didn't know much about him, but I learned after the first patrol we had that he was a great, fearless, and brave fighter. He had served as a rifle platoon leader, ranger platoon leader, assistant personal officer, assistant operation officer, and rifle company commander before he became the company commander for Gator Company at Combat Outpost Monti. He had just transitioned from commanding the Headquarters and Headquarters Company [HHC], 2nd Battalion, 327th Infantry Regiment, 1st Brigade Combat Team before he took over for A Co/2-327th at Monti.

"John, I was in Helmand once, but I didn't like it there," Captain Billig said. Helmand was a safe haven and stronghold for the Taliban and a center of the opium production that allowed the Taliban to make millions of dollars in narcotics and opium trade. This was Captain Billig's fourth combat tour to Afghanistan, and he had years of experience in combat, a deep knowledge of the Taliban and their tactics and a stellar reputation for his leadership. When I was working for Captain Michael, I thought that he was intense in fighting the Taliban, but Captain Billig happened to be even crazier. He was very good at reading and understanding people, which he attributed to his degree in criminology. At the same time, Captain Billig was also familiar with the sensitive parts of the culture and tradition.

"John, why are the people dressed differently than the people in Helmand Province?" he once asked.

"I think we have pretty similar culture and tradition, but clothes vary from state to states."

"I noticed that everyone had turbans in Helmand but not here," Captain Billig added. "I even saw fucking kids had to wear turbans in Helmand."

During CPT Billig's time at Monti in 2011, I became part of every patrol, mission, and operation as his personal interpreter during 2011. He was not only my boss; he quickly became my good friend and was the one who ultimately made my dream of completing my visa paperwork come true.

"John, I promise you, I have done this before and I will do it for you," Captain Billig said when he found out that I decided to leave for FOB Shank, in Logar Province to the east of Kabul, to work again for 1LT Kerr who had been promoted to Captain.

I needed to get my paperwork done before I got killed. It was getting harder to travel to visit my family because of the Taliban checkpoints where they especially searched for interpreters. Because I had been working at Monti for a long time, I was very well known among the local tribal elders and government officials. My work with them led to more and more threatening phone calls and letters from the Taliban and their supporters.

When I finally decided to leave Combat Outpost Monti, it was very hard because I loved everything about it-- the people I worked with and the beautiful high Hindu Kush mountains, the surrounding hills, rivers and heavenly weather. The last piece that I needed was Captain Billig's permission. I found him in his small office, which was filled with a couple of computers, maps, an American flag, an M4 hanger, a few family pictures, and a white writing board with a bunch of markers.

"What's up, John? I heard you are leaving us," Captain Billig greeted me.

"I don't know sir; I like it here but--" While I was talking to Captain Billig, the company fire support officer, LT Blume came in.

"Joe, John is leaving us," Captain Billig told him, "He found someone better than us at FOB Shank."

"Hell no, John is not going anywhere, sir," LT Blume replied.

"It's not about somebody better, sir. I love working here, but I have been working at Monti forever. I just want to get my paperwork done."

"John, we love you buddy; you are one of the best interpreters here at Monti," LT Blume complimented.

"Thank you, sir. That's very nice of you."

"John, you should have told me before," I didn't know you have been trying to get out here." Captain Billig looked at me and asked, "Do you know I got a visa for one of my interpreters while I was in Helmand? Now he is in the States."

"No, I didn't know that sir," I replied with a smile on my face because it was a piece of great news, the news that I had been waiting on forever.

"I will let you work for this other guy, but I don't think he knows as much as I do about the process," Captain Billig said. I am gonna have Joe take care of everything for you."

I was excited that they were going to help me get my paperwork done, and it made me question whether I should leave or continue working with Captain Billig.

"It's a long process, John, but I will make sure I get it done before the end of the deployment," Captain Billig said. "But you are gonna have to get some paperwork from the Afghan government."

"Sounds great, sir. Thank you so much," I responded. They could tell how excited I was.

"No problem, John. You truly deserve it."

I left not knowing what paperwork I needed, but after talking to a few friends, I learned that it was the background check from the Afghan government to make sure I was not involved in any terrorist activities. I was very young when I started working as an interpreter for the U.S. Army, and my family had never had any affiliation with bad people so there was no doubt that I would pass this check. Still, the confirmation letter took more than a month due to the government's bureaucratic system and loads of handwritten paperwork instead of computers, but it finally came. I was excited to let Captain Billig and LT Blume know that I was finally ready to proceed in the process.

I met LT Blume the next day, and he told me that the next step would be to complete the BATS inquiry and BDF [Biometric database] processing to check against the national database and ensure my file was clear of any negative reports and had not been flagged. We couldn't complete this at Monti, we'd have to go to FOB Joyce.

"When do you think we are gonna go to FOB Joyce?" I asked.

Blume laughed and replied, "John, it's the only second day. We are gonna get this done, just like Captain Billig promised. I know, you are excited. We are excited for you too."

I couldn't wait to get everything done. We took care of the biometric data after we got back from our next operation, and it was clear of any negative actions against me. It was a piece of great news, but next, I was a little worried and nervous about my interview with LTC Vowell, the Battalion Commander, even though I had met and interpreted for him a few times.

On January 8, 2011, I was scheduled for an interview with LTC Vowell at FOB Joyce to get his approval and recommendation to complete the requirements for the U.S. government visa process. I was nervous because I had no clue what questions would be asked. Captain Billig tried to reassure me, "Don't worry, John, you will do great. LTC Vowell has heard great things about you, and he wants to help you."

"I don't want to screw this up, sir."

Captain Billig laughed and said, "You won't screw this up."

While I waited for my interview, I met a couple of other soldiers who were also supposed to meet LTC Vowell. One of them was a Puerto Rican-born PFC whose accent was event stronger than mine, and he stuttered over his words when he spoke. Soon, the PFC and I were ushered into our meeting.

"How's it going, John? I heard you are trying to go to the States," LTC Vowell asked as we started our meeting. "What is your plan when you get there?"

"I'd like to join the Army, sir."

"That's awesome. You are gonna be a great soldier." He smiled, "Now it's time to get to the questions. I am gonna ask you two to say, 'The quick brown fox jumps over the lazy dog'. Whoever says it correctly first will win."

I was very familiar with an English pangram sentence containing all of the letters of the alphabet, because that's how I learned how to type. For me, it was a piece of cake, but the PFC struggled a little bit. I eventually beat him in the pronunciation.

LTC Vowell laughed and said, "Good job guys; you both did great-- John, I will write you a letter, and I will talk to COL Poppas, but I don't think you have to meet him," LTC Vowell said.

"Thank you, sir."

"Keep up the great work, John."

When I left his office, I saw Captain Billig waiting outside. "It went really good sir, I won the competition," I told him.

He laughed and asked, "What competition, John? There was no competition, you had an interview. I bet LTC Vowell was messing with you."

I had worried and stressed too much about the interview, because it turned out to be the funniest and easiest interview that I ever had. I couldn't describe how happy I was that I was going to leave Combat Outpost Monti and even Afghanistan for my safety. When I returned to Monti, it became a piece of big news, and everyone congratulated me.

"John, hit me up on Facebook so we can get fucking drunk once you get to the fucking States, man," Sergeant Wartz said.

"Roger, sergeant."

"You better fucking find me on Facebook too," Sergeant Rob Vera added.

"John, fucking John, I heard you are fucking going to the States; that's so fucking awesome brother," Sergeant Roberts chimed in. He had always been the funniest person at Monti, in my opinion.

"Hopefully soon, sergeant."

When I finally made it to the United States after years of waiting, I remained grateful for and thankful to Captain Billig and Captain Blume for their hard work, effort, and the energy that they put into the process. It was their strong belief that I was one of the truly deserving candidates that ultimately allowed me to get my visa.

Ch 39: Bastogne Overwatch

November 2010

On November 6, 2010, Gator Company, 2nd Battalion, 327th Infantry Regiment, 1st Brigade Combat Team, 101st Airborne Division was tasked to overwatch, secure, and protect the supply convoy named "Bastogne Overwatch" in Shal Khowar, known as a safe haven and strongholds of the Taliban militants. It was an air assault mission to stop and prevent the Taliban's attack on supply convoy that was going to pass through Daab Valley the next day.

It was cold and was going to be colder up on the high mountain tops where we were going to be dropped off to watch the Taliban deep in the valley and surrounding villages. We had never had an air assault in an area that had been so dominated and overrun by the Taliban. We were going to fly out of Combat Outpost Monti at 2:00 A.M. "Helos left J-Bad," was the call from the TOC. Everyone geared-up and got ready to fly. It was a full moon with cold breezing hitting our faces, but I was happy that with the moonlight I wouldn't have to worry about falling after we got out of the helicopters because it would be too dark to see. While we were at the HLZ, one of the soldiers ended used his flashlight to find something that he dropped in gravel, forgetting that the enemy could see it.

"Turn off the damn flashlight!" 1SG Ken Bolin yelled at him. We are in the fucking HLZ."

"20 minutes out," SGT Horton shouted.

"Listen up guys! We've done many fuckin missions into Daab Valley, and 2nd platoon just fuckin got shot at there last week," 1SG Bolin said. "But we are not fucking going to Daab Valley; we are going across from it on a fucking mountain top. It's going to be fucking cold; make sure you guys have everything you need."

"Roger, 1SG," everyone responded.

While both Captain Billig and 1SG Bolin were briefing, the UH60 Black Hawks landed on the dirt of the HLZ, and I heard Captain Billig shout, "John, you are with us in the same bird."

"Okay, sir," I shouted back while holding my backpack and stuff to make sure it didn't fly away because it was very windy and the gravel whipped around us.

There was no landing zone up-in the mountain, but the pilots were damn-smart that managed to land in the middle of a forest after a couple of circles, just a few hundred meters away from a small destroyed animal shelter. When we were dropped off into the strongholds of the Taliban, we expected to get shot at, but it turned out to be very quiet in the freezing cold and windy night.

"We need to fucking search this building," 1SG Bolin said. "John, are you fucking ready?"

"I am 1SG," I responded while I was shaking in the cold. We wanted to make sure that there were no weapons and militants hiding from the cold.

It was quite early and very silent in most villages, but after we landed, we noticed lamps and flashlights in some houses in Daab, Shal, and the surrounding villages. The Taliban radios also began chatting about the helicopters, but no one was sure what was going on.

> "*Mujahid, Mujahid, can you hear me? Let me know what is going on*," Omary called.
> "*Omary, I can hear you; I don't know but we heard helicopters flew over Shal*," Mujahid replied
> "*Call Fedai and ask him how is everybody doing. He lives there.*"
> "*I tried to get hold up him but his radio is not working.*"
> "*Okay, I will try to talk to some friends there and ask them about the helicopters*," Omary said. "*It looks like they dropped some people up there.*"
> "*Mujahid, this is Fedai; two helicopters landed on your side of the valley. Make sure everybody is okay.*"

While I was listening to the Taliban's radio, I heard Captain Billig ask about some flashlights that he saw down in the valley.

"Don't they pray after 4:00 A.M.?" SGT Horton asked.

"It's weird, they heard the helicopters, but yes, it's already after 4:00 A.M.," I replied.

"I know, John, it's fucking early for the people to wake up," Captain Billig replied. "Let me know if you hear anything about an attack."

The Taliban was trying to figure out where we had landed and were staying because we were hidden by the trees that surrounded us. We spotted a dozen muzzle flashes in multiple locations deep in the valley, very far from us after multiple speakers went off for a morning prayer call. We did our best to avoid activities that could lead us to disclose our locations in the mountains.

"John, you think they are gonna sneak up here?" SGT Horton asked.

"I don't think so, sergeant, but you never know."

"Is that pre-recorded or he is fucking talking right now?" SGT Horton asked about the Mullah currently preaching.

"Ha, it's not a recording, he's talking now."

"He is non-stop talking man; he must have a ton of energy."

"I bet he does; he has been talking since right after we got here this morning."

"What is he talking about John?" Captain Billig asked.

"Religious stuff," I told him, "but I did hear him mention the infidels."

The preaching and local prayers were routine and part of the religious teachings that followed morning prayer; on Fridays you could hear them in miles. The teaching and preaching went on until the sun slowly crested the eastern portion of the mountain top, and as we listened, the Taliban still couldn't figure out our location.

I listened to them talk back and forth with their friends to get prepared for an attack, but we didn't know where. Around 11:00 A.M., while we were waiting for the convoy to pass through, a few Taliban militants were spotted and engaged by the Apaches on the backside of our location, but it wasn't clear that they were going to attack or the convoy later the day.

Finally, after many hours in the freezing weather, I saw the convoy as it crept through the valley, it still had many miles ahead into the heart and hotbed of the Taliban before arriving to FOB Bostick.

"Qari, the convoy is driving towards your location," Fedai reported.

"Fedai, Fedai, this is Qari; we can see it, but we can't shoot at it."

"Muhajar and his friends got attacked by the wasps and they are taking the high ground," Fedai said. "We've got to do something about the convoy; it's driving by right now."

"We don't know what to do; I don't want to die here," Qari replied.

"Omary, Omary, this his Fedai, are you guys ready? It's coming right now."

"We are ready, but it's pretty crazy here now, I don't think we are going to do anything," Omary responded.

"Mulawi Saab wants us to do something before it's too late," Fedai instructed.

"I don't wanna do anything. Ask him to do it. Muhajir and his friends just got shot. I don't wanna lose anybody here," Qari responded sounding angry.

Gator Company, 2/327th did its best to push the Taliban out of the area. This would be the first time that supply trucks drove through Daab and Shal Valley without getting shot at, and we flew back to Monti at the end of the day without ever engaging the Taliban in a firefight. However, back on base, I heard that as the trucks drove deeper into the district, they were attacked and a couple of truck drivers were killed and a few fuel tankers got burned to the ground in Ghazi Abad

District farther north. But in the fight, the Taliban also lost one of their commanders, Sangary, who had a long history of brutality and ruthless attacks against both Afghans and Americans.

Ch 40: Operation Eagle

Shultan Valley (Halalzoo Village)
January 2011

It was another cold week deep in the Hindu Kush mountains looking for the Taliban and their ammo caches. It was always quite beautiful up in the snow-covered mountains. The Taliban hadn't been operating as much as they used to but, suicide bombing, IEDs, VBIEDs, and rocket attacks directed at Monti were still frequent. PFC Anthony tragically lost his life when his barrack got hit with a 107mm rocket, and another tragedy took the lives of two brave and fearless soldiers-- David Miller and Andrew Looney when a woman approached their checkpoint at the bridge between Halalzoo village and Shultan Valley and detonated herself.

In January 2011, Gator Company, No Slack, 1st Brigade Combat Team, 101st Airborne Division (AASLT), and our Afghan counterparts [ANA] planned to destroy the enemy's rocket positions and ammo caches, and eliminate their supply route along the Durand Line in Shultan Valley, where both HIG and Taliban militants operated and filtered supplies into Kunar Province and Pech Valley. We believed that the insurgents were firing mortars and rockets at Monti and launching attacks against both Afghan and American soldiers along the highway known as MSR California from Shultan Valley. Shultan was a wide valley that was divided into smaller valleys.

"John, tell the ANA that it's going to be fucking cold where we going so make sure you guys get everything you need," 1SG Bolin said during the rehearsal.

"*Turjuman Saab*, we don't care about cold," Qadir, one of the ANA sergeants replied, "We like cold better than hot. When it's cold, you can use the blanket and don't need electricity, but when it's hot, you have to have fan or an air condition system."

1SG Bolin smiled and said, "I agree, but it's gonna be very cold."

We had a rehearsal for the air assault to make sure that everyone was ready to roll. "We are gonna fucking have fun," 1SG Bolin said, "John, ask them if they are excited."

"*Turjuman Saab*, I am very excited; it's going to be my first flight. I had this dream since I was a little kid," Hanif, an ANA soldier, told me.

On January 17th, 2011, the air assault got approved, and we were going to fly out of COP Monti at 2:00 A.M. the next morning.

"Tell Captain Billig that we have to do this mission when it's not too dark," Captain Rasool said during the meeting.

"I know, we talked about this before, but the good thing about this mission is that it's gonna be a full moon," Captain Billig assured him.

We were going into a valley that had the most difficult terrain of steep rocks, and there was a serious risk that we could fall during the search-and-clear mission.

Everyone showed up on time, or even early, because some of the ANA soldiers were so excited to fly in helicopters. Before we departed, we had to do what was called "safety procedure".

"John, tell the ANA that they must not load their weapons until we get out of the helicopters," 1SG Bolin said. "We will do it once we get out."

"John, tell Captain Rasool that we are gonna stay at one of the buildings once we get there," Captain Billig spoke. "But remember there is shit-tons of snow up there."

Captain Rasool laughed and said, "John, ask him if he knows where I am from." I am from the north where we get lots and lots of snow, so much that you can't drive or walk around."

"I bet; I heard that the north of Afghanistan gets many snowfalls in winter," Captain Billig replied. "I've got some money that we can offer to a family if they let us stay in one of the buildings that looks empty."

"That would be a great help; I don't think they would take it due to *Pashtunwali*, but a little bit of money could help us find and identify the Taliban," Captain Rasool told him.

"That's exactly what we gonna do."

Although Captain Rasool was from the north, not every soldier was used to snow or had received their winter gear. We had to be very careful because they could suffer from hypothermia.

We finally took off in the first of two Chinook helicopters to secure the LZ for the rest of the soldiers including the scout team from FOB Joyce. The LZ was up on the steep mountain-top, so we had to make sure that the next flights were secured and safe. When we flew out of Combat Outpost Monti, I noticed the helicopters were flying into Dangam Valley, something we had not discussed with Captain Rasool during the planning of the operation. We had told him that we were going to Shigal Valley, not Dangam, and I worried that he would feel betrayed and that we would lose the trust of him and his soldiers. Suddenly, however, I felt our helicopter take a sharp turn into Shigal. I was so happy that we hadn't lied to Captain Rasool. I had never seen U.S. soldiers salute an Afghan military officer, but the soldiers of Gator Company, 2/327th saluted and respected Captain Rasool at Combat Outpost Monti because he was an irreplaceable fearless fighter, great leader, and friend for life.

We landed on the top of the mountain, in the snow, as planned. Even though it wasn't a flat landing zone, the pilots managed to touch down, and everyone got out of the helicopters safely. Both helicopters took off and returned to Monti to bring the rest of the soldiers while we were secured the LZ. It really was freezing cold.

I was talking to SGT Bolin when we heard a shot. For a second, everyone thought it was enemy fire, but then I heard, "*Turjuman Saab*, our medic shot himself in the foot!"

"You gotta be fucking kidding me," Captain Billig responded.

The ANA medic had loaded his gun days ago and never cleared it, even though we had told the ANA to do it during the rehearsal. He shot himself while playing with the trigger of his M-16 rifle.

When the helicopters returned, they took him to FOB Joyce, and we headed to the building that we believed was empty. It was getting colder and colder.

"John, I am gonna need to speak with the family and let them know we are not gonna hurt them," Captain Billig called me over. "I don't know if they are awake."

The compound wasn't too far from the LZ, but we had to make sure it got searched and cleared before we went in. A squad of ANA soldiers and the third platoon managed to go in and search the entire building, but while they did, the Taliban woke up and began to talk about our helicopters. While I was listening to the radio and waiting for the house to be searched and cleared, Captain Billig asked, "John, do you think should we give the family the money now or later?"

"It's up to you, sir, but it's better to give it now so they can kind of feel happy and satisfied, I think."

While we were discussing, Captain Rasool came over to let us know that his soldiers found an RPG, mortars, and AK-47 with ammo in one of the rooms. It was a game-changer the search-and-clear just got harder. While the others focused in the area where the weapons were found, I went to talk to the owner of the house. He was wide awake with his kids in the cold.

"*Salaam*, how are you?" I asked.

"*Salaam alali kum*, I am sick," he replied, shaking.

I didn't know whether he was sick and shaking or scared or both.

"We are not going to hurt you or your family, but we need a place to stay for tonight if it's okay with you."

"Absolutely, you guys can stay wherever you want; I have a fire stove in the house and you guys can come and use it. It's very cold outside," he replied. The man looked like he was in his late 60s and he was very generous. His wife also came into the room, and was the kindest woman I have ever met.

"Come on in, it's very cold outside; I will make a fire for you guys," she said.

"Thank you so much. My guys are still outside, but they will come in a minute" Captain Billig said. "John, they don't have to do anything; we brought everything with us."

"No, it's okay. We can stay in our other house over there, and I will let you guys stay here; it's very cold outside," the wife said. She was old but the kindest.

"My son and his kids live with us, but right now they are very scared," the man said.

"We are not here to hurt you; we are here to help you," Captain Billig assured him. "John, tell Captain Rasool that we've got to make sure that their son stays here because of the weapons in the house," Captain Billig instructed me. We kept eyes on their son the entire time and never let him walk away because he could expose our mission.

"John, ask Captain Rasool what he thinks about the money," Captain Billig requested.

"Nope, we and Yousaf [the interpreter] found rockets in their house; I don't think we should help them," Captain Rasool replied.

"I agree."

We finally went into the house around 4:00 A.M. It was like going from a freezing shower into a hot bath. But we only had a few hours to enjoy it. We wanted to leave at 7:00 A.M. to search and clear as many qalats as possible, but with more than five inches of snow we didn't manage to conduct our first patrol until 8:00 A.M.

"*Turjuman Saab*, where is the trail?" one of the ANA soldiers asked.

"Just follow us," I replied. We were walking into the valley that was dominated by the Taliban who had been planning to attack since we arrived.

"Where is the fucking Taliban?" 1SG Bolin asked Aziz, the interpreter for the third platoon.

Aziz laughed and responded, "They are hiding right now, 1SG

When we left the house, we had to walk up and down to arrive at the targets because none of the buildings were together. Even though it was more difficult than we expected, the first patrol went very well without getting shot at, and we confiscated some weapons including AK-47s and old English rifles. We returned to the house around noon.

We went back out at 2:30 P.M. to search and clear the remaining houses and buildings, but this time we came under attack. It was a Taliban sniper who we believed to be hiding in one of the houses, but we couldn't tell where the shooting was coming from. We had to crawl in the snow to the nearest building where we could get some cover, but the situation got worse when we arrived at the building. The Taliban launched a massive attack, firing PKMs and small arms, but luckily, we soon spotted the man with PKM at the ridgeline who was shooting at us.

"We fucking got him," 1SG Bolin yelled. He is fucking hiding underneath the trees.

Taliban affiliated-insurgents were also talking on the radio. We didn't know where exactly the Taliban was about to attack, but we tried to guess.

"What do you think, John?" 1SG Bolin asked.

"Sounds like they will attack somewhere between here and the very last compound that we searched yesterday," I replied.

"Are you talking about the one at the ridgeline?"

"Yes, 1SG. The Taliban will try to sneak up on us from the backside of the valley," I responded.

"John, ask Captain Rasool what he thinks about an ambush," Captain Billig directed. While I was translating for Captain Billig, I heard the Taliban radio chats.

> "The helicopter just flew over but couldn't see me," one of the Taliban fighters said.
> "Sangary, Sangary, be careful the helicopters just flew above our friends," Abu Omar said
> "Why is taking so long?
> "We are still walking up," Mulawi answered.

Their conversation gave us good clues to where they were planning their next ambush.

"The ridgeline," Captain Rasool told us.

While we were talking with Captain Rasool, I saw both Aziz and Yousaf running and shouting, "John, did you hear that last conversation? They are right by the house at the very end."

"That's what we are talking about right now."

"Sir, we just heard that they might be by the house at the very end." Yousaf told Captain Billig

"Thanks, Yousaf. I am gonna ask the Apaches to check it out there."

"John, ask Captain Rasool, how many more houses the ANA want to search. The Apaches will need to take off to refuel, and I don't want to get stuck here so we should head back," Captain Billig planned.

"Okay, I can ask my soldiers to stop searching whenever you decide to," Captain Rasool agreed.

"I think they can stop it now; my JTAC is talking to the aircraft," Captain Billig told him.

We stopped our search-and-clear operation and headed back to the house. On our way back, we heard John Norris the JTAC shout, "The aircraft is on the station, sir!"

"John, we need to get out of here. Tell the ANA we are gonna drop bombs but we have to get out of here first," Captain Billig said.

We managed to escape the building for another house that was far enough away for a bomb to be dropped on possible enemy targets. John Norris, the JTAC was working with Captain Billig on a small map, plotting targets for the aircraft that were on station even though we couldn't hear or see them in the sky. After a little while I heard, John Norris begin the countdown, "30 seconds."

"30 fucking seconds," 1SG Bolin shouted.

"Fucking woman power! The Taliban would love that," John Norris-JTAC yelled. I didn't understand what he meant, so I asked.

He laughed and replied," The pilot who just dropped the bomb was a female."

Back on the radio, the Taliban believed that we had some residents of the village and in the valley spying for us.

"Mulawi Saab, there is a spy in the village who reported Mujahidin's location. We need to find this guy and give them the punishment like he has never seen before," Muhajar claimed.

In truth, we didn't have anybody we didn't have anyone spying for us.

The second day our operation was going quite well without enemy engagement, until a couple of soldiers and interpreters got very sick. Yousaf, the interpreter for the third platoon, had a fever, headache, running nose and a very bad cough.

During the day, I listened to the radio outside of the building because it was warm enough and I could hang out with the soldiers who were on guard shift. When the temperature dropped drastically that night, I went back inside and saw Yousaf sleeping like a baby next to the fire stove. It was a small room but we had to fit 10 soldiers inside. Around 1:00 A.M, everyone suddenly awoke in the dark. "Move!

Move!" everyone shouted. I thought we under attack because from the Taliban seeking revenge.

"It's a fucking fire in there!" everyone yelled, trying to get out as quickly as possible. As the others ran out, I had to go back to get Yousaf who was still sleeping.

We didn't know what happened until Yousaf said, "I think I burnt myself."

"What do you mean, Yousaf? Were you dreaming?" I asked him.

"Look at my sleeping bag," He pointed. While he had been asleep next to the hot fire stove, his sleeping bag caught fire and melted a big portion of it. He received a minor burn from the melted plastic, but overall, he was okay.

The last day of a mission always felt great, and got even better when SGT Wartz told us that there was hot coffee.

Hot coffee high up in the snowy Hindu Kush mountains was a dream. I felt like a kid with candy. While we were enjoying the coffee, we received intelligence and the Taliban's radio chats they had traveled from Dangam, Marawara, Lawseen and Gonjgal Valley to launch an intense, large-scale attack, but luckily for us, an air assault was able to successfully eliminate the threat and we were able to return to Monti without an issue.

Ch 41: AH-64 Apache Attack Helicopter

Daab Valley
February 2011

"Did that fuckin scare you, John?" SSG Carlton asked when I returned to Combat Outpost Monti.

"I was freaking scared to death," I replied. "I thought I was done, done."

***

In February 2011, the Taliban ambushed 3rd platoon, Gator Company, Task Force, No Slack in the vicinity of Daab Valley, but fortunately, nobody got hurt. Even after many daily patrols, missions, and operations in Daab Valley, Shall, Barawar Khowar and the surrounding villages, the area still remained a safe haven and stronghold for the Taliban. IED strikes, ambushes, and firefights were the daily business of the Taliban insurgents, and the fear turned the valley into a ghost town on most days. After the latest ambush, Captain Billig decided to conduct a combined operation with his ANA counterparts from the 4th Infantry Battalion, also stationed at Combat Outpost Monti.

Both Captain Billig and Captain Rasool were going to lead the search-and-clear operation deep in Daab valley. The plan was for the American soldiers to clear the area and set up sniper cover before the ANA soldiers were dropped off a couple of miles away from target reference points [TRPs]. We left Combat Outpost Monti around 3:00 P.M. for the short but slow drive, looking out for the Taliban's IEDs under culverts along the road. When we got to the Daab Valley, we sent the drivers back to Monti, trying to manipulate the Taliban into believing that we had left so that we could more safely walk through the valley. Our trick seemed to work when I picked up a radio conversation between militants who were trying to figure out what was going on. We were ready to give them an unexpected surprise.

"John, my guys saw three armed men in the valley," Captain Rasool said. "Next to the qalat's wall." I told Captain Billig and we headed in that direction to check it out. We approached the three-armed men with AK-47s and asked them to put down their weapons before something bad happen. "Don't worry, John, I got your back," SGT Horton-RTO said. I was at the front group so that I could speak to the men as we got closer.

"We are not Taliban; we are not Taliban!" they shouted.

"John, ask them why they tried to escape when they saw us?" Captain Billig responded.

"*Turjumaan Saab*, we got scared," they told me.

"It's normal to be scared, but don't try to run away because we could shoot you," Captain Rasool told them in Dari, so I had to translate it again into Pashtu.

After speaking with them, we decided to arrest them, but then word began to spread around the village that we were there; we had to keep going, it wasn't going to be safe much longer.

"Don't let the infidels and their slaves enter and search any house," The Taliban commander rallied his fighters. "If Allah is willing, they won't make it out of here today!"

We spotted more villagers, including females trying to hide and bury weapons outside of their houses as we continued to search and clear. During that time, we had Apache air cover to keep us safe, but as soon as they left back for Bostick, the Taliban attacked. Luckily the fight didn't last long and none of us were hurt.

As we continued, we saw a group of about 10 men and women gathering in the valley. We soon learned that one of the Taliban's commanders was assassinated in Jalalabad and his body was on the way to arrive to his family in Daab Valley. He was part of the Tablighi, a proselytizing group that is a worldwide network of Deobandi Muslims and he had been involved in many terrorist activities, attacks, and IED strikes against Afghan and American troops.

"John, tell Captain Billig that we should stop operation," Captain Rasool told me.

Captain Billig didn't understand, so Captain Rasool explained,

"It's our culture. There is going to be a funeral ceremony where men, women, and children will participate; I think it's better to stop and head back to Monti."

"Absolutely. We will get out of here," Captain Billig agreed.

The good news was that we would be able to head back without worrying about an attack because of the funeral ceremony. As we hurried to get back to the trucks before dark, we took the trail through the canals; walking on wet and slippery rocks was harder and more complicated than we expected and many of us fell. "God damn it, I broke my fucking ankle," I heard from nearby as one of the soldiers fell. We ended up needing to carry him the rest of the way. The walk also slowed as it got darker and the ANA soldiers didn't have night vision goggles to guide them.

I made it back to the highway where the trucks were supposed to be parked around 9:00 P.M. with Captain Rasool while Captain Billig and the rest of the soldiers were still in the valley carrying the injured soldier. Captain Rasool and the ANA took off to find their trucks and I was left alone in the middle of nowhere with an Ak-47 and four magazines to find my truck in the other direction. I didn't know where to go. I feared that something bad would happen and decided to make sure I saved a few bullets; I wouldn't let the Taliban capture me.

During the search and clear operation in Daab Valley

It was dark on the way to the trucks, and I couldn't see very well. I began walking on the road in the direction that I believed our trucks were parked. I knew that anything could happen while walking by myself in Taliban territory. After about five minutes of walking, there was still no sign of our trucks, but I heard the Apaches flying over the valley; they circled right above me with a spotlight on. I got scared and froze. I stood shaking after they flew away, but soon returned and shot an illumination round [tracer] a couple hundred meters away from me. I thought, "This is it; I am done." I thought that they would shoot me because I had an AK-47. I didn't know that they were trying to help guide me. Even with the illumination round lighting the entire area, I still couldn't see our trucks. Suddenly though, a truck pulled up.

"John, are you okay?" SFC Robinson asked. "We got a call from the pilots saying that you were walking down here by yourself. Where is everybody else?

"I'm okay, sergeant. They are still in the valley, coming right now."

"Did we scare you, John?" SPC Perry asked.

"Yeah, it was freaking scary; I thought I am dead man."

When we got back to Monti, I was in the TOC working on some paperwork when SSG Carlton came in and said, "John, tell us what happened last night."

"I thought I was dead. It was super scary and dangerous."

He laughed and said, "Did you know that I could get in trouble if something happened to you. You should be scared, if something happened to you, we wouldn't know about it."

SSG Carlton, the new manager for the interpreters at Monti, was not happy at all, but Captain Billig, LT Blum, and SFC Wartz laughed so hard at what had happened.

Ch 42: Operation Strong Eagle III

March 2011

At the end of March 2011, TF, No Slack, 1st Brigade Combat Team, 101st Airborne Division (AASLT), conducted an air assault mission called "Strong Eagle III" into several valleys in Kunar Province, located along the Durand Line, between Bajour, the Mohmand tribal agency, and Kunar Province.

"It's going to be a big operation," Captain Billig said. "A battalion-level operation with lots of ANA soldiers." The joint operation's aim was to capture or eliminate the Taliban's notorious commander Qari Ziaurahman, or QZR, in Marawara District. He was a brutal Taliban commander who led foreign fighters, including AQ operatives, along the Durand Line. There was strong evidence that QZR was involved in helping and supporting the fight against that Dakota Meyer and his team in Gonjgal Valley in 2009.

"He was an ordinary kid, born and raised in Asadabad in a very poor family. His father was a blacksmith who helped farmers and other small businesses around the city, and Qari worked with his father," Mangal, a villager, told us. "People bullied and made of fun him because he was a blacksmith.

Once, he was caught stealing and robbing from one of his villagers."

Being a blacksmith was not a profession that many would like for their kids; it was considered a very low-class profession. Nobody in the village would have suspected that someone who used to rob and steal from people would turn into a bigger monster. QZR became everything from a religious leader to a spiritual leader to a holy fighter and hero to the people of his village because they had very little knowledge about their own faith and religion. It's the story of many Taliban fighters.

We flew out of COP Monti late at night on 28 March 2011 with our ANA counterparts for the 3-day air assault, heading to Marawar District to link up with the other forces who were part of the assault. On our way, we were diverted for FOB Joyce and ended up waiting at the HLZ without knowing why. Soon we found out that the others had come under fire as they landed in Marawar. The situation was soon under control, and we were able to continue to the district.

We landed on the top of a mountain that was about 9,000 feet high and covered with snow. It was freezing cold when we got there, but nobody cared about cold and strong wind anymore. It had become a survival mission for everybody after both HHC and Charlie companies got shot at after they landed in the valley. The rain made the steep terrain slippery and most of the soldiers both Afghan and American ended up slipping and falling, but we were still able to set up our security perimeter. We knew that if we lost our air support because of the weather, the Taliban would attack.

Early the next morning, most of the valley, including our location was covered by fog and the visibility was horrible.

"God damn it, we won't be fucking getting air support," SGT Horton-RTO said. "The pilots can't see shit."

Luckily, later in the morning, the clouds cleared up and we were able to observe the majority of the valley. I had been to the valley back in July 2010 with Captain Michael, but it looked different now. We watched families leave their houses in the valley before we headed down to start our search-and-clear operation. The Taliban talked about launching a large-scale attack, including shooting down the helicopters as we worked.

We began clearing the qalats without getting shot at, but we couldn't find a single man in those buildings. The valley had turned into a ghost town. We found recoilless rifles (82mm), PKM, mortar rounds, AK-47s, and RPGs with all sorts of other military stuff and ammunition caches that were buried and hidden outside and inside the buildings. We pushed our patrol even further and searched more qalats, taking advantage of the empty villages. Clouds started coming back in as afternoon approached, and we had to stop our patrol. Everyone headed back to the small post that we established on the top of the hill, surrounded by high mountain peaks and trees; we thought we were probably fairly safe and secure from the enemy's attack. Suddenly, though, we were under Daksha and PKM fire, and while the firefight didn't last for too long, the Dish-Ka never stopped shooting at us for the rest of the day.

By the end of the first day of Operation Strong Eagle III some of our brave soldiers tragically lost their lives. Their deaths did not only shake the 2/327th Battalion but also everybody who knew those soldiers. SFC Ofren was a good friend and fearless soldier who used to work at COP Monti before he moved to the battalion. He was shot in the lower back along with his soldier, SPC Trimm, who tried to grab SFC Ofren by the body armor after he got shot. SPC Trim was shot in the forearms, but continued to fight the enemy after receiving multiple shots in the body armor. While SFC Ofren sadly died from his injuries at the hospital in Asadabad, SPC Trimm survived. SFC Ofren's medic, SPC Jameson, who treated both Afghan and American wounded soldiers, got shot and died while waiting for the MEDEVACs that had been delayed by the weather. That was the bravery and brotherhood I witnessed among both Afghan and American soldiers every day during Operation Enduring Freedom.

SFC Ofren was gone but never forgotten. Everyone talked about him and his incredible leadership while he was the platoon sergeant for 3rd Platoon at Combat Outpost Monti. SFC Ofren always smiled and was super active, I could never keep up while walking with him. He was fit and always ahead of the game during our daily patrol, missions, or operations.

After a couple of days on the hilltop under the Taliban's constant and intensive fire, we decided to leave the hill and move to a more stable location. While we were clearing a building, I heard the Taliban talking about our new location, but our new post was still much safer with no more Dish-Ka and PKM rounds fired at us. However, we knew we couldn't stay there long. We spent the night under trees while it was raining, but the next morning, the Taliban launched a massive attack from our east side with PKM and AK47s. You could hear the rounds snap branches above our heads. It was hard to find a good cover, but we fired back at them without knowing exactly where they were.

"John, let the ANA know that we are going back to the hilltop," Captain Billig said, "and ask Captain Basir if his guys can help us bring down some ammo." A big load of ammo had been dropped off by the helicopters a few hours before along with water and MREs. During the transfer, we ended up leaving some of the ammunition on the hill because we couldn't transport it down the steep, slippery path. What we left behind we stacked so that the helicopter coverage could detonate it, ensuring that the Taliban wouldn't retrieve it.

We made it back to the hilltop while Taliban militants were celebrating and because they thought that they had confiscated a huge stack of ammo that we left behind.

"Mulawi Saab, Mujahidin's captured a lot of ammo," Fedai radioed his boss.

"Allah Akbar, Allah Akbar, it's help from Allah!" Mulawi Saab shouted.

"We are gonna need more help to get it outta here."

"Don't worry, the help is on the way. How many men do you need?" Mulawi asked.

"Probably 10-20."

"I will send them over there, but be careful out there."

"The helicopters are gone. No aircraft here," Fedai said. Americans went back to the hilltop."

Soon the celebration stopped as our bomb hit their newly found ammunitions pile.

We ended up staying on the hill; it was much better than the woods where we couldn't see more than 20 feet in front of us, but Taliban Dish-Ka never stopped shooting at us at the hilltop until LT Blume was able to confirm a fire support mission.

Everyone was super exhausted after a long day in the woods. I couldn't wait to get some sleep, but between the Taliban's radio and the rain, I only slept for an hour at a time. I was soaked, like everyone else, the next morning.

"John, what the fuck is going on here? Talk to your fucking weather friend and tell him that we need some fucking sun," LT Blume joked.

"Hahaha, he doesn't fucking listen to me. Welcome to Afghanistan, sir!" I replied. "Look at me I am soaked too, sir. I need one of those body bag things."

"What the fuck do you need that thing for?" LT Blume surprisingly asked.

"My sleeping bag is soaked and I don't know if I can use it tonight. I figured that the body bag would be good to waterproof the rest of my stuff" I replied.

Unfortunately, we didn't get a resupply all day due to the firefights and Taliban snipers who continued to attack our post the next day. There was a small rocky structure that Captain Billig, LT Blume, SGT Horton and I used for cover while the rest of the soldiers had built their own fighting position and defense mechanism. The walls of the structure were so small so you had to be sitting down at all times in order not to get shot.

"Sit the fuck down, man! They are fucking shooting at us," Captain Billig shouted at LT Blume while he was standing and talking on the radio with fire crew back at Combat Outpost Hanker-Miracle. As Gator Company's fire support officer, LT Blume was calling for an artillery mission [fire support mission] on a dozen of the enemy's possible targets [TRPs] in the mountains.

Then he looked at me and said, "what the fuck are you doing, John?" I had my camera out and was recording where the artillery rounds were going to land.

"John, get out of my fucking way," LT Blume said while I was recording. I moved a little bit to the corner when I heard, "Fuck I got shot. God damn it," LT Blume yelled.

"I fucking told you to get the fuck down," Captain Billig said

"My fucking shoulder!" LT Blume screamed.

"Medic, I need fucking medic here!" Captain Billig yelled. "Take your fucking body armor off."

"It's fucking burning!" LT Blume yelled.

"I fucking told you, but you never fucking listen," Captain Billig told him. "You're a lucky fucking bastard."

It was an enemy PKM round that hit a rock and kicked back hitting LT Blume's shoulder. It burned through his body armor strip while he was standing. Captain Billig tried to medevac him out, but he refused to return to Monti or FOB Joyce.

LT Blume taped the hole in his body armor and stayed for the rest of the mission. When I told him that I got him on camera screaming. He laughed and said, "I fucking need that video. I am going to send it to my girlfriend."

There was a deep cave just above the village that we believed the Taliban used to hide their Dish-Ka. Our next priority was to bomb it because the earlier artillery shells hadn't destroyed it.

"Yah, yah, fuck the Taliban! Fuck the Dish-Ka," the soldiers cheered as the bombs dropped, but the pilots missed the target, and the bomb went off on the ridgeline where there was a village and the mosque.

"John, ask Captain Basir if there is anybody in the qalats down below," JTAC directed. He looked very annoyed and frustrated.

Captain Basir grabbed his binoculars and said, "I don't see anybody in the village; tell him, they are gone."

"We are gonna drop another one," Captain Billig said after the first one went wrong.

"It wasn't my fucking fault; I don't how the hell pilots missed it," the JTAC responded. "They better fucking hit this time."

15 minutes later, the aircraft dropped another bomb, this time, directly hitting the target. The cave was gone and after that we were able to walk around on the post.

Ch 43: Last Air Assault of Strong Eagle III

The ANA were the most excited to go back to Monti after four days in the mountains. The Americans, however, were set to take off that night for the next mission.

We flew out and landed high in the mountains where the battalion TOC was located. It was much safer than where we had just returned from but way colder than we expected.

We were overlooking Bajour City, the Khyber Pukhtunkhwa tribal area that was another safe haven for rebel fighters. Many militants that were involved in fighting against 2/327th during Strong Eagle III infiltrated Marawara from Bajour. The Taliban passed the Durand Line into Kunar Province freely and used Bajour as their casualty collection point [CCP] for their wounded fighters en-route to Pakistani hospitals. One of the biggest challenges that we faced during operation Strong Eagle III was capturing or killing militants before they disappeared into Bajour.

Our new location on the top of the mountain was much safer and drier while other platoons were still taking heavy enemy fire during search-and-clear operations in the valley. Generally, the Taliban were on the run, having lost their morale and motivation of fighting.

Around 8:00 P.M., we received two Black Hawk helicopters delivering ammo, water, and cold weather MREs. As it was taking off, one of the Black Hawks mistakenly fired its common missile warning system [SMWS]. "Fucking fire, sir! Your sleeping bag and backpacks are on fire," SGT Robinson shouted.

"It's the fucking automatic system that went off," Captain Billig said after we searched the entire area for possible enemy's rockets and infiltration.

On the seventh day of Strong Eagle III, we were wrapping up our operations and preparing to return to Combat Outpost Monti when Gator company [BRAVO] received a new mission to go after the Taliban's high-profile commander, QZR. "This is a fucking SEAL mission," I heard someone say in the TOC. Navy SEALs were supposed to carry out the mission later that night, but ISR spotted QZR in a small compound deep in the woods accompanied by women, men and kids. QZR used civilians as human shields to protect himself and his friends. QZR was on the run, and we needed to reach him before he escaped into Pakistan. There was not enough time for Navy SEALs to respond and bombing wasn't an option because the compound was only a few hundred meters away from a Pakistani military post as well as civilians.

At 3:00 P.M., we gathered for our short briefing. "It's going to be fucking dangerous," 1SG Bolin shouted at everybody.

"Roger 1SG," everyone replied. We were going into a very risky and a relatively hostile area, and there is no fucking way that QZR is going to turn himself in.

"QZR has a suicide bomber with him, and fucking explosives around his house. We've got to make sure we don't get fucking blown up. We also have intelligence that he has IEDs inside and outside of the house so we got to be fucking careful once we get there." Captain Billig reported.

Our LZ was close to the Pakistani militia post, along the Durand Line, a few miles away from the compound because we didn't want to let QZR know that we were coming. The plan was walk through the forest to surprise him and his militants. We also knew that we couldn't trust the Pakistanis to support us. At 3:30 P.M., as the sun was about to disappear behind the Hindu Kush, two Black Hawk helicopters approached the LZ. Things were about to get real. SGT Horton-RTO, tapped me on the shoulder and said," John, here is your favorite-shirt that you are always talking about." I looked at him, confused. He handed me the gator shirt that we had talked about a while back, his favorite.

"I know you like it. While I was preparing for this mission, I found it in my backpack, but you need to wash it, SGT Horton told me.

"Oh, thank you so much. I don't care, I wanna put it on right now."

You could feel the soldiers' adrenaline rush as we crowded into Black Hawk Helicopters.

"Let's fucking take care of it!" one of the soldiers yelled.

"Let's fucking do it!"

Our helicopters took off and as we approached our target it was just a tiny single-story building covered by the trees on a rocky hillside. The helicopters circled to get a better area for their landing, right above the steep ridgeline, close to the Pakistani soldiers' outpost and touched down. Soldiers quickly got to work.

We walked over to the Pakistani soldiers who looked very scared and curious. They were all gathered together with no weapons and had no clue was going on.

"*Salaam Alai Kum.*"

"*Wali kum salaam*, how are you?" one of the soldiers responded to me in Pashtu.

"John, tell them not to let anybody cross in and out here," Captain Billig replied.

The soldiers were relieved; they knew that they were guilty of allowing the militants to cross the border freely, and tried to butter-up Captain Billig, "We both have the same enemy, and we will never let anyone cross the border." A Pakistani soldier with a long beard and a trimmed mustache said as he introduced himself as a commander of the post.

He wasn't finished when another soldier interrupted him and yelled in Urdu, "shut up!" He didn't realize that I could also speak Urdu. He was very well-dressed and I thought that he could perhaps be the boss.

"What's going on, John? We don't have time for this. We got to go," Captain Billig interrupted.

"We will do our best to stop and prevent all the movements around here," the well-dressed Pakistani concluded.

"Thank you," Captain Billig replied as we pushed out and continued walking to the target.

"John, how do you like walking in the mountains?" A former Special Forces 1SG who was advising for the Army asked.

"I like it. I was born and raised in Kunar," I responded.

He looked at me like he thought I was joking, "Really? What part of Kunar province? I was in Kunar in 2007."

"Tswaki," I told him.

"I know where Tsawki is. We went to Badil Valley once."

Badil was a remote valley about five miles from my village.

"That's awesome. When I was a kid, we used to go to Badil Valley for firewood."

"I heard it's pretty bad nowadays."

"I haven't been to my village in years."

He was a very nice guy with a ton of battle experiences. "We went to Pech Valley one day, but we didn't have an interpreter and couldn't speak the language; one of the trucks broke down in the middle of a highway and blocked the traffic. I was trying to tell people that our truck was broken but they couldn't understand me," he reflected. "It's a long story but we finally found someone and gave him $100 just to translate a few words for us."

While I was talking to him, I heard somebody call, "John, we need you at the front." I thought, "I am gonna be the fucking first one to get killed in a suicide bomber or an IED", what I didn't know was that I was going to save someone's life.

"John, there is an old man sitting there; we called him but he didn't respond," SGT Frank said.

I saw the old man sitting outside of his house with water in his hand. The man didn't have a weapon on him nor did he look strong enough to fight, but you never knew, he could be a watchman outside for the militants that we believed were hiding in the house with QZR. I shouted to him, but he didn't respond or seem to notice us. I heard one of the soldiers ask, "Why the fuck he is not answering you, John?"

"Do whatever you need to do, John. We need to fucking hurry up," SGT Frank told me.

I threw rock toward the old man, and it landed pretty close to him. He jumped up, looking scared, but he still couldn't find us because we were staying within the bushy forest.

I grabbed another stone and threw it at him again; it landed just a few inches away from him. He stood up and looked around, and I waved at him and shouted.

"You are fine, but we need to talk," I shouted at him.

"Bring him over, we need to fucking talk to him," Captain Billig instructed.

"Be fucking careful," SGT Frank added.

"I got you, John," One of the soldiers with m240 shouted.

I ended up talking the old man, but the entire time, I was still kind of nervous because all of the dangers from the briefing were still on my mind.

"John, let him know that we are going into the house. If he has anybody there, they should come out," Captain Billig said.

"I have my granddaughters and a daughter-in-law in there," the old man said. While I was talking to him, the Apaches engaged a number of insurgents, who ran out of a nearby house and tried to escape on the rocky trail a few hundred yards away.

"You are fine, it's us," I told the old man when we heard the gunshots. We let the old man go to get his grand-daughters and daughter-in-law, while we approached the house. A woman with two kids came out and said, "Brother, brother, there has been a guy in the house since this morning, and we don't know him. He is bleeding very badly."

"Back up, back up! There is a fucking guy in the house," SGT Frank shouted after I translated.

The woman and her kids were scared, "You guys are going to be okay; you are my family, we will take care of you," I told them.

"Brother, we don't know this guy. He came to the house this morning bleeding," The woman said again.

"John, ask her does he have a weapon on him," Captain Billig said.

"We don't know, he is hiding in there," the women told us.

"Listen, there is a fucking guy soaked with fucking blood in the house, we got to be fucking careful. We never know if there could be more than one," Captain Billig briefed as we prepared to breach the house. It was a small two-bedroom house where the family lived in one room with their animals and food. We found the guy soaked in blood, laying on the dirt floor in the guest room next to the living room. He could hardly move.

"We need a fucking medic here," Captain Billig shouted right after we went in. "John, ask him his name and how he got here."

"They brought me here," Gul Wali responded after the medic took care of his wounds and bleeding.

"What do you mean by 'they'?"

"Mulawi Saab," Gul Wali replied.

"Where is Mulawi?" Captain Billig asked.

"He left before you guys came in. I don't know where he went, but he said that they would come back for me."

"John, we can talk to him later, but we got to go now," Captain Billig concluded.

We headed next to the steep trail to assess enemy casualties from the Apache fire we heard earlier. We wanted to make sure that QZR was among them. Instead of bodies, we found cell phones and Pakistani currency equivalent to $3,000 U.S. dollars. We could tell that they were seriously injured from the text messages they had been trying to send asking for reinforcements, but none went through. *"All friends are in very bad condition; we need reinforcements so bad. We just left the house and the Americans came to search it."*

When we returned to the house, everybody was excited about flying back to Combat Outpost Monti because we thought we were done with the air assault mission. Soon however, we found out that we would be staying because QZR was still alive.

I continued talking with Gul Wali while some soldiers pulled out their sleeping bags and crashed on the dirt floor. I couldn't wait to get some rest, but I had to stay awake with Gul Wali until he fell asleep. Finally, he fell asleep in the middle of our questioning, and I curled up for warmth as well. During our search-and-clear operation of the house, we discovered some religious propaganda, books, Taliban flags with strange letters that promoted Jihad against both Afghan and American soldiers-- "Everybody must fight and fulfill the duty of Jihad whether you are a man, woman or kid," one of the letters preached. *"Afghan and American soldiers are infidels who deserve to be killed, murdered and their bodies need to be cut up pieces by pieces."*

"Son! we don't want to fight anybody; I am old and I can't even move, but the Taliban comes to our house and forces us to feed them and do whatever they want us to do," the old man said after we let them back inside the house. While we were talking, his daughter-in-law came back with tea. It was very nice of the family to honor *Pashtunwali*.

"John, don't tell the family, but we are flying out of here tomorrow, and I got some cash for them," Captain Billig told me. "Do you think we should give it to them now or before we fly out? It was nice of them to let us stay in their house."

"They would love that, sir. We can give it to them now," I replied.

The family was happy after they received money from Captain Billig. "Thank you so much. May Allah keep you all safe," the old man put his hands together, raised them above his chest and prayed.

The little girl was thrilled when we also gave her candy; she followed us for the rest of the day. "Uncle, what is it?" she asked. She was probably around seven years-old. "It's candies," I told her in Pashtu. She looked at me and said, "Uncle, nobody ever gave me this before; I like it."

After eight days, Operation Strong Eagle III was about to come to an end. "We fucking fly out of here at 2300 hours," Captain Billig said. "We are not fucking walking back to the LZ, the Chinook is coming to get us here."

Around 11:20 P.M., the Chinook helicopter, escorted by two Apaches, dropped its gapping hatch with just one wheel on the ground, one side of the helicopter was hanging over the cliff. I heard SGT Frank shout, "John, you need to take care of him," pointing to Gul Wali.

Gul Wali refused to get on the helicopter because he had never flown before and had not even seen a helicopter up close. While I was walking with him to the helicopter, he resisted, but we finally managed to get him in. He kept saying, "I am very scared of this thing." When we boarded the helicopter, I noticed that he continued to shake during the whole flight.

"John, we are gonna drop him off at Joyce," Captain Billig said. "We don't need him at Monti. We got S2s [intelligence] waiting for him at the LZ."

After we dropped him off at Joyce, we arrived at Monti around midnight, officially bringing Operation Strong Eagle III to an end.

Ch 44: Welcome to America

My precious and beautiful mom,

I made it to the United States of America after 20 hours and long flights from Kabul to India; India to New York; New York to Houston and finally, Houston to El Paso, Texas. It was a journey full of joy and happiness, but also stress and exhaustion. But I made it. I met my old army combat friend and brother at the airport in El Paso after many, many years.

Mom,

Can you believe that someone who grew up in a small town in the mountains of Kunar Province in the northeast of Afghanistan would make it to the United States? I bet you did because you always believed in me and your kids. I remember that you always said, "I may not be around to see my kids pursuing their dreams," but here you are, still alive and still dreaming for your kids and enjoying time with your grandkids. You still look young and beautiful, are kindhearted like you always have been, and a bit feisty with dad who loves you but never says it. When I was a kid, we couldn't afford to leave our town, even to visit Jalalabad City. But many years later, I made it to the United States of America.

My dearest mom,

I remember the day and time when I had to leave for United States. It still feels like it happened yesterday, as the saying goes, "good memories stay and are remembered." Of course, I was nervous leaving a country that I had never left before, and I even worried about the customs and border police during my departure; I had heard many stories from friends about problems with them.

"*Salaam*, brother, sorry for the late response, I don't get on Facebook much since I have been in the United States," Saleem, a former U.S. Military interpreter, responded my Facebook message. "I can't remember it all, it has been a very long time since I left, but I do remember that the border police ask all sort of questions like date of birth, place of birth and so on."

I heard that the customs and border police are very smart and good at catching people who try to lie. If someone is caught, they are sent back to where they came from. I didn't want to go back, even though I missed everyone so badly, because I didn't want to get killed. These thoughts swirled in my mind as I left the Kabul airport for New Delhi. The Kabul airport was an easy entrance, routine check-in and a few questions that sounded like the customs and border police didn't care. I thought it could be the same along the journey, but it changed when I arrived in New Delhi.

"آپ کا نام اور تاریخ پیدائش کیا ہے"

"Hello, what is your name and date of birth?" An Indian customs and border agent asked while holding my passport in his hand. He spoke Urdu but switched to English right after I responded him with English. He was young and sharp about his work because there was a big line of people that need to go through the checkpoint.

It was a great relief when he handed my passport back to me, but I had a long way to go. I had trouble finding the right terminal, and I spoke English with an American accent so many people at the airport avoided answering my questions or claimed that they couldn't understand me. I had plenty of time, but I felt rushed because I didn't want to miss the flight and be sent back to face the danger in Afghanistan. I bet some of the Indian security personnel, cleaners, airport staff and even other passengers at the airport thought that I was lunatic after watching me staring at everything in the airport. They couldn't know that I had never been to an international airport before. The New Delhi airport was much bigger, more modern and busier than the Kabul airport. For someone who had never left their country, this felt like a big adventure. I felt free physically, emotionally, psychologically, and socially. It was a different feeling, a freedom to approach the world, people and things that I was never told existed. Even though I had to leave everyone behind-- parents, siblings, friends and both good and bad memories, flying away was like a bird being freed from its cage after years. Finally, I was able to find a sign, 'Welcome to American Airlines'. It was a happy moment knowing that I had found where I was supposed to be. "Did I miss the flight? Am I late? What's going on?" all sorts of questions circled in my mind. There was no one at the airline counter to help. Within half an hour, while I was waiting and debating, a young man who appeared to be in his early 20s, very well-dressed with a tie and nice, shiny boots, and long hair that made him look like a Bollywood movie star came to man the desk.

ہیلو ، میرا نام ارجن ہے اور میں امریکن
ائیر لائن کے لئے کام کرتا ہوں

"Hello, my name is Arjun and I am working for American Airlines," I was the only on sitting at the waiting area so he assumed that I was waiting for him.

"آپ کا نام اور تاریخ پیدائش کیا ہے؟"

"What is your name and date of birth?"

مجھے آپ کا ٹکٹ اور باقی کاغذی کام دیکھنے دیں

"Let me see your ticket and the rest of the paperwork," he directed.

I gave him all of my papers, including a sealed packet that I was not allowed to open. The U.S. visa counselor at the embassy in Kabul had told me that I was to present it to the U.S. Customs officials upon my arrival to the country. I was very anxious to find out about what was inside.

Arjun took my papers and disappeared for nearly half an hour. "Thank you and your flight is 10:00 P.M.," he said when he returned with no further explanation.

So far so good, but I had two more stops, both in the U.S. where I was going to deal with tougher customs and border police.

"Let me know if you have any questions," Arjun offered.

"Thank you, brother, I will," I responded. He smiled at me and went back to his small office.

I ended up waiting for more than 6 hours at the airport in New Delhi before departing for the United States.

Finally, after the long wait at the airport in New Delhi, I checked in to make my American dream come true. I couldn't believe it was happening, but got scared when I saw a woman in her early 30s crying while talking with someone on the phone. It was about 40 minutes before we were supposed to depart. Everybody was staring at her, but because I was so close, I could overhear her conversation. She was deported from one of the airports in the U.S. upon her arrival and had been sent back on the next flight because there were problems with her paperwork. It made me nervous that I could face the same fate. She was still there when I left to finally depart to a country and world where people had the right to live peacefully, without explosions and death threats filling their lives.

"Welcome to John F Kennedy Airport"

After a 20-hour flight, I made it to the United States. When we landed on U.S. soil, the flight attendant announced, "Welcome to JFK Airport," over the speaker. It was cold, cloudy, and partially rainy out. I didn't have extra clothes, they were all in my checked luggage, and even then, I didn't have a lot of cloths or stuff, just a few jeans and shirts that I bought in Kabul as well as pre-cooked wheat, similar to popcorn, that my mom made for me in case I got hungry. It was a great snack, but security threw it out in the U.S., but at least it made it to the United States for a short time.

John F. Kennedy Airport was huge, busier and louder than both the Kabul and New Delhi airports. This time, navigating the airport was much easier and comfortable because I could speak with an American accent and be understood.

"U.S. citizens on the left side and non-U.S. citizens on the right please," a big man in a black uniform, equipped with handcuffs, a 9mm pistol, and radio directed at the start of security.

"Where did you come from?" a clean-shaven, thin officer asked me. He reminded me of soldiers that were ready to roll out for daily patrols/missions in Afghanistan.

"Afghanistan," I responded.

"Did you fly from Afghanistan?" he questioned.

"No, No, this flight was from India."

"Oh, I see," he further added.

I was already nervous but got more nervous when he asked about my itinerary. He remained quiet for a bit, but I tried to stay engaged with him.

"You stay out here; I will be right back," he said.

"Thank you!" I said, not fully understanding why I was thanking him for doing his job. I ended up waiting for almost 20 minutes, and every minute felt like an hour. I was getting anxious, restless and scared after every second that something was wrong. My mind ran through my answers during our conversation. "I can't go back; I will die if I do. My paperwork is legit; why is it taking so long?" the questions whizzed through my mind.

Finally, the young officer came out, walking towards me with my passport, and the rest of the paperwork including the packet that I wasn't allowed to open.

"Sorry, I can't say your first name; if it's okay, I'll call you by your last name," he said.

"Yes, of course," I responded.

"Well, we are gonna need to go to the office for some more information and then you will be good to go."

"Sure, but I do have another flight to El Paso, Texas." I told him.

We both went to his small office where two other officers were sitting as well dealing with paperwork.

"Okay, Safi, I bet it was a long flight." The young officer began.

"Yes, indeed, it was. I haven't slept or eaten since yesterday," I told him.

"Do you want coffee, water, anything?" he asked very kindly.

"Water is good," I replied. He helped me pour water from the fountain because I couldn't figure it out.

"How do you say your first name? He asked with smile on his face.

"Nasirullah," I pronounced.

"Na, Nazeerullah," the young officer tried it.

"Very close," I responded.

"I will stick with your last name, Safi," he joked.

"Whatever is easy, sir."

He surprised me when he added, "I know there are some names that I found complicated to say while I was in Afghanistan. I don't remember my interpreter's name, but we called him 'Jakie'. He was a good dude, I really liked him. I remember he brought us Afghan naan; it was so good. I tried to find it here, but never could," he continued, "You were an interpreter too, right?

"Yes, I was for almost 8 years."

"Wow, I can't imagine," he shook his head and looked at his buddies in the office. "That's a commitment, man, and thank you for your service!" Then he looked at me and asked, "Have you ever worked for the 101st, Safi?"

"Of course," I responded. "I worked for the 101st a few times. They were one of my favorite units, after the 10th mountain from Fort Drum, New York. But I also worked for the 173rd Airborne Brigade, 1st Infantry Division, the 4th Infantry Division, the 25th Infantry Division, the 82nd Airborne Division, the 125th Military Police, the OGA and many more that I don't remember."

"I was with the 101st," he responded, "But what's 'OGA'?"

"Other government agency," I replied.

"American, right?" he questioned.

"Yes, but not Army, they are doing secret stuff."

"Oh, I get it. We don't talk about that here," he smiled.

"Okay, we are almost done, and you will on your way soon, but one more question- who is going to pick you up at the airport when you get there?" he asked.

"Sergeant Major Kevin Devine. He was the platoon sergeant that I worked for back in 2009 in Kunar Province with Charlie Company, 1-32, 10th Mountain Division, Afghanistan."

"Alright, Safi, I am done. Welcome to America. I am going to escort you out, but you still need to go to the routine security check where I picked you up earlier. You are gonna have to use the left line, that's for non-U.S. citizens and then you will be good to go. You can pick up your luggage on the other side too," he said. "Nice meeting you, Safi, take care."

He was a very friendly officer and our shared military background helped to put me at ease during the interview.

I couldn't' believe what just happened because I was exhausted and nervous in a place I'd never been. I felt lucky that he didn't ask about my 'birthday' so I didn't have to lie about it once again. Now, after the interview, I felt like I didn't need to worry about anything. His words stuck in my head, *"welcome to America."*

About the Author

Nasirullah "John" Safi was born and raised in the war-torn country of Afghanistan under the Taliban regime. While many schools were closed at that time due to radicalism and extremism, he had a desire to always learn more from a very young age. He began a path to acquire an education no matter how hard the road was. He bounced back and forth between Madrassas and homeschooling to fulfill the dream of becoming a medical doctor, a profession that Safi and his mother chose because she suffered from chronic illness and he wanted to help her. Unfortunately, attending Madrassas wouldn't help him achieve his goals. In 2001, a U.S.-led coalition began the war on terror that not only changed his life for better, it improved the lives of millions of Afghan men, women, and children as well.

Safi joined the U.S. mission in his teens and served both Afghanistan and the United States for many years with dedication and enthusiasm. He worked for both U.S. military personnel and civilians working in other government agencies before he immigrated to the United States of America.

Safi is a multilingual U.S. resident who lives in Oregon, where he attends college to achieve his dream of becoming a medical doctor. He currently has a full-time job and is working on his next writing project, "Life in America: How I Made My Way from the Army to an OGA."

Made in the USA
Las Vegas, NV
27 October 2021